is an excellent starting point for marketers interested in understanding the power of Pinterest.

> —Patrick Shaber, Vice President of Global Marketing at Communications Systems, Inc.

One of the biggest mistakes companies make when a hot new social media channel dominates the headlines is to jump in, feet first, with no plan of action... resulting in no real returns for their brands. Pinterest Marketing: An Hour A Day solves this problem by arming today's marketers with the guidance, best practices, and roadmap they need to create successful, sustainable Pinterest strategies.

> —Christina "CK" Kerley, marketing specialist

You don't get Pinterest? That's okay. Your online audience already does. Half of our brain is devoted to processing visual information. Read this book immediately to harness the explosive growth of this highly-visual social sharing phenomenon for your business!

> —Tim Ash CEO of SiteTuners, chair of Conversion Conference, and bestselling author of Landing Page Optimization

With the explosive growth of Pinterest, every marketer worth their salt is scrambling to figure out how to effectively use the social pinboard giant as a marketing channel. That is why I found this book a must-have resource. Within, Jennifer provides innovative strategies for companies of all sizes looking to effectively promote their brand and/ or products on Pinterest. In fact, whether you are an individual simply using Pinterest to "pin" your favorite things or a marketer looking to tap into its tremendous potential, this resourceful book is sure to amaze and inspire.

> —David Wallace, CEO, SearchRank

This book not only provides valuable tips on how to attract Pinterest traffic but also does a great job in explaining how to effectively monitor campaigns and the appropriate metrics to focus on. Know which campaigns are paying off and your Pinterest campaigns will soar to new heights! This book is a must to compete effectively and take your Pinterest campaigns to the next level.

> —Mona Elesseily, Vice President of Online Marketing, Page Zero Media

There are three or four key reasons why you should read Pinterest Marketing: An Hour A Day by Jennifer Evans Cario. First, Pinterest is one of the top four social media websites along with Facebook, YouTube, and Twitter, according to Experian Hitwise US. Second, Jennifer explains Pinterest's unique appeal and fundamentals, then shows you how to develop a strategic marketing plan, set up an account, curate *winning content, find followers, and track and monitor your Pinterest traffic. Third, her book is written in the popular* An Hour A Day *format, which uses a detailed how-to approach with case studies, tips, and interviews. And fourth, none of the illustrations in her book show Ohio State beating Michigan 26 to 21 this year in "The Game." Since I'm a Wolverine and she's a Buckeye, I'm very grateful that Jennifer didn't "pin" any images, videos and other objects about our football rivalry to her pinboard.*

—GREG JARBOE, President of SEO-PR and author of *YouTube and Video Marketing: An Hour A Day.*

The book is full of tips and helpful suggestions. As a daily Pinterest user I even picked up some great ideas for clients and a non-profit as well. This book is educational, but is a quick and easy read. As with all marketing options one must really study and understand the intricacies of the different platforms. This book will help businesses use Pinterest effectively and help them avoid costly mistakes. A must read!

—MELISSA FACH, Owner, SEO Aware

What makes Pinterest unique? It allows people to visualize and easily capture their dreams, plans, recipes and more. The old adage 'a picture is worth a thousand words' could not be more true—especially in today's fast-paced, content-driven world. And there is no better guide to help people and organizations understand and utilize Pinterest than Jennifer Cario. Jennifer's content marketing, social media and search engine expertise shines through in Pinterest Marketing: An Hour A Day. *Read it and you'll have a sound Pinterest strategy in no time. Happy pinning!*

—BETH HARTE, marketer, blogger and Pinterest fan

As a consultant and educator in the online marketing space, I am consistently advising companies on the best ways to use social media channels to create buzz around their products and services. While most can now get their heads around the value of Facebook and Twitter, the first reaction I get from clients when I suggest they use Pinterest for business is almost always 'But isn't Pinterest just for scrapbookers?' Now, instead of exasperated sighs and my usual lecture about what a fabulous and underestimated marketing tool Pinterest is, I'll just be able to hand them a copy of Jennifer's book!

—KALENA JORDAN, Founder, Search Engine College

Jennifer Cario is an expert in online community building and this book illustrates that perfectly. With over 15 years of online marketing experience, I've read many expert books. Jennifer's knowledge of Pinterest and its practical applications allow this book to stand out among the best in the industry. Pinterest is a powerhouse website and Jennifer packs this book with nuggets of great information for companies of all sizes.

—JOHN ELLIS, CEO, Crescent Interactive

Jennifer is and always has been a foremost leader in the social media realm. Her new book, Pinterest Marketing: An Hour A Day *shows that social media leadership to a T. If you have a visual product you should read this book. If you don't think you have a visual product you should* **definitely** *read this book. Jennifer will help you understand how to use Pinterest in ways you had never thought of before.*

—Sage Lewis, President, SageRock Web Marketing Agency

Pinterest arrived on the scene with little fanfare, and serious marketers initially ignored the "visual scrapbooking" site, viewing it as a novelty with limited appeal. Jennifer was one of the first to see its potential to drive high volumes of quality traffic, and started writing Pinterest Marketing *even before the site caught fire and became a valuable resource for tens of millions of users. The marketing world is still warming up to Pinterest, so early readers of this book can get a huge head-start on their competition. Online marketers: read it now or fall behind!*

—David Szetela, speaker, consultant and author of *PPC SEM: An Hour A Day.*

As the new kid on the social media block, Pinterest is very different from the old standbys like Twitter and Facebook. At first glance it's not self-evident how to use it effectively either personally or as a marketing channel for businesses. Jennifer does a great job of explaining all there is to know about Pinterest, while providing numerous creative ways that companies have used it to enhance their brands. As an online marketer who didn't think Pinterest would be of much use for my type of business, I came away with many ideas that I'll be trying out ASAP!

—Jill Whalen, Founder & CEO, High Rankings

The hockey stick growth of Pinterest has both brands and consumers salivating. In her new book, Jennifer shows how Pinterest has changed the game of visual search, and how marketers can leverage the behavior to lead customers astray and directly into a conversion funnel! From board optimization and finding followers, to contests and mind mapping, this is a Must Read for anyone looking to make Pinterest brand integration work!

—Lisa Barone, Vice President of Strategy at Overit Media

If you're a small business owner who wants to understand how Pinterest could help your business – this is the book for you. Jennifer has a wonderful grasp of what it takes to be successful on Pinterest and walks you through the process in her clear, easy to understand style.

—Marty Diamond, Diamond Website Conversion

I have had the pleasure of speaking with Jennifer multiple times at various top search marketing conferences around the country and simply put, she "gets" marketing.

I am always impressed with the takeaways, actionable information and knowledge that Jennifer shares with the audience. This book is reflective of that, too. If you are interested in learning how to market your business with Pinterest this is the book I'd recommend.

—MATT SILTALA, President, AvalaunchMedia.com

Jen's research illustrates how Pinterest is a surprisingly powerful marketing tool. When added to a social marketing strategy, the sort of data gathered focuses on user choices made naturally by browsing and pinning items they like or want to save for later. Jennifer's passion and friendly writing style will inspire you to try out Pinterest yourself.

—KIM KRAUSE BERG, Owner Cre8pc forums

This book will give any size brand the guidance and tools to easily gain more online visibility using Pinterest and be part of the visual marketing movement.

—LISA BUYER, President and CEO of The Buyer Group

What is Pinterest? How does it work? Why is it important to your business? And, most importantly, how can you make money from Pinterest? All of these questions are expertly answered in Pinterest Marketing: An Hour A Day, *with the later answered in a series of easy to follow, detailed steps.*

—ANDY BEAL, coauthor Radically Transparent: Monitoring & Managing Reputations Online

If you thought that Facebook helps level the playing field for small business, wait till you read Jennifer's Cario's advice on Understanding Pinterest for your ecommerce business. Not only can you leverage crowd sourcing but you can create an army of raving fans to drive very relevant traffic to your website. Pinterest today is what Google Adwords was in 2004 with the best price tag "FREE".

—SHIRLEY TAN, EcommerceSystems.com

Jennifer possesses the unique ability to identify actionable trends in online marketing. This same ability allowed her to create a social media book in a timely fashion for a platform that is still ripe with opportunity. If you want to know how to market using Pinterest —this is your guide.

—TODD MALICOAT, Online Marketing Consultant at Stuntdubl.com

In the years that I have known her, Jennifer has always been on the forefront of understanding new technology and how it can positively (or negatively) affect online marketing, and this book proves it again. Jennifer makes a strong case for the value of this new community and photograph-based technology, when she defends her prediction that Pinterest "has all the makings of a long-term social media player."

*This books acts as an early barometer showing what companies are using and suc-
ceeding with Pinterest, and provides outstanding guidance for small, medium, and
large organization to consider when developing their integrated digital marketing
plans.*
 —CHRIS BOGGS, Director at Rosetta and Chairman of SEMPO

*Because of its visual nature and core user base, Pinterest offers online marketers a
new unmet challenge. Jennifer Cairo resolves the myths and shows us all how we can
drive traffic and results through this major social network.*
 —GEOFF LIVINGSTON, author and marketing strategist

*More parents are turning to Pinterest to help organize their busy lives, so it's no
surprise the site is becoming an increasingly important source of traffic for us.
Through a wide range of examples, Jennifer Evans Cario's* Pinterest Marketing: An
Hour A Day *reinforced some of our current strategies and offered up a number of
new ideas to test and measure. I wouldn't be surprised to see this book on the desks
of editorial, social, marketing and product folks alike.*
 —MATT LAW, Parenting.com Senior Producer

*Jennifer is a highly respected and well known member of the Internet marketing com-
munity. Witty, precise, practical and most importantly easily understood, Jennifer has
successfully tried and tested everything she writes about. In an environment where
making missteps is common, Jennifer's experiences can save you time and make you
money.*
 —JIM HEDGER, Creative Partner, Digital Always Media, Inc.

*Jennifer Cario has been my editor at the Search Engine Guide blog for years, so I am
very familiar with her ability to explain new and challenging concepts in marketing
so that normal people can change what they are doing. If your company needs to take
advantage of Pinterest, this is the book for you.*
 —MIKE MORAN, Chief Strategist at Converseon

*Let's face it, most small business owners and social media managers are so busy it's
hard to imagine taking on another social network. Jennifer does an excellent job of
providing practical bite-sized steps that won't overwhelm and will have your business
pinning its way to success in no time!*
 —KATHY GRAY, Web Content Manager at Stark County Convention &
 Visitors Bureau

*In first establishing the value of Pinterest as a marketing channel by using real-world
examples, and then laying out an actionable week-by-week plan for implement-
ing your Pinterest marketing, Jennifer writes with the credibility of a social media*

veteran that can only be earned through years of work and experience. She gets Business, and she gets Social Media, and no author or trainer excels more at bringing the two together. You won't find vapid theories or empty conjecture here, this is social media marketing for real businesses presented in a manner that every business needs: there is now no excuse for not running a successful Pinterest campaign!

—RYAN FREEMAN, Strider Search Marketing

Pinterest is a powerful tool for the visual. Jennifer takes her knowledge of this network and makes it easy to use, understand, and execute. A must read for those serious in using Pinterest.

—TAMAR WEINBERG, Techipedia and author of *The New Community Rules*, Social Media Strategist

Jennifer's book is essential to anyone looking to learn about Pinterest and use it as a marketing medium. She covers all aspects from the grass to the clouds in an easy-to-understand manner that'll have you building your presences in no time. Highly recommended reading if you're targeting Pinterest!

—DUANE FORRESTER, author of How to Make Money with Your Blog and Turn Click into Customers, and Sr. Product Marketing Manager, Microsoft

Jennifer Cario uses her own unique techniques to allow brands an opportunity to visualize and execute a plan to engage an audience using Pinterest. She provides more than just a how-to, she also expertly answers the question of "Why?".

—CRAIG SUTTON, Owner at Ikon Marketing Group

Thinking about taking the Pinterest plunge? Jennifer Cario's engaging writing style makes it easy to set up, manage and measure your Pinterest campaigns. You'll have people clicking your "Pin It" buttons in no time—and driving new (and profitable) traffic to your site. Don't wait—buy this fantastic go-to guide today!

—HEATHER LLOYD-MARTIN, President and CEO, SuccessWorks Search Marketing

For over a decade, Jennifer has been paving the road for marketers as they navigate new marketing channels. This book is another great example of her amazing ability to demystify disruptive mediums and educate marketers on how to take advantage of them. Jenn breaks down what Pinterest is and gives the reader clear next steps on how to use Pinterest to increase sales, improve engagement, and build communities. It's an absolute must-read for today's marketer.

—JOANNA LORD, VP of Growth Marketing, SEOMoz

This book is proof that there's no need to fly blind when it comes to learning how to successfully incorporate Pinterest into your marketing strategy. Jennifer Cario has brilliantly captured the opportunity Pinterest is creating for businesses and professionals

alike. The icing on the cake? By the end of the book you'll feel prepared and inspired to rev up your own Pinterest strategy —get ready to read, learn, pin and repeat!
—TORI TAIT, Senior Community Manager at DailyGrommet.com

Jennifer paints a jargon-free practical guide for executives, marketers and managers who are ready to rapidly take their social marketing to a new level. Each chapter has surprising insights even for the most seasoned social marketers. Jennifer captures all the key aspects of the Pinterest phenomena. With multiple illustrated references, current trending examples and the biggest take-away is that you will know how to rock Pinterest in one week! This goes beyond basic understanding of Pinterest and unleashes power to engage. It incorporates advance strategy and tools, and it saves months of ineffective work. You will see your results within days.
—REBECCA RYAN, Senior VP of Social Media at Click Media Agency, LLC.

Pinterest™
Marketing:

An Hour A Day

Pinterest™ Marketing:

An Hour A Day

Jennifer Evans Cario

John Wiley & Sons, Inc.

Senior Acquisitions Editor: WILLEM KNIBBE
Development Editor: AMY BREGUET
Technical Editor: KATIE OSKIN
Production Editor: REBECCA ANDERSON
Copy Editor: ELIZABETH WELCH
Editorial Manager: PETE GAUGHAN
Production Manager: TIM TATE
Vice President and Executive Group Publisher: RICHARD SWADLEY
Vice President and Publisher: NEIL EDDE
Book Designer: FRANZ BAUMHACKL
Proofreader: REBECCA RIDER
Indexer: TED LAUX
Project Coordinator, Cover: KATHERINE CROCKER
Cover Designer: RYAN SNEED
Cover Image: © SKYNESHER / ISTOCKPHOTO

Copyright © 2013 by John Wiley & Sons, Inc., Indianapolis, Indiana

Published simultaneously in Canada

ISBN: 978-1-118-40345-7
ISBN: 978-1-118-42189-5 (ebk.)
ISBN: 978-1-118-41767-6 (ebk.)
ISBN: 978-1-118-60563-9 (ebk.)

For general information on our other products and services or to obtain technical support, please contact our Customer Care Department within the U.S. at (877) 762-2974, outside the U.S. at (317) 572-3993 or fax (317) 572-4002.

Wiley publishes in a variety of print and electronic formats and by print-on-demand. Some material included with standard print versions of this book may not be included in e-books or in print-on-demand. If this book refers to media such as a CD or DVD that is not included in the version you purchased, you may download this material at http://booksupport.wiley.com. For more information about Wiley products, visit www.wiley.com.

Library of Congress Control Number: 2012952211

10 9 8 7 6 5 4 3 2 1

Dear Reader,

Thank you for choosing *Pinterest Marketing: An Hour A Day*. This book is part of a family of premium-quality Sybex books, all of which are written by outstanding authors who combine practical experience with a gift for teaching.

Sybex was founded in 1976. More than 30 years later, we're still committed to producing consistently exceptional books. With each of our titles, we're working hard to set a new standard for the industry. From the paper we print on, to the authors we work with, our goal is to bring you the best books available.

I hope you see all that reflected in these pages. I'd be very interested to hear your comments and get your feedback on how we're doing. Feel free to let me know what you think about this or any other Sybex book by sending me an email at nedde@wiley.com. If you think you've found a technical error in this book, please visit http://sybex.custhelp.com. Customer feedback is critical to our efforts at Sybex.

Best regards,

Neil Edde
Vice President and Publisher
Sybex, an Imprint of Wiley

To Mr. Williams, who first made me believe I could write, and to

Mrs. Leet, who loves books and learning as much as I do.

 # Acknowledgments

Thank you to Willem Knibbe for absorbing my enthusiasm for Pinterest before it had really exploded and to the entire team at Sybex/Wiley for believing in both of us and giving this book the green light. You've not only helped me bring sustainable Pinterest strategy to businesses of all sizes, you've also helped me check an item off my bucket list. Thank you for trusting me with this book.

Thank you to Pete, Amy, Becca, Liz, and the entire editing and production team for taking my words and making them even better. Thank you for your patience and persistence throughout the entire process.

To Katie Oskin, you have not only been a fantastic technical editor, you've also become a dear friend. I am so blessed to have you in my life, whether it's to help make this book better or to help make the world around me better. Thank you for your love and friendship.

Love and thanks to Robert Clough, who not only gave me my break in the industry by bringing me on board as Editor-in-Chief of Search Engine Guide, but who also became like a brother to me in the process.

To everyone at the Market Motive offices: You have given me my dream job and allowed me to spend my days doing what I love. Thank you, Michael and John, for bringing me into the mix, and thank you, Scott, for being not only a slave driver but also a friend. Additional thanks to Avinash, Brad, Todd, Matt, Greg, Jamie, and Bryan for helping make Market Motive shine.

My thanks also go out to every last industry contact who ever blogged, retweeted, or shared my content with the world. You all know who you are and I appreciate you immensely.

To Delores…you helped me find my path and for that I will be forever grateful.

To my "West Coast Family" Michael and Karen: Sometimes God makes deep connections we would never expect and you two fall into this category. Thank you for being an inspiration to me as a couple, as parents, and as business owners. You will never know just how much you have helped me in life. I love you both!

Elnora, Emmitt, and Eli: Without you this book never would have happened. Even before you were born, I knew more than anything that I would want to be home with you, loving you, playing with you, teaching you, and absorbing every minute of your childhood I could. Without you, I never would have followed the path I have and I never would have been in a position to write this book. You are all my favorites and I can't imagine life without you.

To my parents: It has not always been an easy road, but you have always believed in me. Thank you for supporting me when I've had to make the hard choices in life. I love you both and appreciate you so very much.

Rachel, for 18 years you have been my rock. Few people in life are blessed enough to have a friendship like ours, and I thank God daily for allowing me to have you in my life. You've been an integral part of every major moment of my life, and it's been a better life because of it. Thank you for loving me, supporting me, and for always helping me to be a better version of myself.

Finally, and most importantly, to my husband Matt. No words in a book could ever tell you what you actually mean to me. Your love, support, and encouragement have meant the world to me. Your willingness to take on extra tasks around the house and with the kids to give me the time I needed to write was a Godsend. And you never once complained about it. This book never could have happened if it hadn't been for your willingness to have my back at every turn. You've shown me what it is to be loved, cherished, and cared for. I couldn't ask for a better business partner or for a better partner in life. Your willingness to put our family first and your knowledge of what truly matters in life make you a man so worthy of respect that I am proud to call you my husband. I love you, baby!

About the Author

Jennifer Evans Cario has made a career out of finding unique and creative ways to connect with consumers without spending a fortune in marketing dollars, making Pinterest a natural fit in her social media arsenal.

Recognized as an industry leader in content-driven social media strategies, Jennifer is known for using real language and a commonsense approach that delivers solid results while still allowing her clients to fully understand and participate in the process.

An industry veteran of more than 15 years, Jennifer founded SugarSpun Marketing in 2010 to serve the strategic social media development needs of small to mid-sized businesses. Her husband Matt joined the business in 2012 as Director of Operations to oversee project management, web analytics, and new business development.

Jennifer spent six years as Editor-in-Chief of Search Engine Guide, a popular industry site focused on educating small businesses about the various aspects of online marketing. She now serves as Social Media faculty chair for Market Motive, a premier online training facility, and as Adjunct Faculty for Rutgers University's MiniMBA Program. She also spends a decent amount of time on the road speaking at a wide range of conferences, including Search Engine Strategies, Search Marketing Expo (SMX), PubCon, and a variety of regional and specialized events.

Jennifer first caught the Pinterest bug as a consumer in the late summer of 2011. Within a few weeks of joining, she began experimenting with test sites to better understand the marketing potential of the platform. Her complete and total Pinterest addiction meant nearly every screen shot captured for this book included the distraction of pinning or repinning several items spotted during the day's research.

You'll find her pinning recipes, kid projects, and homesteading content onto a wide range of Pinterest boards at www.pinterest.com/aflexiblelife.

When she's not writing or pinning, Jennifer lives on a 22-acre micro-farm in Western Pennsylvania with her husband Matt and their children Elnora, Emmitt, and Eli. They often spend summer days exploring fields, woods, and waterfalls.

She strongly believes in "kitchen therapy" and can often be found in her baking kitchen testing out new recipes. She makes the best cinnamon rolls you'll ever eat in your life and is a closet sci-fi buff who will be more than happy to rattle off Firefly quotes or explain exactly why BSG is actually cooler than Star Wars.

Contents

Chapter 4   **Week 1—Set Up a Pinterest Account**   **57**

Chapter 5   **Week 2—Curating Content with Pinterest**   **79**

Introduction

Despite quietly growing an audience of middle-American moms and crafters for several years prior, Pinterest first exploded onto the national scene in late 2011. That's when marketers and site owners first started noticing impressive amounts of traffic streaming into their sites from this little-known social channel. Before long, site owners were clamoring for a better understanding of "this thing called Pinterest" and the media was buzzing about social media's newest darling. As press mentions grew, more users streamed into the site and traffic referrals continued to climb.

With more than 25 million active users, Pinterest has fast become a major player in the world of social media, ranking as the third most popular social network behind Facebook and Twitter. In a world where 91 percent of adults use social media "regularly" and 15 percent of online visits were to social media sites (according to Experian's 2012 Digital Marketer: Benchmark and Trend Report), those figures are worth paying attention to.

Pinterest made its mark on the Internet by allowing web users to create image-based archives of web content organized by topics and themes. Pinterest basically took the concept of web-based bookmarks, made it visual, and allowed people to share their streams with other members of the service. These days, you'll be hard-pressed to find a 25–40-year-old American woman who hasn't heard of the service, and interest from men and other countries is growing steadily.

For websites and brands targeting the female demographic, Pinterest is fast becoming an essential component of a solid social media strategy. Even male-focused brands and the business-to-business market have begun to embrace and explore the service, opening the doors to an entirely new way of reaching consumers on the Web.

Learning how to get your brand proper exposure on Pinterest is becoming an essential skill for anyone tasked with overseeing online marketing.

Who Should Read This Book

This book is designed for anyone involved in social media marketing or online marketing. Such people probably fall into three basic groups:

- Website owners and bloggers who are looking for ways to leverage Pinterest to drive new and qualified traffic to their websites. These people are probably already familiar with the traffic potential of Pinterest but are looking to better understand how to channel that traffic more specifically and how to use Pinterest to boost awareness of their sites and blogs.

- Brand managers and content managers who are looking to better understand the role Pinterest plays in the everyday lives of their target audience and who want to learn to better target that audience through the curation of brand-supporting pinboards and content. These people will benefit most from understanding how Pinterest can help boost or solidify their brand identities and how Pinterest can provide valuable consumer insight on their target audiences.

- Social media marketers and strategists who want to stay on top of the ever-changing world of social media to make sure their clients are maximizing exposure channels. These people will be looking to understand the best tactics for approaching Pinterest as a direct marketing channel. They'll be looking at what types of images perform best, what types of content or interactive contests have the most potential, and how best to integrate Pinterest into existing social media plans for their clients.

The great news is that Pinterest has a low learning curve. Most companies can be up and running on Pinterest in an afternoon and can easily have a starter-level strategy in place for testing in a matter of days. This book provides a comprehensive and accessible overview of the best ways to build a brand presence on Pinterest as well as how to leverage it for both traffic development and consumer insight. It features numerous case studies, examples, and ideas that you can immediately put to work for your website or your clients' websites.

A huge benefit to getting involved with Pinterest marketing right now is the wide open landscape this new channel presents. As of this writing, Pinterest's Terms of Service were extremely open and had very few limitations on how the service can be leveraged by websites, brands, and marketers. As a result, marketing blogs and discussion forums are chock-full of stories, examples, and ideas of how best to get rolling with your own Pinterest campaigns. Taking advantage of the resources listed in Appendix A of this book will help you keep up-to-date on the latest ideas being kicked around the Web. The newness of this medium also provides inventive social media strategists with an excellent chance to carve out new business niches for themselves and gives brand managers the chance to score impressive wins with creative new tactics.

With *Pinterest Marketing: An Hour A Day,* my goal is to provide not only a step-by-step guide to help you get started with your Pinterest marketing plan, but also to get you thinking about the many ways that Pinterest can be used to improve your website, your content efforts, and even your company as a whole. I hope you will be inspired to create amazing content and to take advantage of the trails created within Pinterest to find and reach out to your brand's biggest evangelists on Pinterest and across the Web.

There are several ways you can use this book. The most straightforward is to start at the beginning and follow each chapter as a step-by-step guide to building, leveraging, measuring, and refining your Pinterest strategy. Alternately, if you've already been using Pinterest and have a solid grasp of the basics, you can skip around from chapter to chapter to absorb the ideas and suggestions for making your Pinterest presence even stronger. However you choose to approach the book, pay special attention to Chapters 8 and 14, which focus heavily on measuring and refining your approach to Pinterest over time. It is with this knowledge that you will be able to create and improve upon your own ideas to make Pinterest a powerful part of your ongoing social media marketing efforts.

What You Will Learn

Pinterest is about more than pretty graphics and do-it-yourself content. It's a place where people go to collect, organize, and share the content that matters to them. It's a source of inspiration and a haven for ideas. This book will help you look past any preconceived notions you may have of Pinterest and will allow you to see it for what it is: an amazingly effective resource that gives companies valuable insight into what matters most to their target audience.

I'll teach you the fundamentals of building a Pinterest presence, but I'll also help you understand how to structure it in a way that allows you to reach a wide and varied audience while still keeping them highly engaged.

I'll also detail the best practices used to attract attention in the extremely competitive world of gathering repins and will help you learn how to increase the potential that your content will be consumed, shared, and archived for future interactions. I'll show which types of contests and which methods of engagement will be the best fit for your style of company and will offer tips and ideas for making even the least sexy brands fare well on this image-based website.

Finally, you'll explore the best ways to measure and refine your efforts over time, focusing in on common problems with Pinterest campaigns and how to combat them. You'll even take a look at the future of Pinterest to explore how this growing channel could impact not only the way people consume content online, but even how search engines value content in the future. Overall, I'll help you view Pinterest as more than just another social media channel so you can grasp the full impact it can have on the way your company does business on the Web.

What You Need

The only thing you really need to get rolling with Pinterest is an Internet connection and a Pinterest account. That said, if you are looking to properly leverage Pinterest as a marketing channel, it's a good idea to have a working knowledge of a solid analytics program (like Google Analytics), access to some image-editing software, and the ability to create or outsource strong content development.

What Is Covered in This Book

Pinterest Marketing: An Hour A Day is organized to provide you with a step by step approach to building a sustainable Pinterest marketing plan.

Chapter 1, "Understanding Pinterest" Unlike social networks designed to help people connect based on relationships, Pinterest serves to connect users based on shared interests and images. This chapter explores what Pinterest is and how and why so many people are using it.

Chapter 2, "Who Uses Pinterest for Marketing and Why?" In Chapter 2, you'll learn why companies are so drawn to Pinterest. I'll talk about how it allows them to engage users and build their brand in a unique way and examine the various types of companies that are most apt to benefit from investing time there.

Chapter 3, "What Makes Pinterest Valuable?" Pinterest is basically a bookmarking site. Those are nothing new; Furl, del.icio.us, and others have been around and popular for quite some time, but Pinterest plays off the collector in all of us.

Chapter 4, "Week 1—Set Up a Pinterest Account" Setting up a Pinterest account and making your first pin takes less than five minutes. I'll walk you through the process step by step and get you ready to start sharing content in no time.

Chapter 5, "Week 2—Curating Content with Pinterest" Pinterest is a powerful online filing system that gives you visual access to the content you might wish to use down the road. This chapter focuses on the many ways to pin content to your account.

Chapter 6, "Week 3—Find and Attract Followers" In this chapter, we'll take a look at the world of user-to-user interactions. You'll learn how to build a following and how to find people of value to follow. We'll also explore how your use of boards can play a strong role in building up your Pinterest presence.

Chapter 7, "Week 4—Purposely Propagating Pins on Pinterest" In this chapter, our focus is on learning how to increase the chances of having your pins propagate through the Pinterest community.

Chapter 8, "Week 5—Track and Monitor Pinterest Traffic" Before we dig too deeply into leveraging Pinterest as a traffic generator and brand building, it's essential to take a look at some of the metrics and measurement behind a good Pinterest campaign.

Chapter 9, "Week 6—Developing a Successful Pinterest Strategy" So far you've built a solid understanding of what Pinterest is, how and why people use it, and what you need to do in order to get your business up and running on it. Now it's time to start exploring the strategy behind Pinterest.

Chapter 10, "Week 7—Leveraging Boards for Better Reach" In this chapter we'll be tackling board structure. We'll look at how and when to rearrange the order, how to organize the boards themselves, how to leverage evangelists and marketing teams for better board content, and how to make use of seasonal and situational boards for short-term marketing efforts.

Chapter 11, "Week 8—Using Pinterest to Attract Traffic"   In this chapter, we'll dive into some of the specific tactics brands and organizations are using to leverage Pinterest for traffic and brand building.

Chapter 12, "Week 9—Using Pinterest to Engage with Fans"   One of the single most powerful forces propelling Pinterest's phenomenal growth is the impressive ability of images to strike at the passion points of people's heartstrings. An essential part of any Pinterest-based social media strategy is an understanding of how to leverage those passion points to better engage with customers and fans.

Chapter 13, "Week 10— Pinterest Marketing Through Contests"   In this chapter, we'll explore the idea of Pinterest contests and how they can benefit your brand while digging through several great examples of what some brands are already doing.

Chapter 14, "Week 11—Measure and Refine Your Strategy"   It's not enough to learn how to leverage Pinterest as a marketing channel; you also have to learn how to refine your approach over time based on how your audience is reacting to your content. This chapter helps you understand how to improve your Pinterest efforts over time.

Chapter 15, "The Future of Pinterest Marketing"   In this chapter, we'll wrap things up by exploring the likely future for Pinterest and by taking a look at just how heavily it's already influenced social media and web culture as a whole.

How to Contact the Author

Jennifer welcomes feedback from you about this book or any questions you may have after reading it. She travels frequently for training and speaking events and welcomes inquiries about having her speak at your upcoming conference or training event. You can reach Jennifer by writing to Jennifer@sugarspunmarketing.com. For more information about her work, please visit her website at www.sugarspunmarketing.com.

Sybex strives to keep you supplied with the latest tools and information you need for your work. Please check their website at www.sybex.com, where we'll post additional content and updates that supplement this book if the need arises. Enter **Pinterest** in the Search box (or type the book's ISBN—9781118403457), and click Go to get to the book's update page.

Understanding Pinterest

As one of the fastest-growing social media channels ever, Pinterest is probably something you've heard plenty of buzz about. "I saw it on Pinterest" is becoming a common answer to the question "where did you learn how to do that?" You might also have heard other website owners or businesses talking about a huge influx of traffic from Pinterest. No matter how Pinterest made it onto your radar, you know you need to learn more about it to best leverage it as part of your social media plan. But first, you have to understand it. In this chapter, we'll explore what Pinterest is and how and why so many people are using it.

Chapter Contents

What Is Pinterest?

Pinterest refers to itself as a "virtual pinboard." Of course if you don't know what a virtual pinboard is, that title doesn't help you very much.

Think of it this way. If you've ever seen someone pull out a card box filled with recipe clippings or a binder full of wedding ideas or inspiration for their next home remodel, you've got the general idea.

Pinterest simply takes that concept and moves it to a socially based online environment. Now users can collect those wedding ideas in a web-based environment where each picture also features a link back to the original source of the content. Pinterest users can connect with and follow the pins of other users who have posted content they find interesting.

Pinterest essentially becomes a community bound together by interests rather than existing personal connections.

Visual Bookmarking

One of the great things about the Internet is the ability to use it to find ideas, inspiration, and guides for nearly any topic known to humankind. Whether you're looking to make insanely great waffles, rebuild the engine on a 1988 Ferrari F40, or create the ultimate bucket list, the Web is a user's best friend.

The problem comes when you stumble across information that's valuable but for which you have no immediate use. This is why web browsers allow users to save pages into collections known as bookmarks. While it's certainly possible for users to categorize and tag these bookmarks, it requires them to read through their listings to find just the right information.

For many users, browser-based bookmarks eventually become a jumbled mess of listings that resemble the previously mentioned box of recipe clippings, as you can see in Figure 1.1.

This obviously harms the user experience because all that great content gets lost in the virtual bottom of the box and users never find their way back.

Pinterest addresses this problem by turning bookmarks into a visual medium. Users can create topical boards and pin the images that inspired them to these boards along with a description and the URL of where they found the information, as shown in Figure 1.2.

This way, instead of trying to read through a jumbled collection of saved title tags, users can spot the content they're looking for by simply browsing the pictures they've pinned to a topical pinboard and immediately clicking through to the content. For web users, Pinterest becomes an ever evolving collection of the things that interest them.

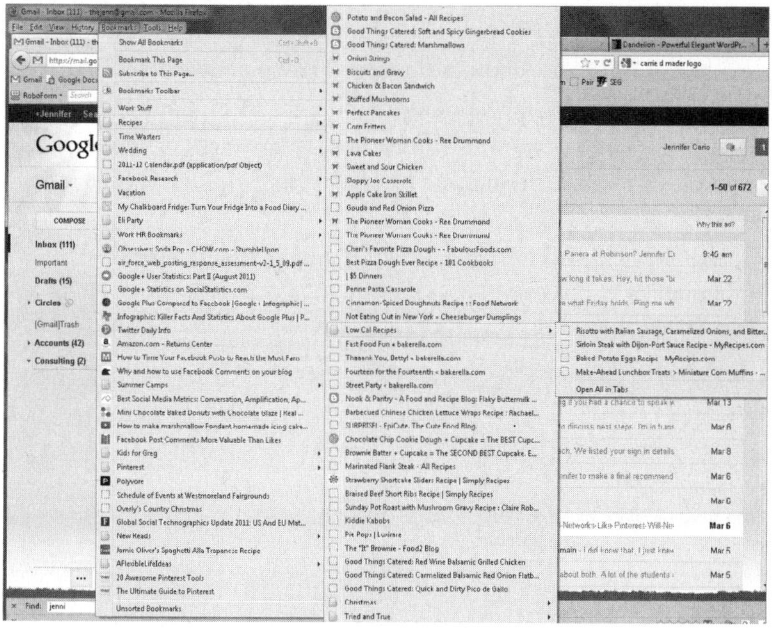

Figure 1.1 The average web user has a large collection of bookmarks that actually tell them very little about what links they've saved.

Figure 1.2 Pinterest boards make it easy for web users to find saved content at a glance.

Visual Idea Searching

Another key differentiator of Pinterest is how it changes the way people search for information. Although search engines like Google and Bing do an excellent job of indexing the billions of pages of content on the Web, they still leave users with the somewhat exhausting task of sorting through listing after listing looking for the information they want.

A standard Google search for birthday cake ideas might turn up a page of results like those shown in Figure 1.3.

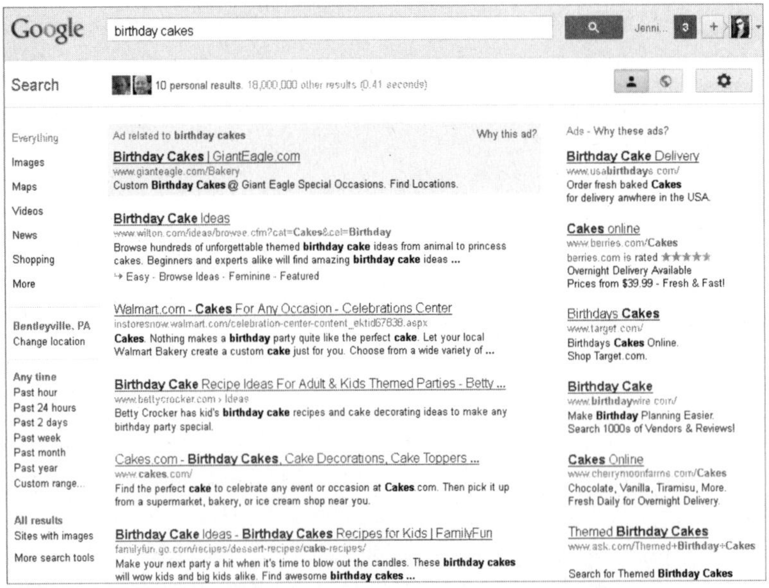

Figure 1.3 Traditional search results are text heavy and image light, requiring users to click on each result to see if it's a fit.

Users are forced to read through the titles and descriptions of various web pages to find the content that will be visually appealing to them. While most search engines integrate image listings into the results, those images are often a mishmash of related and unrelated content.

In the world of Pinterest, keyword searches can be used to search for individual users, topical boards, or individual pins (see Figure 1.4). Using Pinterest to run the same search often turns up a virtual smorgasbord of options and ideas.

The difference in terms of user experience is clear. Search engines deliver up text-based content based on algorithms. Pinterest serves up full visuals based on the content other people have found to be worthwhile.

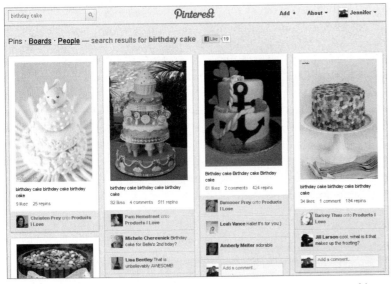

Figure 1.4 Pinterest search results allow users to quickly scroll through visual representations of the content behind the click.

The History of Pinterest

While Pinterest was originally launched as an invitation-only beta in the spring of 2010, it took a while for it to gain notice among social media marketers and mainstream web users. In fact, in December 2010, Pinterest was home to only about 10,000 users.

A full year after its launch, marketers could still be forgiven for their unfamiliarity with the service. After all, Pinterest was a bit like a sneaky, lovable cat—the kind of cat that curls up in the lap of its owner to give warm fuzzies while they pet it but remains quietly invisible to anyone not already in the know. People either knew of Pinterest and used it daily, or had no idea it even existed.

That all changed in the latter half of 2011 when Pinterest started showing up as a strong source of referral traffic for both retail and content-driven websites.

Note: For many content-based sites, Pinterest has quickly become a key source of referral traffic. Shannon King, general manager of *Real Simple* magazine, claimed that Pinterest was responsible for more referral traffic than Facebook during the month of October 2011. In an interview with *AdAge*, King explained that *Real Simple* viewed Pinterest as "an important part of our social media strategy."

Time magazine named Pinterest as one of the "50 Best Websites of 2011" in August of that year, and user and marketer interest quickly picked up steam.

By the end of 2011, the cat was out of the bag and everyone was stepping up for some love. The site reported more than 11 million unique visits per week by the end of 2011, making it a top-10 social media site and the fastest site ever to top 10 million users.

Pinterest's Quietly Explosive Growth

One of the things that makes Pinterest unique from other popular social media sites is the organic nature with which traffic grew and flourished. While most social media sites that perform well in the United States tend to attract early adoption from the coasts, which then expands inward to the general populace, Pinterest followed a different pattern.

An Organically Formed Community

Rather than launching among techies and marketers, Pinterest first attracted crafters and brides-to-be in the heartland of the United States. These users shared the site with their friends via social media channels like Facebook, Twitter, and blogs and quietly built a thriving community of users with little to no influence from big brands or marketers.

In fact, Pinterest founder Ben Silbermann explained in an interview with *The New York Times* that he launched the service in his hometown of Des Moines, Iowa, and by reaching out to crafters and hobby bloggers via the Web.

> **Note:** Silbermann's inspiration for the site came from his penchant for collecting items as a child. "It's like, when you go to a friend's house, you're always excited to see what's on their bookshelf," he said in a March 11, 2012 *New York Times* article. "Behind Pinterest was the idea that if you can put that online, it'd be really exciting for folks."

During the first year the site was in operation, the user base grew primarily by word of mouth and online invitation. Brides-to-be mentioned the site on wedding-oriented forums and talked it up as a great place to collect ideas. Crafting bloggers started mentioning it as a great source of inspiration and shared do-it-yourself (DIY) style ideas. Foodies started uploading food porn and collecting the recipes they wanted to try.

As more users joined in, they talked the site up to their friends or mentioned "I found the idea on Pinterest" on their blog, and legions more signed up.

Silbermann created a product that didn't have to be hyped by the tech-savvy influencers of the Web. In fact, while the tech world was talking about Google+, the rest of America was quietly adopting Pinterest and using it to change the way they use the Web.

Demographics

Part of the big appeal of Pinterest for marketers is the current demographic makeup of the site. The average user is a female between the ages of 25 and 34 who hails from middle America. Half of them have children and nearly a third of them are from families with household incomes of more than $100,000 per year.

According to data from DoubleClick (Figure 1.5), the site skews heavily toward women, a fact that isn't surprising given that food and crafts are currently the most popular topics on the site.

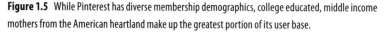

Sources: ComScore, Experian Hitwise, Alexa

Figure 1.5 While Pinterest has diverse membership demographics, college educated, middle income mothers from the American heartland make up the greatest portion of its user base.

Although men have begun streaming into the site as it's risen in popularity, women still make up the greatest majority of the active user base. In fact, 97 percent of Pinterest's followers on Facebook are female.

These are the same women who make the greatest majority of purchasing decisions in the retail market, making Pinterest an extremely attractive place for brands to build connections with consumers.

Perhaps the biggest differentiator of Pinterest demographics compared to other popular social media sites is the geographical breakdown. While most social media sites have high adoption rates in major metropolitan areas and the East and West coasts, Pinterest's most active users are from America's heartland.

States like Utah, Alabama, Oklahoma, and Tennessee lead the way among active Pinterest users. This makes Pinterest an especially attractive social media channel for advertisers who are already successfully engaging with coastal and metropolitan users on other social media channels but have not yet been able to fully tap the Middle America market.

How Pinterest Makes Money

Like most social media channels, Pinterest was launched with a focus on user experience and growth. While Pinterest has had no problem attracting angel investors to power its development machine, Pinterest had no clear-cut revenue model in place when this book went to print.

On the Pinterest Help page (http://pinterest.com/about/help/), the site explains its revenue model this way:

> *Right now, we are focused on growing Pinterest and making it more valuable. To fund these efforts, we have taken outside investment from entrepreneurs and venture capitalists. In the past, we've tested a few different approaches to making money such as affiliate links. We might also try adding advertisements, but we haven't done this yet.*
>
> *Even though making money isn't our top priority right now, it is a long term goal. After all, we want Pinterest to be here to stay!*

Affiliate Links

One of the more public ways Pinterest has explored monetization as the site has grown has been to explore the use of affiliate links to generate small portions of revenue each time a user follows a relevant link and makes a product purchase. Pinterest accomplished this via what they called a "test run" with the company Skimlinks.

Skimlinks helped Pinterest monetize the site by searching for pinned images that linked to websites featuring an affiliate program. If no affiliate code was included in the link when it was originally pinned, Skimlinks would automatically generate and insert the appropriate affiliate code.

As the volume of activity on Pinterest increased, Skimlinks allowed the site to pull in ongoing revenue from user activity without the need for intrusive ads or premium accounts.

In January 2012, several bloggers made note that their pins were being edited by the inclusion of affiliate links. In the firestorm of conversation and controversy that followed, Pinterest announced that it had already terminated its relationship with Skimlinks and was exploring other ways of monetizing the site.

Ad Platform Potential

A natural source of revenue for Pinterest to explore will be targeted advertising opportunities. Much like Google, Facebook, and Twitter before it, Pinterest has the potential to gather an extraordinary amount of insight and data on its users.

In fact, Facebook's foray into the world of paid advertising has demonstrated the lucrative ad market potential for a company that can aggregate specific data on what its users like best and how they interact with their social media–based connections.

Chances are high that Pinterest will work to develop a targeted ad platform that focuses on the benefits derived from the site, including the following:

Contextual Advertising Advertisers could easily match ads to specific topics, displaying them when users run searches or browse certain categories.

Premium Pins   Pinterest could allow brands and users to pay a fee to promote their pins to the top of category listings or to be permanently listed at the tops of the boards they are pinned to.

Sponsored Pins   Following the style of sponsored posts on blogs and sponsored tweets, Pinterest could allow power users the option of receiving payment for highlighting pins from advertisers.

Board-Based Advertising   With boards so carefully curated by topic and tagged as part of Pinterest's overall categorization system, advertisers could easily buy topical space at the top of users' boards.

Premium Account Potential

Most social media sites have shied away from subscription-based models, but several have successfully generated revenue from users by offering "freemium: and premium versions of a similar user experience.

Flickr, a popular social media–based image-sharing site that flourished in the early 2000s, offered a premium model that removed the cap on the number and size of the images that could be posted. Millions of users paid $25 a year to have unlimited access to the service.

It is possible Pinterest could consider placing limitations on the number of boards a user could curate unless they paid for a premium membership. It is also possible Pinterest could allow users to opt out of any advertising models by paying a yearly subscription fee for the service.

Pinterest's Long-Term Potential

The single biggest question marketers tend to have when new social media channels experience explosive growth is whether or not the channel has the potential to go the distance. After all, the big risk of being an early adopter is wasting time building a presence for an audience that never materializes.

While Pinterest experienced steady growth during the first 18 months of its existence, the sudden explosion in exposure and interest at the end of 2011 has led many to wonder if Pinterest is simply the latest in a series of sites that will flourish and then fade away. As someone who has been in the online marketing industry since the late 1990s, I've seen many companies rise to the spotlight before fading away as the "ooh shiny" mentality wears off and people move on to the next new thing. When I consider the qualities present in the social media channels that go the distance, I believe Pinterest has all the makings of a long-term social media player.

Early-to-Market Advantage

Perhaps the single biggest advantage Pinterest has in the realm of social media image duration is the fact that it got there first. The years have shown that the first company to reach critical mass on a newly developed social media channel tends to rule the roost for the long haul.

Dozens of sites have challenged YouTube without ever coming close to capturing a high percentage of the video market. The same can be said for Twitter's many challengers. While Facebook did need to beat out MySpace to take the reigning position as the king of social networking, it managed to do so while social networking channels were still in their infancy.

Pinterest rose to popularity with a product that provided what no other site was offering: an excellent user experience that allowed members to do something no other site did. There are bound to be challengers, but it's mighty hard to knock the king off the hill once that hill has become Mt. Everest.

Third-Party Integration

When you consider the sheer amount of data being collected by Pinterest right now, it's a bit staggering. Millions upon millions of individuals are actively cataloging their likes, their plans, and their sources of inspiration on a single website. Pinterest's server system is poised to become one of the largest consumer insight machines that has ever been put together.

A key difference between Pinterest and other social media sites is that Pinterest doesn't just track the information consumers deem worthy of actively sharing with their connections. Social networks like Facebook and microblogging platforms like Twitter are designed to give users a place to broadcast content. It's where users go to showcase the best of the best of what they've discovered online. It's where they stake their personal reputation on the idea that other people will also be interested in a piece of content.

Pinterest is an entirely different type of website. It's where users focus on collecting ideas and information for themselves. They just happen to be doing it in an environment where their contacts are free to take a peek. This opens the door for a very different type of user data for advertisers.

While sites like Facebook and Twitter allowed advertisers to learn who consumers interacted with and sites like Foursquare allowed them to understand the retail locations they frequented, Pinterest gives advertisers the ability to understand what sparks passion in their users.

Overlaying the data being collected at Pinterest with the data available via other social media channels leads to powerful advertising potential. Consider the following scenarios:

> **A retail store** receives notification via a social check-in app that a user has entered the store. The app integrates with Pinterest's interest graph data on that customer and takes note of any products from the store's retail site that have been pinned. A discount on those products is offered to the individual.

An ad network partners with both Facebook and Pinterest and overlays the user data from each site to create a highly targeted ad system. Advertisers would know an individual user's age, geographical location, employment status, social connection level, and propensity for sharing content or engaging with shared content along with a fully cataloged listing of every topic, item, and concept they've chosen to archive.

Gathering and understanding demographics has gotten easier and easier as social networks have emerged and analytical technology has improved. Adding psychographic data to the mix offers up a powerful combination for companies looking to reach highly targeted customers.

Sustainability for Users

A key factor likely to contribute to the ongoing growth and future stability of Pinterest is the ease of use for the system. There's no need to devote much time and effort to the service. Few users generate original content. There's no need to create and edit videos to upload or to research and write blog posts. In fact, there's not even a reason for users to leave the site.

The greatest majority of pin activity comes from "repins," meaning users are simply taking images that have been pinned by other users and adding them to their own categories. This makes Pinterest more of a time killer than a time sink, unless users get completely caught up in browsing original content.

Pinterest is one of the few social media channels that requires absolutely no content creation by its users. This makes it one of the least time consuming of all social media channels. It also makes it extremely attractive to both busy consumers and thinly stretched marketing departments.

Who Uses Pinterest for Marketing and Why?

Every now and then a social media channel comes along that allows people to express themselves in an entirely new way.

Pinterest appeals to users because it allows them to collect and curate the things that interest them in a way no other service has done. At a basic level, it appeals to marketers because it appeals to users.

Of course, it's more complicated than that. In this chapter, we'll explore why companies are so drawn to Pinterest. We'll talk about how it allows them to engage users and build their brand in a unique way, and we'll examine the various types of companies that are most apt to benefit from investing time there.

Chapter Contents

Why Are Companies Using Pinterest?

This is the single most important question you need to ask yourself before setting up a Pinterest strategy for your business. Why do you want to be there? What do you hope to gain? Otherwise, Pinterest runs the risk of becoming yet another well-intentioned time sink for your social media team.

Despite its relatively young status as an emerging social media channel, Pinterest has already demonstrated a wide range of possibilities for companies looking to drive traffic, gain consumer insight, and build stronger ties with their customer base. Learning how to best leverage Pinterest for your brand starts with understanding how other brands are already using it.

To Drive Traffic

If there is one thing Pinterest has demonstrated in its reasonably short social media life, it's an ability to generate an astonishing amount of traffic. In fact, only a few months after marketers first took notice of the service, Pinterest started showing up in the top-10 referrers listing for major retailers and content publishers across the Web.

In the summer of 2011, MarthaStewartWeddings.com claimed that Pinterest was sending more traffic to their website than Facebook and Twitter combined. By the spring of 2012, *Cooking Light* was receiving three times the traffic from Pinterest than it was from Facebook, making Pinterest second only to Google in terms of how much traffic it was feeding in to the site.

Even in a world where only a very small portion of websites have explored the idea of encouraging pins, Pinterest sends very impressive amounts of traffic. In a survey of over 200,000 publishers by Shareaholic, Pinterest was found to send more referral traffic than Twitter, making it second only to Facebook in terms of the amount of traffic it sends to the average website (see Figure 2.1).

April 2012 All Traffic Sources Report			
Source	Share of Visits - January	Share of Visits - February	Share of Visits March	Share of Visits- April
Google (Organic)	48.9%	48.81%	48.48%	48.88%
Direct	19.44%	18.20%	18.32%	18.44%
Facebook	6.92%	6.38%	6.08%	6.10%
Yahoo	1.60%	1.61%	1.67%	1.67%
Bing	1.24%	1.21%	1.27%	1.29%
StumbleUpon	1.30%	1.29%	1.05%	1.13%
Google (Referral)	.68%	0.91%	.99%	1.05%
Twitter	.88%	.82%	.85%	.85%
Pinterest	.85%	1.05%	.80%	.74%

Presented by:

Figure 2.1 Pinterest is quickly overtaking long established social media sites as a powerful traffic source.

It's not just large publishers and online retailers that are experiencing traffic bumps from Pinterest. Small businesses and independent bloggers are also reaping the benefits of what can often lead to phenomenal amounts of traffic.

Christina Refford of The Fairly Odd Mother found out exactly what Pinterest is capable of in early 2012. Christina's blog, which she'd been plugging away at for over six years, averaged 150 or so visitors per day. Until Pinterest happened.

One day Christina's blog received a mostly average 120 visitors; the next day traffic exploded to more than 25,000 visitors. An additional 15,000 visitors followed the very next day (see Figure 2.2).

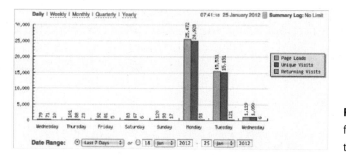

Figure 2.2 Pinterest was responsible for an astonishing spike in traffic over the course of a single day.

What caused the spike? A single blog post that turned into a Pinterest frenzy. Christina had made a post about setting aside a $5 bill every time she came across one and then sharing her year-end tally. The idea struck a chord with Pinterest users and the blog post was pinned, repinned, and repinned again. A total of more than 8,500 pins came in for that one post, as shown in Figure 2.3. And traffic exploded accordingly. Christina saw more than 60,000 page loads occur in the week that followed. That's quite a traffic bump for a small blog that normally only pulls a few thousand visitors per month.

Figure 2.3 Christina's blog post was pinned dozens of times and repinned thousands of times.

It wasn't just a short-term spike either. More than two months later, Christina was still seeing regular traffic levels of around 450 page views per day, roughly three to four times higher than her pre-Pinterest levels. A large portion of those visitors are still being traced to Pinterest as new people find, pin, and revisit the blog.

The challenge in all this traffic is learning how to retain it and how to leverage it toward conversion opportunities, but we'll talk more about that in Chapter 9, "Week 6–Developing a Successful Pinterest Strategy."

To Generate (and Track) Loyalty

When it comes to marketing, it's essential to look past traffic alone as a goal for your marketing plan. For many companies, Pinterest becomes an ideal way to generate and even track loyalty to their brand.

Consumers tend to enjoy receiving information in the environments they are comfortable in. In the early days of social media, tools like Really Simple Syndication (RSS) readers allowed users to quickly scan through the latest posts from all the blogs they were following. RSS feeds eventually gave way to Twitter feeds, as users realized they'd rather hear about the specific articles being read and enjoyed by their trusted network.

When Facebook came into its own, brands quickly realized the need to tie their feeds into their Facebook pages so fans and brand loyalists could consume brand-based content in an environment where they were already spending time.

As Pinterest use has grown, users are programmed to seek out content from other Pinterest users who share their tastes and interests. In many cases, this includes brands. After all, the outdoor adventurer will probably be very interested in the latest adventure gear and camping advice from REI (see Figure 2.4) or Patagonia. Even more so, they're interested in the travel destinations, training tips, and how-to guides provided by trusted brands—especially if the brands are carrying an appropriate balance of self-promoting content to third-party content.

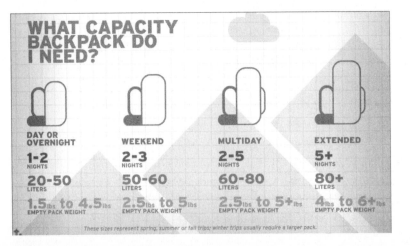

Figure 2.4 REI offers pinned content showing how to choose the proper size backpack for a camping trip

Pinterest provides the opportunity to relate to consumers in a completely new way. It gives brands the chance to demonstrate the value they can bring to the everyday life of a customer by offering up the things that customer is seeking. It also gives them a chance to build consumer loyalty by positioning themselves as a go-to resource for the things related to their line of business.

The other side of the loyalty angle comes in the ability to see which users are most loyal to your brand in more practical terms. Because Pinterest allows brands to monitor content being pinned from their domain, it is possible for brands to see which users repeatedly pin content from the brand's website, as shown in Figure 2.5.

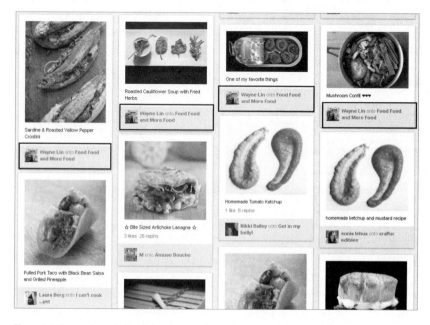

Figure 2.5 By examining the list of pinned content from a domain, you can see which users are pinning multiple items of content from the site.

It's important to keep in mind that simply pinning multiple pieces of content doesn't always signify a loyal reader. When content is posted in immediate succession, it's quite likely a visitor spent time going through the site pinning the items that struck their interest and then never returned. That's why it's important to look at the bigger picture to see who repeatedly pins new content over longer periods of time.

Note: It's interesting to note that the ultimate number of repins a post receives rarely correlates to how many followers a Pinterest user has. Because so many Pinterest users explore the topical streams, it's not at all uncommon to see a brand-new Pinterest user generate a pin that gets repinned 5,000+ or more times.

Similarly, it's not just about pinning the content when it comes to measuring impactful loyalty. It's about learning which Pinterest users pin content that gets repinned and results in traffic. That's why it's also important to look at the number of repins on an individual pin to see which pinners make posts that go the distance (see Figure 2.6).

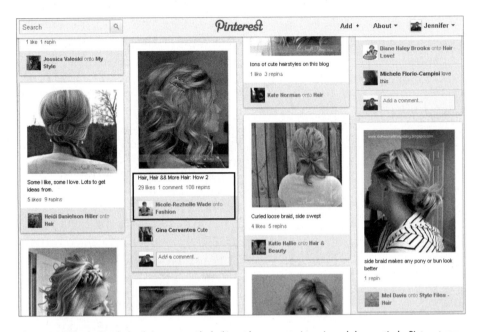

Figure 2.6 When looking for loyal pinners, consider looking at how many repins a pin made by a particular Pinterest user receives to help determine value.

As Pinterest metrics and analysis programs continue to grow, learning which users create the most pin activity and drive the most traffic back to a website will become even easier.

To Demonstrate Product Potential

One of the most powerful ways brands are leveraging Pinterest is to show their product being used in different scenarios. The quest to display product potential is nothing new on the Social Web. Product reviews on major retail sites like Amazon, Target, and Wal-Mart have long been used by Internet consumers to gain a better understanding of how a product fares in the real world. Video-based social sites like YouTube are regularly leveraged for demonstration-based product reviews, and consumers regularly turn to sites like Twitter and Facebook to ask for input on product purchases before making them.

The benefit of leveraging Pinterest when it comes to product potential is the freedom of both the brand and consumers to work together to showcase a product's potential.

The popular Greek yogurt brand Chobani was one of the first retail brands to start exploring ways to leverage Pinterest. Demonstrating product potential is one of the key opportunities they hit on from the start. With pinboards like "Chobaniac Creations" and "Simple Swaps," Chobani has built a Pinterest presence around showing the various ways their product can be integrated into a healthy lifestyle.

Their Chobaniac Creations board features recipes the Chobani team has found posted on the Web using Chobani products as ingredients (see Figure 2.7).

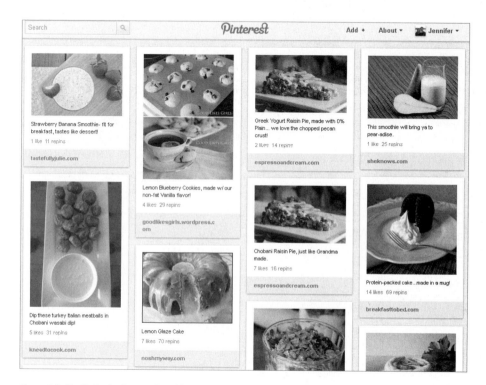

Figure 2.7 The Chobaniac Creations board features recipes from across the Web that incorporate Chobani products.

Chobani has been able to pair this strategy with outreach efforts to bloggers. In early 2012, Chobani sent packages of their latest flavors to food and mom bloggers and invited them to get creative with the ingredients. The resulting flood of blog posts resulted in tons of pinnable fodder for the Chobani branded boards.

Not satisfied to simply showcase the people already using their product, the team has creatively set up an additional board featuring non-Chobani recipes. The pins made to this board include descriptive instructions telling users which ingredients they can swap out for various Chobani products (see Figure 2.8).

Figure 2.8 The Simple Swaps board expands on the Chobani recipe options by explaining where to make substitutions.

The potential for a strategy like this extends to quite a wide range of brands and companies. Fashion brands are already beginning to set up boards featuring the complete look created by customers using their products. Home improvement and gardening brands could easily set up showcase-style pinboards. Even business-to-business (B2B)-based businesses could link to implementation and integration images showing their products or ideas at work.

To Better Understand Consumers

One of the key areas of interest and exploration for many brands when it comes to Pinterest is the idea of gaining additional consumer insight. While web analytics have long allowed companies to have insight on how consumers interact with their brand online, Pinterest opens the door to additional observations.

When it comes to understanding how and why consumers choose to interact with and or share your content, Pinterest allows site owners and content developers to better understand what catches the eye of their readers.

What Picture Do They Pin?

In a world like Pinterest where visual impact matters greatly, there's amazing opportunity to test various approaches to image delivery. This holds especially true for content you've created that may include several variations of the same image or concept.

Do they pin the finished project, or specific steps along the way? Do they pin images with text or images that have been left to speak for themselves? Looking at the list of pins from your specific website can make it easy to tell at a glance if a certain type of photograph is playing well with your audience (see Figure 2.9).

Figure 2.9 When Shannon Brown featured a blog post about giving a year of dates to her husband, pinners chose several different images for their pins but favored a picture of the gift basket itself.

During my own testing with one particular client site, we were able to see several dozen pins come in for the finished product image of a particular how-to style post. Upon building and submitting a collage-style image of the most important steps, that number skyrocketed to hundreds of pins in a matter of an hour or two. Since traffic click-through rates were strong for both types of pin, it quickly became apparent there was great value in taking the time to create Pinterest-specific images for certain types of posts.

On Which Area of the Article Were They Focused?

Another useful bit of analysis that can come from exploring pins is the level of activity around certain images in compilation posts. If your brand has made a post about 10 ways to spruce up your backyard on a budget and the greatest majority of pins to that post include one specific image, it's generally safe to assume your customers would like more ideas of that variety.

This is an area where Pinterest offers insight that most standard web analytics packages do not. With the rare exception of companies who use eye tracking software, it's next to impossible to tell which area of an article a user paused to investigate. With Pinterest, those interest levels clearly show through in the choice of image made by the user when pinning content.

This is also useful for exploring how Pinterest users and consumers like to see your product in use. Are they caught up in dreams while they look at your product in high-end design showcases? Or do they focus more on how your high-ticket item is used in more cost-effective designs to allow for a balanced budget?

What Are the Names of Their Pinboards?

One of the most surprising things to me during my early days on Pinterest was watching content I'd meant for one audience be collected and archived by someone with a different use in mind.

For example, I posted images and a detailed step-by-step blog post of how I built a prop wall photo booth for my wedding. As the pins started rolling in, I fully expected them to be filed away under boards like "wedding ideas" and "photo booths." Instead, the greatest majority of activity was from moms who were filing the picture in boards marked "Joey's birthday party" and "Summer Camp ideas."

Taking the time to see how users are classifying your content can go a long way toward helping you understand why it appealed to them. If your low-fat and low-calorie recipes are continually being pinned to boards titled "Weight Watchers" and "WW recipes," you'd better make sure you invest in calculating and listing the Weight Watchers points with your recipes.

To Establish Brand Personality

One of the primary ways companies have benefited from social media is in the ability to take what appears to be a nameless, faceless company and portray it as an entity that has taste, vision, and opinions. Giving a "voice" to a business has been one of the primary reasons companies have turned to social media. That voice can then be used to engage in dialogue with customers and to lead them down the path to conversion.

Businesses have long worked to establish a "feeling" or "perception" of the personality for their brand. Whether it's about the clean-cut professional image of a women's clothing store like Ann Taylor or the sense of fearless exploration associated with outdoor adventure retailer REI, businesses want their customers to relate to them in a specific way.

Because Pinterest focuses so heavily on the collection of images and ideas in a categorized manner, companies have the chance to showcase both content related to their businesses as well as content that supports their brand. In other words, they can use Pinterest in much the same way an individual can to shore up the imagery or relation of the brand with things potential customers are interested in.

Modern furniture design company West Elm uses Pinterest to showcase the kind of style and design its customers crave. They've curated boards featuring urban backyards or creative reuse of old products to appeal to the general style of customers, but they haven't stopped there. They've also worked to build and curate boards around various design themes (see Figure 2.10).

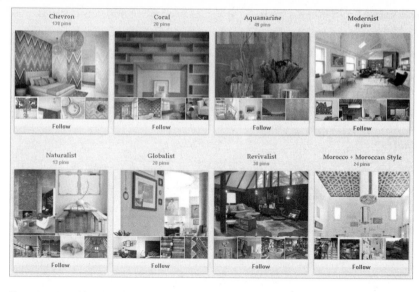

Figure 2.10 West Elm curates design boards around various colors and themes.

This helps cement West Elm as a go-to resource for design inspiration and creative color and pattern usage. Pinterest becomes an extension of the content strategy that drives more brand blogs. Share a little bit about yourself and share a lot about the things that interest your customers. Following this technique allows blogging brands to occasionally work in the appropriate product plug. Following this technique on Pinterest has the same effect (see Figure 2.11).

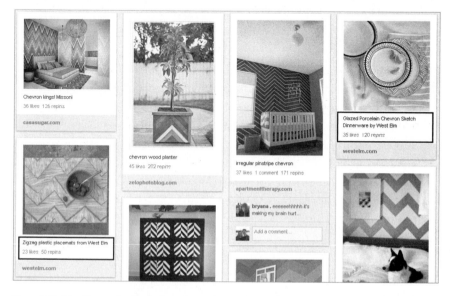

Figure 2.11 West Elm occasionally pins items from its lineup into topically curated design boards.

For brands exploring Pinterest and asking themselves why consumers would want to connect with them in this environment, the topical boards of established Pinterest brands should serve as inspiration. Ask yourself what your brand represents and what the people who buy from you love, and then build boards around those concepts to attract a loyal following.

What Types of Companies Can Benefit from Using Pinterest?

It would be a mistake to write Pinterest off as the type of social media channel that works best for any one type of company. The truth is, companies of all sizes and focuses are finding ways to build community, connect with customers, and support their brand identities via Pinterest.

While each type of company or organization may have different areas that will benefit them most clearly, Pinterest presents a new frontier for creative marketers to both build and leverage additional audiences.

Bloggers

Outside of individual users flocking to the service to find inspiration and collect ideas, bloggers were among the first to see the potential value of Pinterest. Clearly the potential for dramatically increasing their traffic was a driving factor, but for most bloggers, the value of Pinterest goes deeper.

In a world where bloggers are continually searching for new topics to write about, new approaches to old problems, and better insight into what's striking the world's fancy at any particular moment, Pinterest offers a world of insight and inspiration.

Inspiration for Projects and Blog Posts

Whether it's home improvement ideas, places to travel next summer, or a new knitting technique, bloggers are turning to Pinterest and building inspiration boards for the very things they spend their days blogging about.

Pinterest becomes the perfect place to set up a holding ground of ideas. Whether it's storing up recipes, gathering birthday party ideas, or sorting through various techniques to build a new deck, Pinterest makes it easier for bloggers to keep track of ideas they'd like to try down the road. Pinterest's search features also give bloggers the chance to search for different approaches or take on a specific topic and to gather them for future testing.

When you are browsing through boards, it's not uncommon to see one category for future ideas (such as Recipes/Desserts) and another for tested and approved ideas (such as Tried and True Recipes), as shown in Figure 2.12.

Figure 2.12 Many bloggers use Pinterest to store ideas for future use and subsequent blog posts.

Watching the trend in topics or approaches on Pinterest can also be a great way for bloggers to identify hot topics for their own blogs. Food bloggers noticed a non-stop parade of cake batter–flavored recipes come strolling through their Pinterest radar in early 2012. Experimental food bloggers then set to work inventing every variation of cake batter dip, fudge, ice cream, popcorn, and so on, that could be imagined.

Almost overnight, Pinterest gave birth to (and helped shape) a brand-new flavor obsession. Bloggers who had their eyes open were able to get in on the trend early and reap the benefit of future pins and traffic.

Compilation Post Potential

Another popular way bloggers utilize Pinterest is for the creation of compilation posts. Bloggers have long worked to gather different takes on a single topic from around the Web in order to create monster-size posts designed to attract links and traffic. Prior to Pinterest, doing so involved long hours slugging through search results and jumping from one blog to another.

In the era of Pinterest, it can be as simple as making a blog post out of the boards you've been putting together. A Pinterest user who loads up on kid-friendly Easter crafts during the current Easter season can easily tap that board the next March to prepare a post about "21 Easy Easter Crafts & Activities" prior to the holiday (see Figure 2.13). Compilation blog posts are also a great way to introduce readers to a new board to increase Pinterest followers.

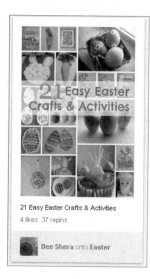

Figure 2.13 Pinterest offers excellent fodder for compilation posts.

Expanding Their Blog Community

For bloggers who are seeking to increase their contacts with other bloggers in the same topical communities, Pinterest is a great way to connect. Much like Twitter, Pinterest opens the door for topical searches and daisy-chain connections that can lead to the discovery of other bloggers who are active in social media circles.

Retail Stores

For retailers who target the primary Pinterest demographic of middle American women, Pinterest provides a key opportunity to match product to consumer. Users don't just pin links to recipes and how-to posts; they also actively pin and repin their favorite products and gift ideas.

For that reason, retailers were among the first to start noticing an increase in direct traffic and ultimate conversions from Pinterest. As Pinterest grew in grassroots popularity, major retailers like West Elm, Nordstrom, and ModCloth noticed inbound traffic and began exploring ways to leverage the site to drive additional traffic and sales.

By early 2012, Pinterest was one of the top social media sites across the board in terms of referrer traffic to major retailers. Retailers are leveraging Pinterest in a variety of creative ways.

Pinning Products with Gift Designations

Pinterest's product listing feature adds a price tag overlay to any pin that includes a price in its description (see Figure 2.14). Pinterest also includes a category called Gifts that segments listings by price point.

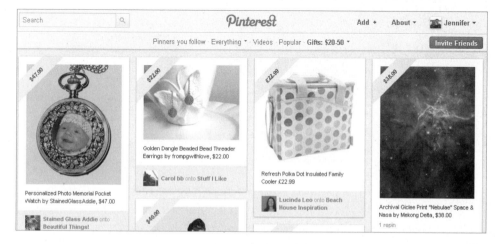

Figure 2.14 Pinterest adds a price tag to any pin that features a dollar amount in the description.

As Pinterest grows in popularity and more consumers turn to Pinterest boards to hunt for gift ideas and product solutions, brands will need to increase their focus on motivating customers to pin their favorite products.

Encouraging Customers to Pin Their Favorite Products

Another way brands are driving traffic and sales is by encouraging existing customers and shoppers to share their favorite items via Pinterest. In fact, as Pinterest referrer levels have started to rise, online retailers have moved to add "Pin it" buttons to their product pages.

Big-name retail sites like Etsy, Aeropostale, Barneys New York, and Hanes are now including "Pin it" buttons alongside other top-tier social sharing buttons from Facebook and Twitter (see Figure 2.15).

Figure 2.15 Barneys New York product pages all include a "Pin it" button alongside other major social sharing options.

While many Pinterest users are already actively pinning their favorite products to boards, several retailers have taken the push a step further and sponsored contests oriented around board curation and product pinning.

Showcasing New Products

It's important to note that successful sharing of retail products on Pinterest requires the same balance seen in other forms of social media. Brands that focus exclusively on promotion will have a hard time attracting followers and gaining credibility with the community. That's why retailers like Frederick's of Hollywood are finding balance by showcasing their new catalog products alongside pinboards designed to boost the brand (see Figure 2.16).

Other retail sites push their partnership with services like Polyvore, a site allowing consumers to create a collage of their favorite products from a variety of retailers to present a complete outfit (see Figure 2.17). These collages are then shared via social media sites like Pinterest where they, in turn, lead additional consumers back to the site to find out where each product can be purchased online.

Figure 2.16 Frederick's of Hollywood showcases vintage ads and vintage Hollywood photos to gain traction and audience for their new catalog items.

Figure 2.17 Collage creation services like Polyvore allow Pinterest users to incorporate several different products into a single pin.

Online Publications

One type of business that has seen a massive amount of benefit from Pinterest has been online publications. Because these ad-driven sites can focus on driving traffic without always having to worry about eventual conversion, Pinterest holds a great deal of potential.

Magazines like *Martha Stewart Living*, *Cooking Light*, and *Country Living* receive a large portion of their social media–based traffic from Pinterest. *Real Simple* reported in early 2012 that it was receiving more referral traffic from Pinterest than it was from Facebook. To understand this trend, you need to know what makes an image-based network like Pinterest so well suited to content sites.

Pinterest users value the ability to scan through ideas and inspiration in image form. In many cases, they save images simply because they can. They build boards full of images of the places they might like to visit or the things that make them smile. At the same time, they're often busy curating boards filled with photos of things they want to do. They're looking for new recipes, new ways to approach fashion, and new tips and ideas for organizing their lives. In other words, they're looking for the exact type of content served up by online magazines and content networks.

That makes Pinterest an ideal place to market content to a target audience that may not already be familiar with your site. It also makes Pinterest an ideal channel to leverage your existing audience.

Actively Encourage Pins

While adding the "Pin it" button to content pages can help, actively encouraging users to pin content to their favorite boards as they research ideas and look for inspiration can also increase Pinterest activity.

Reminders attached to new article series, specially crafted Pinterest-friendly images, and the occasional callout within page content can go a long way toward reminding users to share content with their Pinterest network.

Cross-Promote Your Pinterest Boards

An excellent way to use existing content as a Pinterest launch board is to create a pinboard tied to an article series or content feature. *Health* magazine did this when they created a Jillian Michaels–themed pinboard to coincide with Michaels' appearance as the March cover model (see Figure 2.18).

Figure 2.18 *Health* magazine's Jillian Michaels–themed pinboard featured images of the fitness guru as well as pins to content from the magazine.

Health magazine then hosted a 45-minute Facebook chat with Michaels, which it cross-promoted via Twitter. Both conversations referenced and pointed users to the newly created pinboard.

Consider Contests

It's not just about making your site Pinterest friendly; it's also about figuring out creative ways to increase the engagement and activity levels of your target audience. One online publisher who has done this effectively is *Better Homes & Gardens*. The brand ran a "Pin & Win" contest in the spring of 2012 asking fans to create a pinboard called "My Better Homes and Gardens Dream Home" (see Figure 2.19).

Figure 2.19 More than one thousand Pinterest users created new pinboards to enter the *Better Homes & Gardens* Pin & Win contest.

These boards were required to feature at least 10 pins from the BHG.com website, and entrants had to register their contest pinboard with *Better Homes & Gardens* to enter. Finalists were awarded cash prizes toward their remodeling projects, and *Better Homes & Gardens* was rewarded with a flood of new pins pointing toward their site.

Big Brands

Pinterest has also opened a new door of opportunity for big brands when it comes to better engaging their loyal followers as well as reaching out to consumers who may not yet be tied to the brand. Companies like Coke, Disney, and PlayStation have already built monstrous followings on Facebook as a way to stay top of mind with consumers. Now these brands have a way to move past the continued pressure of engagement and into a world of sharing and collecting on a new channel.

Several brands are already finding ways to further cement the emotional and topical ties to their name by cleverly curating brand-supportive boards.

Go for the Obvious Tie-in

Coupled with Pinterest, visually intensive brands like HGTV are a match made in Marketing Heaven. Between pinned images from the latest seasons of their various TV shows to themed boards targeting the DIY crowd, the TV network focuses on delivering up the same content people tune into their shows for (see Figure 2.20).

Figure 2.20 HGTV has focused on curating content related to their shows, magazine, and overall brand image.

For many businesses, Pinterest offers a world of easy opportunity. Most brands can consider the way people use their products or services and pin content related to those concepts. For others, Pinterest offers more challenge.

Focus on the Lifestyle of Your Customers

There are some brands that have become as much a business for who they are as they are for what they sell.

Companies like Coca-Cola and Kodak are using Pinterest to reinforce the iconic nature of their brands. Coca-Cola curates boards focused on life like "Be Together" and "Be Giving." Kodak plays off their role in helping people share memories with boards titled "Photos That Help Us Remember" and "Photo Story Telling."

In these instances, pinboards become yet another way to reinforce the visuals, emotions, and images brands work so hard to associate with their names.

Focus on Becoming a Resource

There's a distinct challenge in approaching Pinterest successfully for non-sexy brands. It's easy enough to show people various ways to use your products or to entice them with inspiring images that relate to the lifestyle they want to live. It's another thing entirely to wow them with your sexy…knowledge.

That's where brands like Mashable have done well. By curating boards like "Infographics," "Web Humor," and "Tip and Tricks" (see Figure 2.21), Mashable has been able to gain a loyal following with an audience interested in staying up-to-date on the latest web-related news.

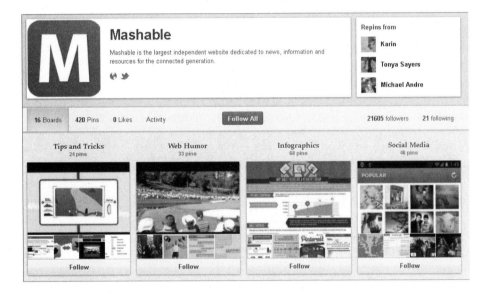

Figure 2.21 Mashable regularly pins content related to the topics they cover.

Small Business

For small businesses, Pinterest offers yet another way to showcase their personality and to build stronger emotional connections and loyalty levels with customers. Pinterest offers all the benefits listed earlier for larger brands and retailers, but it holds a few extra enticements for small businesses.

A Social Media Channel That Doesn't Require Babysitting

One of the single biggest reasons Pinterest appeals to small business owners is because of the amount of time required (or rather *not* required) to properly maintain an account. In a world where staffing and budget are already stretched paper thin, new social media channels are rarely welcomed with open arms. Pinterest rocks the boat a bit in terms of what's expected of the user.

Pinterest is more about curating and sharing than it is about having conversations. There's no need for immediate response when someone pins or repins your content. Best of all, there's no need to invest time daily to maintain an interest level from your audience.

For small businesses looking for a way to build followers, be viewed as a resource, and establish a brand identity, Pinterest can be a dream come true. A company's Pinterest manager can do the work of repinning content during a five-minute break from their smartphone. They can also pin content as they run across it during the normal course of their workday. As long as they can avoid the sucking draw of addiction, Pinterest can add impact without requiring much additional time.

The Opportunity to Recruit Help

Another primary reason Pinterest appeals to small business owners is because of the ability to recruit help with pinboards. Pinterest allows boards to be curated and managed by multiple users. That means brands can open specific boards to trusted evangelists and loyal customers and let them do the work on behalf of the brand.

In many cases, bloggers or topically related social media users will band together to co-curate a board related to their interests (see Figure 2.22). Small businesses can use this same technique to allow their customers to help them better represent the business.

Figure 2.22 More than 100 craft bloggers have banded together to curate the Kid Blogger Network Activities & Crafts board on Pinterest.

Use Pinterest to Supplement Other Efforts

Because pinboards are designed to store information and inspiration, they become the perfect place to point people for additional insight. Giving a speech to the local Chamber of Commerce? Use a Pinterest board to store links to the resources and supportive content you discovered while preparing it. Link users to the Pinterest board at the end of your speech and encourage them to follow the board for additional updates.

Offering a how-to class or a live demonstration at one of your stores? Pair the event with a board and promote it to attendees as a way to continue their learning experience after the event.

Nonprofits

Pinterest is a natural fit for nonprofits and charity-based organizations. These types of organizations are focused on sparking passion in people to motivate them to get involved in or donate to a cause. Images are one of the most compelling ways to spark this passion, and Pinterest is all about images.

Additionally, Pinterest usage patterns show users have a high propensity for sharing images that strike an emotional chord with them. They pin photos of cute animals, they collect images of children laughing and playing, and they build boards to house inspirational quotes and sayings. All of these things open the door of opportunity for nonprofits.

Put a Personality Behind the People You're Helping

A key way nonprofits reach out and spark passion in supporters is by making it about the impact on individual people rather than the big picture. Pinterest provides an ideal way for these groups to showcase those individuals. Organizations like UNICEF build boards that feature images taken by their team members around the world (see Figure 2.23).

Figure 2.23 UNICEF curates more than a dozen boards featuring the individuals their programs help.

Each pin provides the opportunity to share insight about the person or people being featured and to link Pinterest users back to the full story on the UNICEF website (see Figure 2.24).

Syrian Arab Republic, 2012 - A woman and her child stand inside their house after it was damaged by bombing, in a city affected by the conflict. The light on the top centre of the wall behind them comes through a hole caused by a mortar shell. - © UNICEF/NYHQ2012-0213/Alessio Romenzi - **www.unicef.org**

1 like 3 repins

Uploaded by user

Figure 2.24 UNICEF links some pins back to additional information and resources on their website.

Strike Passion in Your Audience

What would a nonprofit be without passion? When your product is the difference you make in the world or in the life of an individual person, it's essential to strike an emotional chord with your members to motivate them to keep the funding flowing. Pictures speak a thousand words, and using a site like Pinterest to share and paint pictures of the work you are doing can speak volumes.

The Monmouth County SPCA in Eatontown, New Jersey has perfected the art of playing to supporters emotions with Pinterest. They feature the obvious boards showcasing dogs and cats available for adoption. They also collect animal-related quotes and the ever popular "Cute Animals & Animal Humor" (see Figure 2.25).

Figure 2.25 Cute animal pictures are among the most popular types of content on Pinterest.

Nonprofits need to think about what motivates people to volunteer or donate to their organization. They must consider what the underlying passion points are for their audience. Then they should build and curate boards that play to those passions.

Leverage the Pinterest Gift Tag

It's important for nonprofits not to shy away from the retail side of Pinterest. The gift categories are a popular browsing channel for people looking for unique and creative ideas for their loved ones. Setting up a specific donation goal and posting the dollar amount to a pin that links back to a donation page can be a compelling way to remind people to take action.

For charities and organizations that provide specific donation goals like buying a goat for a third-world family or supplying medication to an impoverished child, it makes perfect sense to leverage Pinterest to tell the story.

By this point, you should have some ideas rolling around in your head regarding how your business or organization might be able to leverage Pinterest. Now that we've tackled the idea of which businesses are a good fit for Pinterest, we're ready to start exploring why Pinterest has made such an impact on the social media world and why it's likely to go the distance as a social media channel.

What Makes Pinterest Valuable?

Pinterest is basically a bookmarking site. Those are nothing new; Furl, del.icio.us., and so on have been around and popular for quite some time. Pinterest plays off the collector in all of us.

At the same time, Pinterest puts a brand new spin on the idea of collecting. It allows us to collect content we find online and keep it organized in a way that makes the most sense to us. Better still, it allows us to share those collections with others and to see their collections in return. In this chapter, we'll look at the many reasons Pinterest has resonated so well with its audience.

Chapter Contents

Pinterest Plays Off the Impact of Imagery

Understanding what makes Pinterest stand out so prevalently in a sea of social media channels competing for attention is fairly simple. Just open your eyes.

It's been said that "a picture is worth a thousand words," and for good reason. It takes mere seconds for a still photograph to convey a complex scenario that might take hundreds or even thousands of words to describe in a text-only environment. This concept is what allowed Pinterest to break through the clutter to capture the attention of millions of users.

While many sites (such as Furl and del.icio.us) have tried to play off the collector in us, and many sites (such as Flickr and Photobucket) have played off our love of images, Pinterest is the first to effectively combine the two.

Consider the way we seek out and manage information online. Historically, we've run searches on search engines, visited content sites we're familiar with, and maybe read information posted by friends and family or bloggers we follow. We might read about the beauty of the tiny villages perched along the Cinque Terre in Italy. We might even read some reviews of the dazzling array of colors in the cities and how they hang on cliffs perched on the edge of the Ligurian Sea (see Figure 3.1).

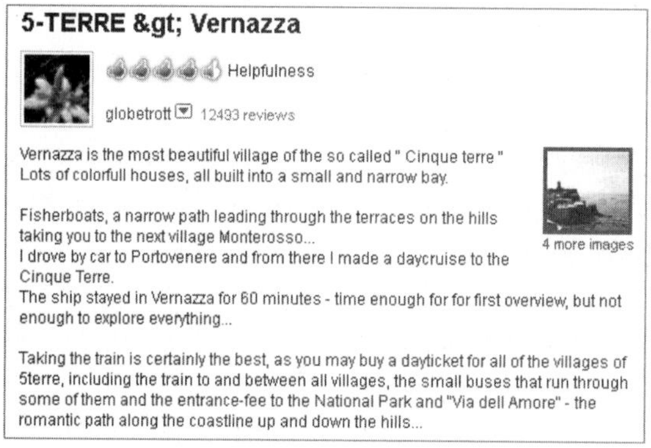

5-TERRE > Vernazza

Helpfulness

globetrott 12493 reviews

Vernazza is the most beautiful village of the so called " Cinque terre ".
Lots of colorfull houses, all built into a small and narrow bay.

Fisherboats, a narrow path leading through the terraces on the hills taking you to the next village Monterosso...
I drove by car to Portovenere and from there I made a daycruise to the Cinque Terre.
The ship stayed in Vernazza for 60 minutes - time enough for for first overview, but not enough to explore everything...

Taking the train is certainly the best, as you may buy a dayticket for all of the villages of 5terre, including the train to and between all villages, the small buses that run through some of them and the entrance-fee to the National Park and "Via dell Amore" - the romantic path along the coastline up and down the hills...

4 more images

Figure 3.1 A web-based review of the Cinque Terre will speak of its beauty but will rarely display its full imagery.

The words in those reviews do little to explain the full impact of the breathtaking Cinque Terre for the beauty-seeking traveler of Italy. It's the images that convey the impact (see Figure 3.2).

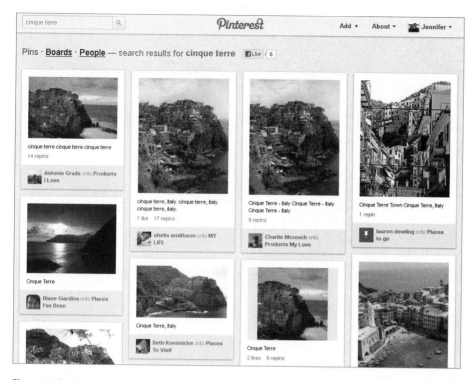

Figure 3.2 Travel planners, dreamers, and explorers continually pin images of the Cinque Terre in all its beauty.

Pinterest allows users to take in a far greater amount of information and to make more concrete decisions about what they're interested in quickly. Although someone planning their next vacation might spend weeks or even months reading reviews and researching various destinations on blogs and travel sites, it might take only a few moments to fall in love with a destination while browsing through the "Travel and Places" category on Pinterest.

Pinterest recognizes the level of that visual impact and plays to it effectively. Pinterest boasts one of the cleanest designs on the Web, with nothing to take away focus from the images until users decide to roll their cursor over them to start interacting (see Figure 3.3).

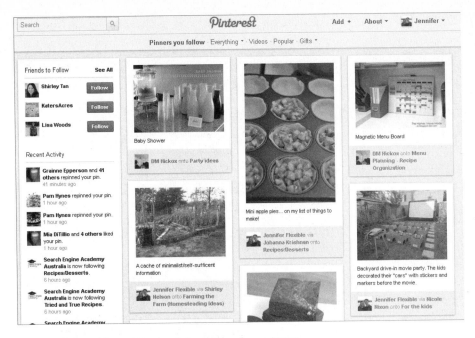

Figure 3.3 Pinterest is known for its clean design and heavy focus on images.

Pinterest isn't just about saving images to categorized boards; it's about sharing visual representations of ideas: the various cakes you might make for your son's next birthday, the kitchen cabinet organization idea that will make your life easier, the collection of infographics you're gathering for your next big presentation.

Visual Bookmarking

The idea of saving links to resources, ideas, and inspiration is nothing new. For as long as there have been web browsers, Internet users have had the ability to "save" a link so they can revisit it later. Even the idea of "social bookmarking"—saving links in a public environment so others can also see and follow the links—isn't new. Text-based social media sites like Furl and del.icio.us have been operating since 2003.

These sites were founded on the idea that users could store their bookmarks in a public location where they could share access with their friends. Additionally, these sites would keep track of how many times a particular website or URL was bookmarked, using that data to judge the relevance and popularity of any given resource.

The difference Pinterest brings to the mix is the addition of imagery to the curated items. In a social media–heavy world where Internet users are choosing to consume more and more information in less time, Pinterest serves a very useful purpose. Ideas can be gathered and pinned to topical boards where they can easily be revisited and either pruned or researched over time.

Let's say you are considering building a chicken coop in your backyard. You could spend hours running searches on Google, clicking through the results to find the ones you like best and bookmarking the contenders for later review. When you go back to review them, you'll have to click through each result to get a look at the coop and to have an idea of which one is which.

Or, you could pin each of the coops you are considering to a newly created pin-board. You could tag the coops with notes on the number of chickens it would hold, what it might cost to build, or what feature you liked best (see Figure 3.4). When it's time to revisit your research, you can tell, at a glance, which links you'd like to click on.

Figure 3.4 A quick glance at pinned resources tells you exactly which one you are looking for.

This style of visual bookmarking can be an absolute boon for the sites and companies that produce Pinterest-friendly images related to topics that are popular with pinners.

Saved Images for Later Exploration

In some cases, it's not about bookmarking resources. It's about wanting to revisit an image that inspires, intrigues, or downright confuses. That's part of why Pinterest is filled with boards that have titles like "Places I Dream Of" or "What in the World?"

These boards are filled with pictures, illustrations, and infographics designed to capture people's attention. They feature the weird, the wonderful, and the inspirational. Sometimes they also simply feature the "I don't have time for this right now."

Think of the mom planning a birthday party for her six-year-old. She won't have time to make all her decisions at once, but Pinterest gives her a place to save images related to the party. The same goes for the bride considering centerpiece ideas or the interior designer looking for fall color palettes.

Note: It's interesting to note that most Pinterest users search for and repin content from within the system. According to Flowtown, in an infographic released in the spring of 2012, 80 percent of the pins on the site are repins. Compare this to Twitter, where only 1.4 percent of tweets are re-tweets. Pinterest users are more interested in exploring other people's discoveries than making their own.

In trying to understand the appeal of collected images, it's essential to understand why Pinterest stands out. I've explained why Pinterest differs from social bookmarking services like Furl and del.icio.us, but it's also important to understand how it differs from once popular image-based social-sharing sites like Flickr and Photobucket.

For years, Flickr was the reigning image-based social media site. It was the number-one social media channel for viewing and sharing images. But with Flickr, it was all about sharing your *own* images, images you'd taken or created. Pinterest's upgrade is the idea of the images being tied to something more—that the image is the reminder or trigger of the inspiration, the way to allow people to instinctively grab something that causes a reaction in them and save it for later absorption and action.

Pinterest opened up the world of image-based social media to the masses by removing the qualifiers. You don't have to be a stunning photographer to be an active contributor to Pinterest. Flickr was about sharing your own photos. Pinterest is about sharing the images that lead you to something of value.

Driven by Impulse Clicks

One of the reasons Pinterest has flourished is because it appeals to two key instincts in humans: the desire to collect and the desire to act impulsively. From a very young age, we're encouraged to "collect them all!" when we stumble across something we love.

Hundreds of years before people were collecting stamps, they were collecting shells. Hundreds of years before that, they were probably collecting sabertooth tiger teeth or mammoth tusks. Collecting is part of who we are, but so is an attraction to whatever is new and shiny.

Pinterest appeals because it removes the need to surf the Web looking for ideas and inspiration. Those ideas are served up on a beautiful-looking platter every time you log in. Repinning the images for future reference and inspiration is as simple as clicking a button.

This allows content to spread quickly and to spread broadly in a very short amount of time. Pinterest users log in for a few minutes in the morning before checking email, or from a phone while they're waiting in line, or from a tablet while they're watching television, and then repin the content that strikes their fancy.

In fact, there hasn't been a screen shot yet I've captured for this book that didn't result in at least one repin when I went to Pinterest to capture the image. We are impulsive people, and both Pinterest and Pinterest marketers take full advantage of it.

Pinterest Has a Low Barrier to Entry

Perhaps the single biggest attraction of Pinterest for businesses is just how easy it is to use. Twitter alone rivals Pinterest in terms of start-up investment, daily time requirements, and ease of use.

Social media channels like Facebook require setup time, customization, app development, and thanks to an ever-changing interface, plenty of ongoing education. The same can be said for setting up a blog or building a YouTube channel. Even Twitter, with its almost instantaneous access, requires a time investment to find and solicit followers in order to gain enough traction to leverage the channel.

Not so with Pinterest. A few minutes in setup time can be enough to get you rolling and to start attracting followers. Beyond that, the average Pinterest account can be built and managed in less than 15 minutes a day. That makes Pinterest an extremely attractive option for big businesses that need to justify every minute of time spent as well as for small businesses that don't have more than a few minutes of time to invest.

Easy Account Setup

Setting up your Pinterest account is as simple as using an existing Facebook or Twitter account to sign on.

Note: It takes less than 10 minutes to get a Pinterest account up and running and to make your first pin, making Pinterest one of the lowest barrier-to-entry sites in all of social media.

Pinterest will walk you through the steps to get your account up and running and you'll have access to start pinning within five minutes or so. Few other social media channels can boast ease of access to rival Pinterest. This makes it easy to set an account up and do a little exploring. If it turns out Pinterest isn't a fit for you or your business, you haven't wasted much time. If it carries appeal, you're all ready to start leveraging it.

Minimal Account Management

Another selling point for Pinterest is how easy it is to use and manage your account. Pinterest has been repeatedly lauded for its user-friendly interface. Adding boards, editing pins, customizing your personal profile, and using the system are extremely easy.

In addition, there's no need to worry about approving or managing followers. Much like Twitter, Pinterest accounts are open access. People simply choose to follow you or one of your pinboards, and Pinterest sends you a notification about the new follower. Absolutely no action is required unless you want to take the time to check out a new follower to decide whether to follow them back.

Freedom from Publishing Schedules

Perhaps the single biggest differentiator between Pinterest and other social media channels is the lack of need for a publishing schedule. This one difference makes Pinterest appeal to a broad range of businesses that otherwise have trouble making time for social media involvement.

Consider the time required to maintain a strong Facebook presence. You need to find or generate content on a daily basis, format it and upload it to the site, monitor it for responses, reply when appropriate, and then start the entire process over again. An average company can spend anywhere from one employee spending an hour a day on this to using a team of individuals to monitor the site full time. The same can be said of Twitter or blogs, where publishing schedules are expected to stay consistent and responses are expected almost immediately.

Pinterest opens up a new type of interaction with followers. Because users are sharing content rather than creating it, there's less expectation of daily posts or updates. Users pin content when they have time to pin content. That might mean a five-minute burst today followed by a 20-minute burst of activity four days from now.

It should come as no surprise that the highest usage on Pinterest comes before and after standard work hours, with an additional spike around lunchtime. TotalPinterest.com shared data in March 2012 that reverse-engineered server response time to determine when the highest volumes of usage occur. Peak time occurs between 5 a.m. and 7 a.m. and between 7 p.m. and 9 p.m. Eastern Standard Time.

When marketers first started leveraging Pinterest, any and all pins and repins were fed directly into the category stream. This made pinning during peak hours a vital part of any Pinterest strategy. As Pinterest has started refining its algorithm, the number of pins from any one user that get fed into the category stream has dropped dramatically. With most accounts landing only a single pin in the category stream every 24 hours or so, the opportunity for mass exposure during peak hours has dropped dramatically.

Still, for Pinterest users wishing to gain a high volume of views, it's a good idea to time your first pin of the day to hit during peak hours. Subsequent pins are less impacted by time since they'll feed only into the streams of users who have subscribed to your pinboards. Since users often scroll through a day's worth of pins when they log in to their feed, your chances of gaining exposure remain fairly high no matter what time of day you pin your content.

This makes Pinterest a social media channel that can be used as time allows, rather than yet another channel to bog down your team with time-intensive updates and monitoring. That said, it's a good idea to run some testing to find out if time of the day or day of the week makes a difference in terms of both repins and click-throughs on any original pins you upload to your pinboards.

Pinterest Provides an Outlet for Content Curators

One of the ways in which Pinterest turns traditional social media on its head is by creating a system where curators are rewarded as much, or more than, content creators. Channels like Facebook, YouTube, and blogs require companies to invest time and effort into creating engaging content strategies, whereas Pinterest operates off a platform of shared resources.

Becoming a Pinterest power player requires nothing more than an eye for good content and an ability to categorize it properly. Some of the most popular Pinterest users never generate a single piece of unique content on the Internet. They simply serve up a consistent dose of curation that attracts legions of followers who want to share in their discovery.

Users and Businesses Can Share without Flooding Streams

Pinterest is a place for people to save ideas and to share those ideas with other people in a way they can't do on any other social network.

Imagine logging in to Facebook and seeing 27 shared photos of various centerpieces from one of your friends in a single afternoon. More than likely, you'd be a little annoyed. You might even block them from your newsfeed. Picture a stream of 30 or 40 tweets from someone you follow, all of which link to DIY instructions for chicken coops. You'd probably be a bit miffed.

With Pinterest, those rules of sharing are out the window. Suddenly people are free to share whatever they want while archiving it for themselves. Pinterest users can set up that board to feature all the centerpiece ideas they are considering (see Figure 3.5) with the confidence that only people who subscribe to it will see them.

Figure 3.5 Pinterest users can share as many images as they want without taking over social networks like Facebook or Twitter.

This also means companies are free to share content as they find it. People often digest information in chunks. You might spend a few minutes looking for just the right super hero–themed birthday cake during which time you might find half a dozen or more options. You might start out researching organic foods and end up finding and saving a wide range of content on the benefits of local honey.

Pinterest allows for that type of mass digestion by creating an environment where it's safe to collect and share content as you come across it without fear of repercussion by uninterested followers.

Provides Businesses with Freedom to Share More Content

Just as there's less cause for concern over sharing too much content on any one topic at a given time, Pinterest also allows for companies to open up the breadth and amount of content they choose to share.

On standard social media channels like Twitter and Facebook, every follower receives every update. Get too involved on a specific topic or spend too much time engaging with any one user and you risk alienating the rest of your followers.

This is an especially big concern for small business owners who doesn't want to take the time to manage multiple accounts but also don't want to risk alienating their clients with too much talk about their love of all things Star Wars or their massive collection of Battlestar Galactica bobbleheads.

Pinterest does a brilliant job of solving this problem by allowing users to set up topical boards and, more importantly, by allowing other Pinterest users to selectively follow boards rather than following all content from a specific individual. This leads us to one of Pinterest's most powerful features.

Pinterest Offers Content Segmentation to Users

Imagine the difficulty of a brand that appeals to multiple demographics for multiple reasons. The 62-year-old woman who loves Advil for the arthritis relief it brings after a long day of gardening has completely different interests than the 28-year-old distance runner who uses Advil to deal with pain from a sprained ankle.

Generating content that appears to these wildly different demographics has been an ever-present challenge in the world of social media. Blog readers or Twitter followers get blasted with a wide range of content that may or may not interest them. This can cause even stronger damage on a network like Facebook whose algorithm actually harms the visibility of brands that send out updates that are not well received.

On Pinterest, one brand can captivate and entertain dozens of different demographics by creating pinboards targeted to each of them. Advil could easily set up a board focused on gardening for their 62-year-old customer who struggles with arthritis pain. They could also set up a board filled with inspirational running quotes, images of the best locations to run, and other content targeted toward the 28-year-old distance runner.

AMD is an example of a company that walks this line extremely effectively. They curate nearly 30 boards designed to appeal to a broad set of demographics (see Figure 3.6). They have the expected boards featuring AMD Technology and showcasing photos from CES, but they also curate boards with titles like PC Gaming, Organization, and Gadgets to appeal to gamers, women, and techies.

Each user could check out Advil's Pinterest account and pick which categories to follow, guaranteeing that only the content they are most interested in will be served up via that channel.

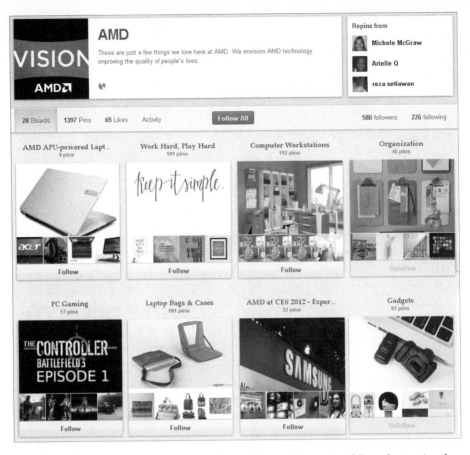

Figure 3.6 AMD curates nearly 30 boards covering a wide range of topics so they can attract followers from a variety of demographics.

Pinterest Serves as a Gateway Rather Than a Destination

A very important thing to understand about Pinterest and why it can drive so much traffic is the concept of Pinterest as a social media gateway rather than as a social media destination. When people visit a site like Facebook, they are visiting to connect with friends, to share photos and videos and to generally socialize in an online environment. When people visit a site like Pinterest, they are looking for ideas, for inspiration, and for a place to store information for later.

Consider the differences between the two sites, as shown in Figure 3.7.

When a bride visits Facebook, she might mention that she went cake tasting. She might even check in on Facebook at the location she visited. When that same bride visits Pinterest, she starts saving and archiving images of the cakes designs she likes. These images are then discovered by other users and ultimately become public data as they enter the Pinterest Wedding stream and as users search for wedding cake images.

The images become a launch point to visit the sites they were pinned from so users can learn more about their options.

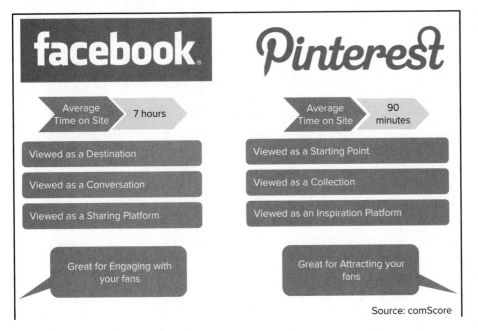

Figure 3.7 Unlike Facebook, which is designed to retain visitors, Pinterest helps lead users to resources *off* the site.

Pinterest becomes a gateway to ideas and information, with pins and boards serving as the starting point and websites serving as the destination. Traffic flows out of Pinterest as fast or as often as it flows in. Leaving the site is part of the experience of using the site.

Better Than Bookmarks for Users and Businesses

I've already explained the numerous ways that Pinterest is superior to standard Internet bookmarking in terms of revisiting saved links and digesting information. What's also important to understand is how this benefit increases exponentially in an environment like Pinterest designed for sharing.

Consider the businesses you follow online. Perhaps you're a fan of Trader Joe's or Whole Foods because eating organic and whole foods is important to you. Chances are good these companies will build up a Pinterest-based set of "bookmarks" that will also interest you.

What's more, Pinterest's search feature allows users to search for individual pins, Pinterest users, or pinboards (see Figure 3.8). That means you can actually search for the topical collections of links being curated by other users. It's not just the individual bookmarks that are available—it's the entire categories.

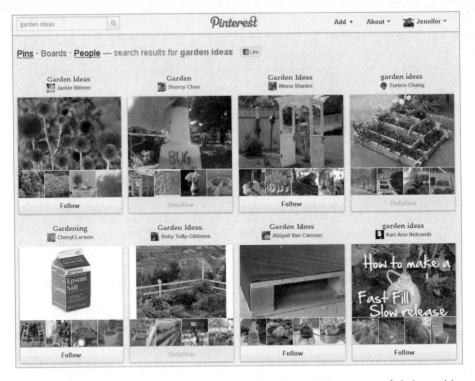

Figure 3.8 Pinterest allows users to search for Pinterest boards based on keywords. It's a great way to find other people's visual bookmarks.

Pinterest Works Off Latent Click Conversions

One of the interesting ways that Pinterest differs from other popular social media sites is in the often present gap between discovery and engagement.

On other social media channels, users tend to stumble across a link to a resource or article and then immediately click it. They read it, digest it, make a decision on whether or not to share it, and occasionally bookmark it for future reference. On Pinterest, the process works a little differently (see Figure 3.9).

Because so many Pinterest users repin content as opposed to finding and pinning original content, there's not always a need to click through to digest the final materials before taking action. Many users will spend a small amount of time on the site looking for ideas to repin to their boards without ever bothering to click on the links prior to the pin.

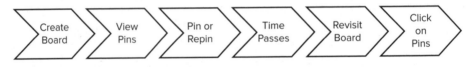

Figure 3.9 While Pinterest users sometimes pin content as they discover it, a large portion of Pinterest clicks are latent.

These users tend to return to specific boards at a later time to make decisions about which pins to click on and which resources to investigate further. The user who spends weeks pinning and repinning images of chicken coop designs may not actually click on any of the links until months down the road when they're ready to come up with a building plan.

This is why it's important to understand that there is not always a direct correlation between the number of pins and repins a piece of content receives and the amount of resulting traffic that flows into the site from Pinterest.

Increased Opportunity for Traffic

Isn't this what it all boils down to? The potential for traffic? This is where Pinterest wins on so many fronts. It's an area of discovery...people are coming to the site with a specific intent to find new resources. Unlike other social media channels where people are engaged in conversation and networking and your attempt to lure them in to view your content is sometimes unwelcome, Pinterest users come to the site expecting to be led astray.

This works heavily in favor of the companies that figure out how to leverage Pinterest either by becoming active members of the service or by encouraging their existing fan base to help feed their content into the network. We'll explore more of the techniques for growing your traffic via Pinterest in Chapter 7, "Week 4–Purposely Propagating Pins on Pinterest."

Pinterest Puts All Users on an Equal Playing Field

One of the things that made Pinterest so attractive to new users and to early adopters in the business world was the equality of posting potential. Much like Twitter, individual users and small businesses were every bit as likely as big brands and large corporations to have a strong base of followers.

Pinterest represents another new frontier in social media—one that has not yet (and likely won't be for at least a year or more) been overrun by business. Money doesn't buy fancy third-party apps or snazzy designs for Pinterest users. Everyone competes with the same set of tools and the same potential. That makes it prime territory for creatively enterprising brands.

Both Big and Small Companies Have Equal Leverage Potential

Social media was supposed to be the great equalizer, and in many ways it still is. Small companies and start-ups are often able to marshal powerful followings on sites like Twitter and Facebook, and creative companies can often leverage YouTube to reach millions without spending much capital.

Unfortunately, the longer a social media channel exists, the more segregated the offerings become. Advertising programs, premium accounts, and promoted posts and tweets get opened to the largest brands first and only sometimes filter down to the smaller companies. This makes it increasingly difficult to build a strong grass-roots following and leaves budget-minded businesses scanning the horizon for the next frontier.

For now, Pinterest offers some attractive real estate. Every business—large or small, capital heavy or budget minded—has the same chance to build their following and promote their stream. Pinterest becomes more about what you can offer than how much money you have to push your agenda. In a world where marketing purse strings are forever tightening, that makes Pinterest a welcome addition to a brand's social media arsenal.

How Pins Get Fed into the Stream

For the first two years of Pinterest's existence, its algorithm was fairly simple. As long as a pin was added to a board that was properly associated with an existing Pinterest category, that pin would show up at the top of the category page (see Figure 3.10).

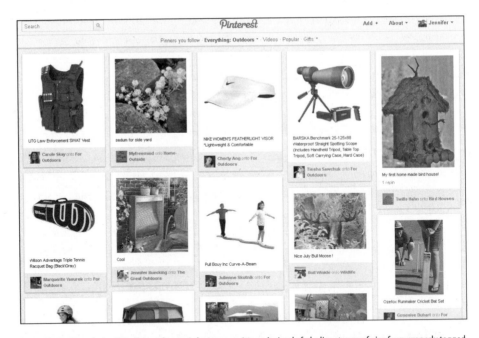

Figure 3.10 Pinterest's original algorithm was almost nonexistent. It simply fed a live stream of pins from properly tagged boards into each category.

In other words, Pinterest delivered a steady stream of live pins, showing exactly what its users were interested in at any point in time. This made it extremely easy for new users to break into the system and capture both followers and repins. All it took was one intriguing piece of content pinned at the right time of day to capture users' attention.

Unfortunately, as with many social media channels, spammers became such an issue as the site rose in popularity that adjustments to the algorithm became necessary.

After launching as a site that took virtually every pin made and pushed it to the category stream, Pinterest ran into quite a bit of trouble with spammers. Affiliate marketers and site owners alike took advantage of the "every pin gets promoted to the category" algorithm to virtually flood the channels with their own content, prompting Pinterest to take steps to tighten up their algorithm. These days, Pinterest has locked its algorithm down significantly, limiting the number of pins from each user that get promoted to the category stream.

At the time of publication, Pinterest appeared to be letting only a handful of pins per user, per day into the category stream. This means it's extremely important to make sure your first pin of the day is the one you'd most like to see propagate though the system.

Down the road as Pinterest's algorithmic abilities improve, we can expect to see them take several factors into consideration when deciding which pins to promote. Most likely, Pinterest will focus on the number of repins and likes a Pinterest user receives on average and will use that data to help compel more content from respected pinners into the category streams.

Potential Benefit of More Traffic with Followers

With Pinterest's algorithm no longer feeding pins directly into the stream as they are uploaded to the site, it has become slightly more difficult to capture the attention of users. This is where it become beneficial to invest time in building a strong Pinterest following.

Clearly pins that are fed out to thousands of followers will have a higher chance of being repinned and propagating through the system than pins that are launched to only a handful of followers. (More on this in Chapter 5, "Week 2–Curating Content with Pinterest.") Similarly, websites that already have high traffic numbers will enjoy much stronger results from adding the "Pin It" button to their content than smaller publishers will.

This is why it's important to focus on building up your Pinterest following the same way you might seek to build your Twitter, Facebook, or YouTube followers. More people subscribing to your content equals more potential for repins and increased exposure.

We'll explore more about how to fine-tune your curation skills to attract more followers in Chapter 6, "Week 3—Find and Attract Followers," and look at several ways to help you gather more repins in Chapter 7.

Equality in Ultimate Pins Based on Size of Posting Account

Despite the obvious benefit that comes with having a larger number of followers or higher traffic numbers to your existing website, Pinterest is a place of surprising equality. It's not at all unusual to see a Pinterest user with fewer than a hundred followers pin a piece of content that gets repined thousands of times.

Being the first to pin something of high quality or that makes up a unique offering seems to have far more to do with the ultimate reach of a pin than who pinned it in the first place.

It's not even remotely uncommon to find an image with thousands of pins (see Figure 3.11) and hundreds of likes on Pinterest.

Cutie
629 likes   24 comments   2977 repins

Figure 3.11 This pin has been repinned nearly three thousand times and has hundreds of likes.

It's also not even remotely uncommon to check out the profile of the person who originally pinned the immensely popular post and to learn they have only a handful of followers (see Figure 3.12).

Lorna Carolyn

📍 Kolkata, India

Repins from

Virginia Stevenson

Lori Shimer

Hana selly

5 Boards   53 Pins   4 Likes   Activity   Follow All   15 followers   15 following

Figure 3.12 While this user pinned a piece of content that received thousands of repins, she only has 15 followers.

Because Pinterest activity is so visual and impulse driven, the image has more to do with whether the content gains traction than the status of the pinner does.

Week 1—Set Up a Pinterest Account

4

Fair warning: Pinterest is addictive. I joined up in the fall of 2011 when I noticed Pin It buttons showing up on crafting and food blogs. I've been an almost daily visitor ever since.

While I use it for my own projects and clients, it's also great for a web-based diversion. It's my new time killer when I'm waiting in line or need a distraction at the end of a long day. It's my source (and storage) for inspiration on food, my home, and a huge portion of the things I do in my everyday life.

It's best to spend at least a few weeks using the site before you begin exploring the idea of using it as a marketing tool, so grab a cup of coffee, get ready to set up an account, and prepare for a new addiction.

Chapter Contents

Monday: Create an Account
Tuesday: Understand the Category System
Wednesday: Understand the Search System
Thursday: Create and Organize Your Boards
Friday: Start Pinning!

Monday: Create an Account

The first thing you'll need to do to get rolling with Pinterest is create an account. Signing up only takes a few minutes. If you don't already have an account, let's spend today in front of the computer joining yet another social media network. I promise you won't regret this one…unless the regret stems from how much time you spend collecting ideas.

Registering for an Account

The first thing you'll see when you visit Pinterest.com is the Pinterest dashboard with a big yellow box at the top suggesting you join Pinterest or log in (see Figure 4.1). While this option works great for individual users, businesses and organizations looking to create a branded presence will need to sign up through Pinterest's business portal. We'll discuss that option later in the chapter. For now, we can focus on setting up a personal account.

Figure 4.1 New Pinterest users can't miss the "Join Pinterest" option at the top of the page.

Clicking the Join Pinterest button will take you to a new screen where you'll be asked to connect your account with an existing Facebook or Twitter account. Pinterest will also give you the option to register using an email address, but if you plan to connect with friends on the service, it's a good idea to register using one of the offered social media accounts (see Figure 4.2).

Figure 4.2 The Pinterest registration page asks you to connect your account with Facebook or Twitter.

Choosing whether to opt for Facebook or Twitter is mostly a personal preference. Pinterest will only share your pins via those networks if you ask it to. For the purpose of this book, we'll go with Facebook. Clicking on the Facebook icon will take you to your Facebook sign-in page (see Figure 4.3).

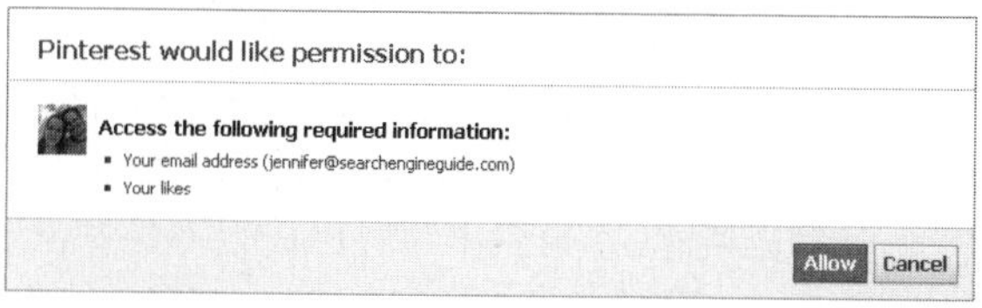

Figure 4.3 You'll need to give Facebook permission to share your data with Pinterest.

Once you're signed in, you'll need to approve the app to work in Facebook. Consider whether you want to leave things set to display to all your Facebook friends or if you want to narrow the friend group and then click through to move along. From there, it's on to finally setting up your Pinterest account.

Note: Although it's easy enough to allow Pinterest to publish your activity stream to Facebook or Twitter, it's generally not advised. Part of the freedom of Pinterest is the ability to pin and repin as much content as you want without fear of alienating your followers. Allowing Pinterest to publish your activity feed to other channels sort of defeats the purpose.

You'll need to select a username, supply your email address, and establish a password. In the future, you can use either the username and password you create here or your Facebook account to log into the site.

Once you've finished this step, Pinterest will try to get you started with some people to follow. They'll start by asking you to click through a wide range of topics, selecting a few boards to follow as you go (see Figure 4.4).

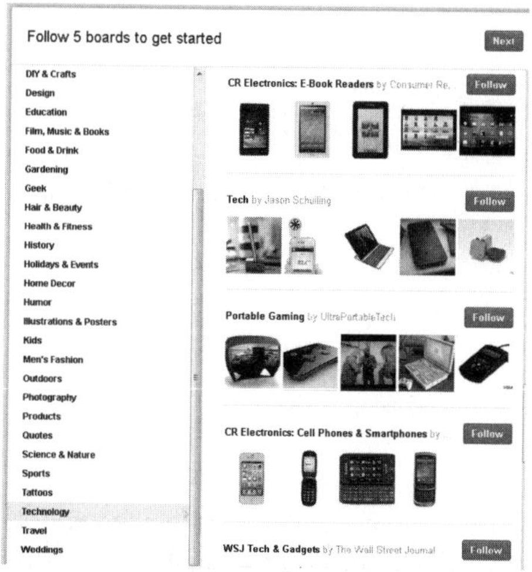

Figure 4.4 Pinterest will lead you through the process of selecting a few boards to follow to help fill your initial Pinterest stream.

Your next step in the process is to create some boards (see Figure 4.5). Boards are Pinterest's version of visual filing cabinets. They are usually topical and give you a chance to categorize your pins for easy access. Take a minute to set up one or two, but rest assured we'll cover more on this later on this week.

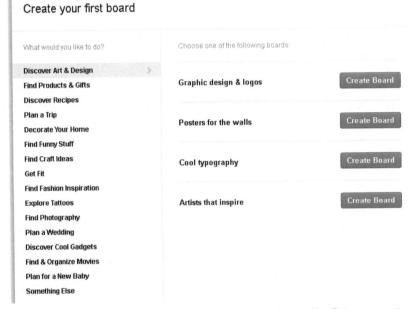

Figure 4.5 Pinterest will guide you through the process of creating your first board by offering up suggestions based on your areas of interest.

Once you've set up your starter categories, you're ready to get going. At this point, you'll be able to view your Pinterest stream. In this case, that stream will be made up of recent pins from the people your account is following.

Of course chances are high you'll see a lot of things you aren't interested in. Just because you're friends with someone on Facebook doesn't mean you're interested in every little thing they want to save in their scrapbooks. There are a few ways to work around this, but we'll cover that in Chapter 6, "Week 3—Find and Attract Followers."

Setting Up Your Profile

Once you've established your account, you'll need to do a little bit of setup to ensure your profile isn't a barren wasteland. After all, you'll want to give people a reason to follow you if and when they stop by to view your account.

To customize your profile, you'll need to visit Pinterest.com and look for the Settings link underneath your name in the top-right corner of the page (see Figure 4.6).

Figure 4.6 You can access your profile settings by clicking the drop-down menu under your username in the top-right corner of the Pinterest dashboard.

The top of the page will be filled with the standard forms for changing your email address, your name, and even your username. Further down the page, you'll see the options for adding a bit of personality to your listing (see Figure 4.7).

About	3 kids, 2 kitchens, 1 husband and 22 acres in Western Pennsylvania. Small business owner, author, speaker and lover of all things food related! Curating food, crafts, projects and general merriment
Location	Western Pennsylvania e.g. Palo Alto, CA
Website	http://www.aflexiblelife.com
Image	Upload an Image Refresh from Facebook Refresh from Twitter

Figure 4.7 Taking the time to write a creative and/or descriptive About section can help increase followers.

Once you've uploaded a profile image and written a description of yourself or your account, you can revisit your profile page to see your account as others will (see Figure 4.8).

Figure 4.8 Your avatar and self-description are your way to set expectations for people visiting your profile and deciding whether to follow you.

If you look further down the Settings page, you'll also notice some options regarding linking your account to Facebook and Twitter, as well as the ability to make your profile available to or hidden from search engines (see Figure 4.9).

Facebook	ON	Link to Facebook
	OFF	Add Pinterest to Facebook Timeline
	Find Facebook Friends on Pinterest	
Twitter	ON	Link to Twitter
Hide	OFF	Hide your Pinterest profile from search engines
Delete	Delete Account	

Figure 4.9 Pinterest allows you to toggle sharing to Twitter and Facebook. It also allows you to hide your Pinterest profile from search engines.

It's important to give some consideration to these settings. They can have an impact on how your Pinterest content is distributed elsewhere.

Personal Name vs. Company Name

One of the challenges many Pinterest users have when setting up their account is deciding whether to use their business or blog name or to use their actual name. It's the same dilemma experienced on sites like Twitter where credibility often comes with establishing a solidly recognized presence.

My recommendation is to make this choice based on the size and power of your brand. If you're setting up a Pinterest account for a company, brand, or organization, use the official name. This is especially true if you plan to have multiple contributors working together to curate your boards.

If you're setting up a Pinterest account for yourself, your hobby blog, or a solo consulting-style business, go ahead and set up the account using your actual name.

Setting up a Business Account

While it did not originally distinguish between business and personal accounts Pinterest added business accounts to the mix in November of 2012. The idea, according to Pinterest was to enable businesses, brands and organizations to embrace the service while also taking advantage of free tools and resources designed just for companies.

Splitting accounts into personal and business also allowed Pinterest to create a Terms of Service specifically for businesses. The Business Terms of Service (http://business.pinterest.com/tos/) clearly outline the acceptable use policy for business accounts as well as the copyright policies and legal disclaimers surrounding how content is shared.

Existing account holders can quickly and easily upgrade their accounts from personal ones to business ones and new accounts can now be set up as official business profiles from the start. No matter which route you need to take, you can get things rolling by visiting the Pinterest Business site at http://business.pinterest.com/.

Converting an Existing Account

Because Pinterest introduced business accounts a few years after the service launched, many companies will need to go through the process of converting an existing personal account to an official business account.

When you first log in to the Pinterest Business site, you'll be asked whether you wish to convert an existing account or join up to create a new account (see Figure 4.10). Those of you who originally set up your business account as a personal account will want to start the conversion process.

Make sure you are logged into Pinterest with the account you wish to convert before starting this process.

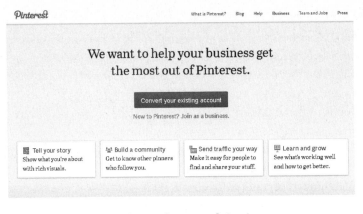

Figure 4.10 Existing Pinterest account holders can't miss the big red "Convert your existing account" button at the top of the page.

Clicking this button will bring you to a screen titled "Convert to Business Account" (see Figure 4.11). You'll need to select your business type from one of nine different options. You'll also need to designate contact information, your business name and create a new "about" description.

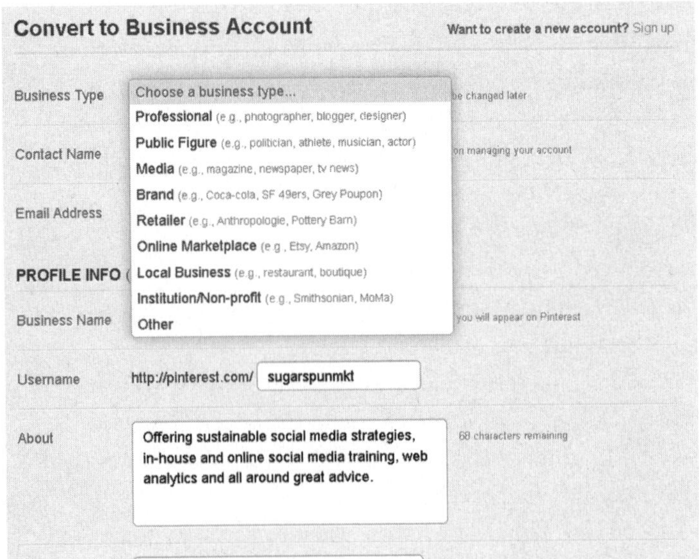

Convert to Business Account   Want to create a new account? Sign up

Business Type	Choose a business type...	be changed later
Contact Name	Professional (e.g., photographer, blogger, designer)	on managing your account
	Public Figure (e.g., politician, athlete, musician, actor)	
Email Address	Media (e.g., magazine, newspaper, tv news)	
	Brand (e.g., Coca-cola, SF 49ers, Grey Poupon)	
PROFILE INFO	Retailer (e.g., Anthropologie, Pottery Barn)	
	Online Marketplace (e.g., Etsy, Amazon)	
Business Name	Local Business (e.g., restaurant, boutique)	you will appear on Pinterest
	Institution/Non-profit (e.g., Smithsonian, MoMa)	
	Other	

Username   http://pinterest.com/ sugarspunmkt

About   Offering sustainable social media strategies, in-house and online social media training, web analytics and all around great advice.   68 characters remaining

Website   www.sugarspunmarketing.com   ex: yourwebsite.com

Figure 4.11 You'll need to designate the type of business you have as well as updating contact information and your "about us" section.

Once you've made the transition, you'll be returned to your Pinterest page and a new set of links to help you make the most of your business account (see Figure 4.12).

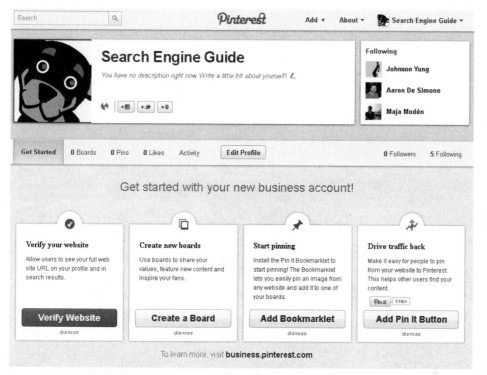

Figure 4.12 Pinterest will direct you to verify your web site, add the Pinterest bookmarklet to your browser, install the Pin it Button and Follow Us buttons on your web site.

If you don't see the "Verify your web site" option included in the list at this point, do not be concerned. This simply means you, or someone else on the team has already verified your account.

Set up a New Business Account

The process for setting up a new account is pretty similar to the process for converting an account. Simply go to the Pinterest business page (`http://business .pinterest.com`) and select the "New to Pinterest? Join as Business" link from the page (see Figure 4.13).

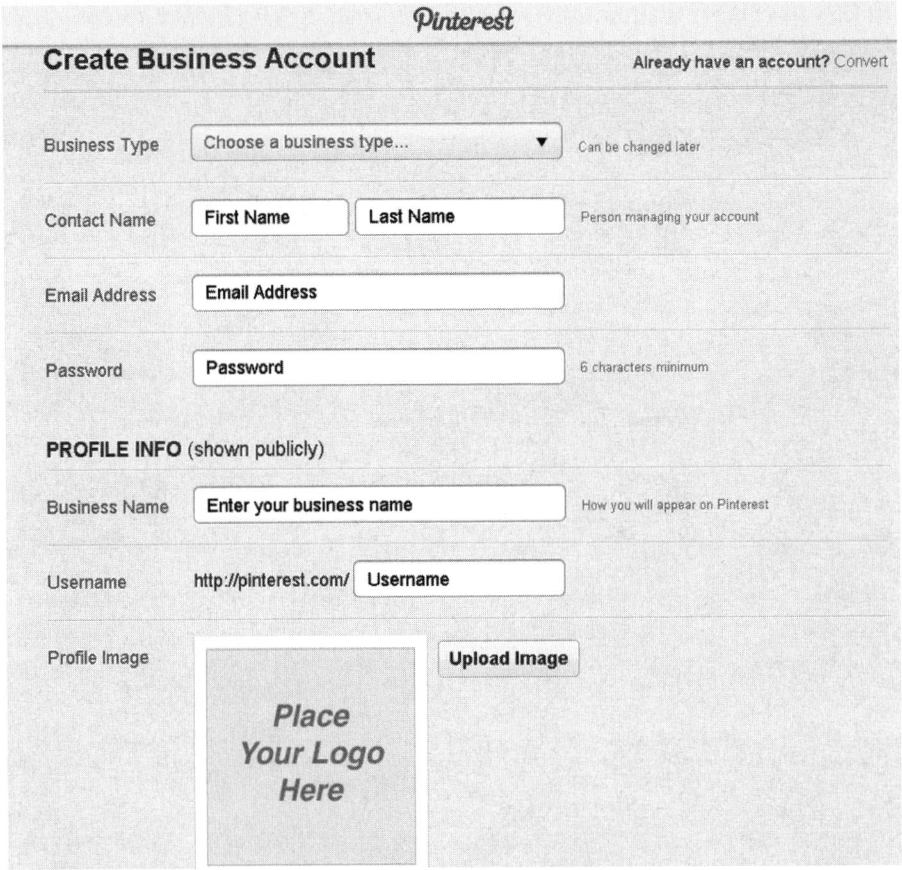

Figure 4.13 To open a new business account on Pinterest, select the "New to Pinterest" link from the Pinterest Business home page.

The primary difference you'll see with setting up a new account as opposed to converting an existing account is the need to upload a profile image. Once you've filled out this form and hit the submit button, you'll find the rest of the process nearly identical to setting up a personal account.

Walk through the steps of finding some boards to follow and setting up your first board and you'll be ready to start pinning.

Tuesday: Understand the Category System

Pinterest displays content to Pinterest users in one of two ways: by aggregating the feeds of the users and pinboards you choose to follow and by dividing the pins into topical categories. (We'll talk more about how to attract followers in Chapter 6.)

Today, we're going to focus on the Pinterest Category system. We'll explore what the categories are, why they are essential to a good Pinterest strategy, and how to leverage categories as you look to build a strong Pinterest stream.

What Are the Pinterest Categories?

When you log in to Pinterest, you'll notice a list of links across the top of the page. One of them reads "Categories." Hovering over this link will open up a drop-down menu of the 33 categories Pinterest was using as of this writing (see Figure 4.14).

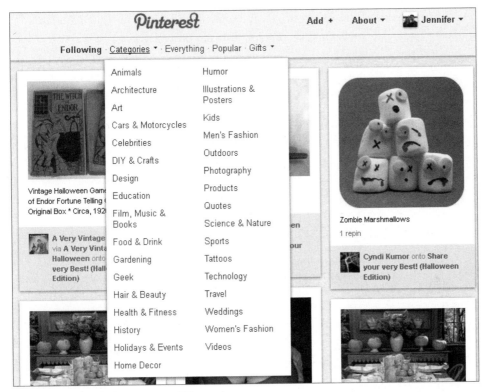

Figure 4.14 Pinterest divides pins into one of 33 categories.

These categories are Pinterest's way of helping users browse other pins they might be interested in. Some categories like "Weddings" or "Gardening" are fairly self-explanatory. Other categories like "Humor" and "Geek" are slightly more subjective and can contain any number and variety of pins.

It's important to realize that you aren't limited to setting up boards with these category names and that you don't even have to associate any of your pins with these categories. However, if you choose not to associate your content with Pinterest's predefined categories, your content will only show up for the people who have chosen to follow your Pinterest account.

Why Do You Need to Use Pinterest's Categories?

The single biggest reason to make use of Pinterest's categories is for exposure, pure and simple. Getting a pin listed on a Pinterest category page is the ideal way to gain exposure, gather repins, and get yourself on the radar of other Pinterest users who are looking for people to follow.

Consider it this way. When you post a pin without a category, it exists in a bit of a vacuum. It will only display to the people who have elected to follow the content on the board you've pinned it to. That means you're limiting the number of chances you have for the content to be repinned.

When you utilize the Pinterest Category system and match up your pinboards with one of Pinterest's predefined categories, your pin propagates in two ways. It will still show for the people who have chosen to follow your board, but it will also have a chance to show on the appropriate category page, giving you access to a much larger number of potential repinners (see Figure 4.15).

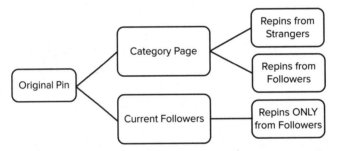

Figure 4.15 Taking the time to match categories to your Pinterest boards dramatically increases the exposure of your pins.

Browsing Categories

It's a very good idea to take some time to sit down and work your way through the Pinterest categories. At the very least, you should look through the categories most closely related to your business or your offerings to get an idea of what types of content get pinned and repinned.

For example, if you're in the travel business, you might want to spend some time scrolling through the Travel category searching for content that has been repinned. This can be an excellent way to get an idea of what types of content may perform well for your business on Pinterest.

It's also helpful when browsing categories to take a look at the names of the pinboards people are pinning their content to. The person who pins pictures of beautiful places into boards titled "Places to Visit" are likely just collecting dreams and ideas. On the other hand, the person who pins a picture of the seating chart of a 747 to a board titled "Vietnam/Thailand Trip 2012" is probably using Pinterest to plan an actual trip and might be worth reaching out to with some strong original content.

Take some time today to look around Pinterest. Explore the various categories and see what the popular topics and ideas are in each of them. You'll quickly learn that knitters, upcyclers, and paper craft types have a strong presence in the DIY & Crafts category or that homesteaders and disaster-preparedness types can sometimes overpower the Gardening and Outdoors categories. Investing the time to understand the pulse of Pinterest can go a long way toward helping you develop a plan to create content for it.

Wednesday: Understand the Search System

Another way Pinterest has revolutionized the way people do research and discover information via the Social Web is by offering an alternative to standard search engines. Universal Search has done an excellent job of bringing more visual elements to the search results at sites like Google, but most users will need to click on and visit several listings to find what they're looking for (see Figure 4.16).

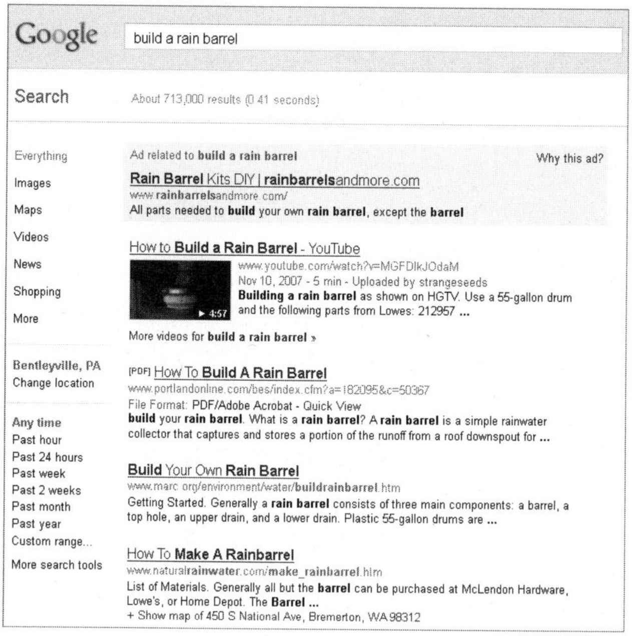

Figure 4.16 Standard search results from a search engine require time spent reading link descriptions and clicking through for a view.

Consider the results when running the same search on Pinterest (see Figure 4.17). Pinterest shows users a list of image-based results with short descriptions of the content and an indicator of how popular each particular pin is.

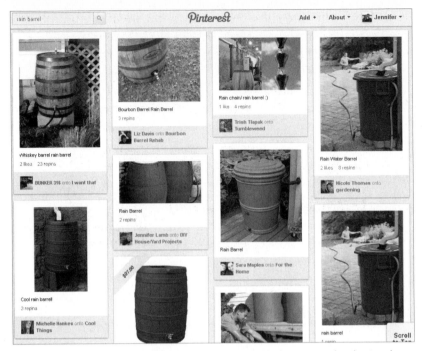

Figure 4.17 Pinterest search results offer visual listings accompanied by descriptions and total repin and likes count.

The complicated piece of Pinterest's search results are that no definable algorithm has been detected yet. Running the same search on different days or even from different systems can return dramatically different results. Additionally, the results can range from listings with high numbers of repins to single postings and can come from Pinterest users with anywhere from zero followers to several thousand followers.

Even though marketers are not yet able to fully understand the Pinterest search algorithm, there's still plenty of benefit to be had in using Pinterest search.

Searching for Pins

The first type of search you'll need to understand is the Pin Search. This is the default search option on the site and will return a list of individual pins related to the keyword or phrase you've entered into the search box.

To get started, take a look at the top-left side of the Pinterest home page and you'll spot the search box (see Figure 4.18).

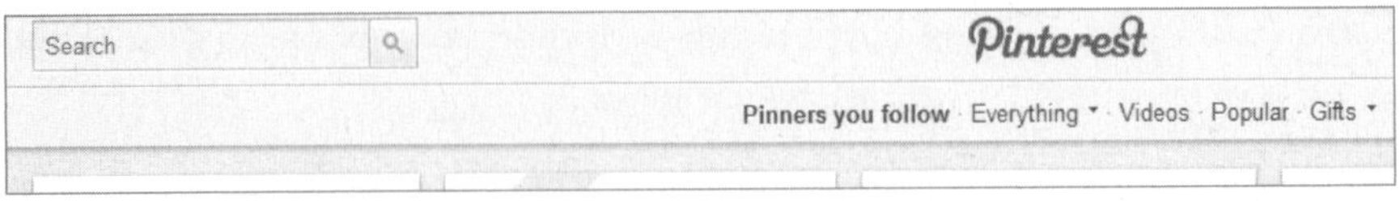

Figure 4.18 The Pinterest search box is found in the upper-left corner of the site.

Typing a keyword or phrase into this box will generate a list of pins related to your search query. At the top of the search results will also be links to refine the search to look for "Boards" or "People" (see Figure 4.19).

Figure 4.19 Pinterest search results default to pin listings but allow users to refine the search to show Boards or People.

Running searches for pins can be a great way, as an individual user, to find a lot of content on a single topic. Although it's a good strategy to pin as much unique content as you are able, there are also times when it makes sense to search for a specific topic to help flesh out a board you've just started.

Searching for People

Of course if you are looking for a particular brand, person, or website, you can simply select the People option from just below the search box. This will narrow down the results to any applicable people who fit your search criteria (see Figure 4.20).

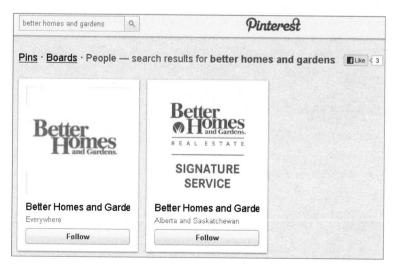

Figure 4.20 Pinterest allows users to search for individual users, an ideal way to locate your favorite brand or website.

Searching for Boards

The final way to search Pinterest is also one of the most beneficial. Selecting the Boards link to refine your search results can be a great way to explore the pinboards set up by other users on the system.

When you consider the fact that Pinterest allows you to follow an individual pinboard for a user rather than forcing you to follow every piece of content they pin, searching for boards becomes an excellent way to find new people to follow and connect with.

Consider the Pinterest search for "bento box" I ran back in Figure 4.19. If we click the Boards qualifier on the search results page, we switch to seeing the boards set up by other users about this topic (see Figure 4.21). What makes these search results even more useful is that you can choose to follow each listing right there on the search results page.

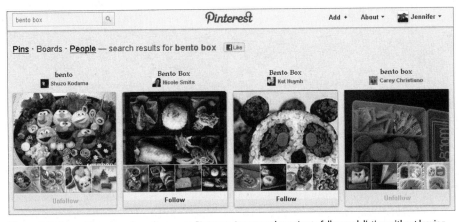

Figure 4.21 A board-based search results page on Pinterest gives users the option to follow each listing without leaving the results page.

Running these types of searches can be an excellent way to expand your network. Searching for topics you're interested in gives you access to more users and more pins, and gets you on the radar of the people you choose to follow.

Thursday: Create and Organize Your Boards

One of the most important parts of setting up a strong Pinterest account is building and managing boards properly. You set up a few starter boards back in Chapter 3, "What Makes Pinterest Valuable?," when you were opening your accounts. Now it's time to do a little bit of refinement to maximize their potential.

How to Create a Pinboard

There are two primary ways to create a new pinboard once you have your account up and running. You can set them up while you're pinning or repinning an item, or you can set them up within your profile.

The most common way to set them up is while you're pinning items. This is because many people don't even realize they want or need a specific pinboard until they have a piece of content they'd like to pin and no idea where to pin it.

Setting up new boards while pinning works a little something like this. First, spot an item you'd like to pin and select the Pin It button or, on Pinterest itself, select the Repin option. When the boards pops up allowing you to edit the description and select a pinboard, scroll to the bottom of your list of boards and look for the Create New Board form (see Figure 4.22). Type in the name of your new pinboard and click Create. The board will be created and the pin you made will be published onto it.

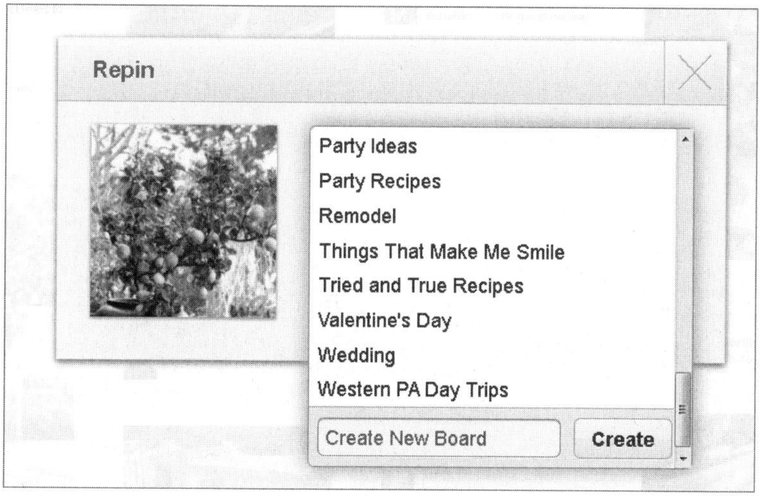

Repin

- Party Ideas
- Party Recipes
- Remodel
- Things That Make Me Smile
- Tried and True Recipes
- Valentine's Day
- Wedding
- Western PA Day Trips

Create New Board   **Create**

Figure 4.22 You can create a new pinboard while pinning items.

There's one big problem with creating pinboards this way, though. They don't have categories tied with them yet, which means any pin you place onto the board does not have the chance to get fed into the primary category feeds. This can cost you dearly in terms of missed opportunities for repins and exposures.

The better way to create a new pinboard is right on Pinterest itself. To create a board from within Pinterest, look for the "Add +" link in the menu system at the top of the page (see Figure 4.23).

Search   *Pinterest*   Add +   About ▾   Jennifer ▾

Pinners you follow Everything ▾ · Videos Popular Gifts ▾

Figure 4.23 The "Add +" button at the top of your Pinterest profile allows you to create a new pinboard.

Once you've clicked the "Add +" button, you'll get a pop-up window asking you to select one of three choices (see Figure 4.24). The last of these choices is "Create a Board." This is the one you'll want to click.

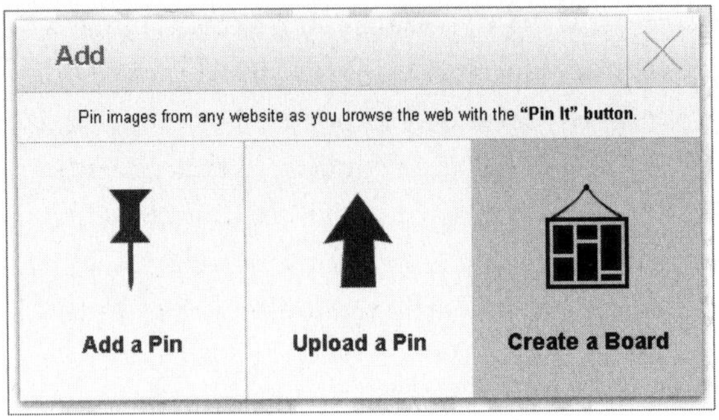

Figure 4.24 Select "Create a Board" to build and categorize a new pinboard on Pinterest.

At this point, Pinterest will pop up a new window asking you to name your new board, select a category to place it in, and specify who can pin to the board (see Figure 4.25). If you plan to use it on your own, leave the default set to your name. If you're setting up a collaborative pinboard, you can add other pinners during the creation process. (You'll learn more about collaborative pinning in Chapter 9, "Week 6—Developing a Successful Pinterest Strategy.")

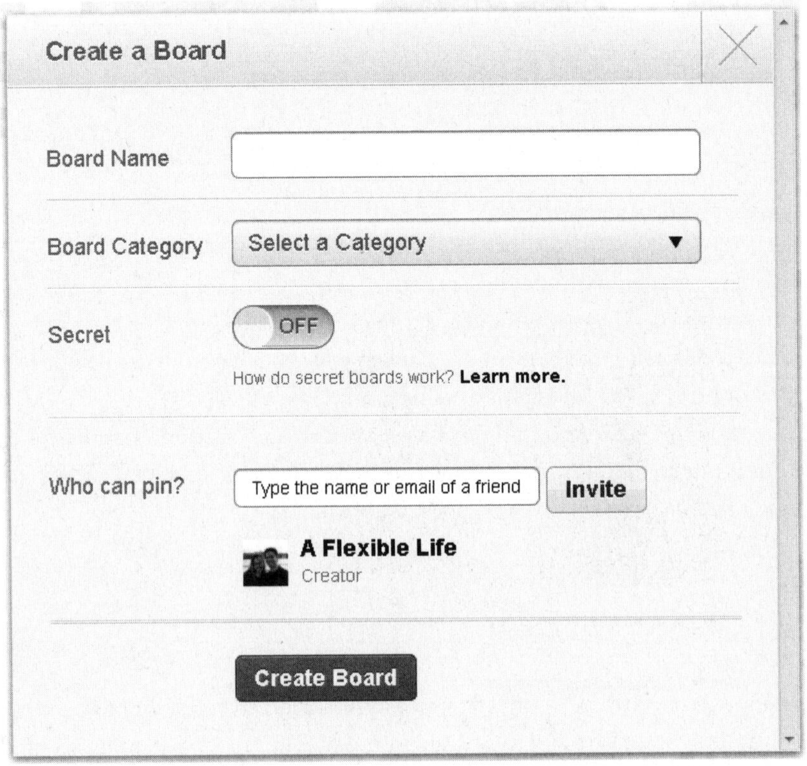

Figure 4.25 Selecting the name, category, and pinners you would like associated with your new pinboard

You also have the option of making your board "secret." Pinterest allows you to have up to three secret pinboards at a time, though you can be part of additional pinboards if they have been created by another user. Once you've created a secret board, you can edit that board's settings to invite other users to participate in these boards.

Selecting a category during setup is an important part of this process. Let's explore why.

Naming and Categorizing Pinboards

A pinboard without a name or category is nothing more than an aimless collection of images no one's ever likely to see. In fact, any content pinned to a board that is not associated with a category will only show up to Pinterest users who have specifically chosen to follow the user or the board it's been posted to.

This is why it's essential to properly name and categorize any pinboard you set up on Pinterest. The easiest way to categorize your board is during setup, as shown in the previous section. The second way to categorize a board is by visiting the pinboard in question and taking advantage of the handy little reminder Pinterest gives you right there on the board's page (see Figure 4.26).

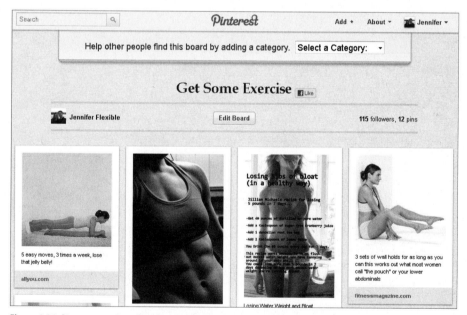

Figure 4.26 Pinterest provides a drop-down category option for any board not already tied to a category.

It's also a good idea to think about the names you assign to your Pinterest boards. Keep in mind those names will influence both whether or not you show up in search results and whether or not people click the follow button when they view your pinboards.

For this reason, it's important to give your boards descriptive names that are still easily understandable and take into account keyword-friendly words and phrases. This is why board names like "Kid Party Ideas" will likely gather more followers than "Kayden's Third Birthday."

Organizing Pinboard Display

Another important thing to consider about your Pinterest profile is the display of your pinboards. When a Pinterest user visits your profile to consider whether or not to follow you, your boards are what create your first impression.

If your board listings are haphazard, empty, or otherwise unattractive, there's not much there to encourage people to sign up for more (see Figure 4.27).

Figure 4.27 Featuring empty boards at the top of your profile can drive away potential followers.

On the other hand, if people visit your account and quickly see a wide range of interesting topics and well-curated pinboards, there's a very good chance they'll both follow some boards and scroll down further to see what else you have to offer (see Figure 4.28).

Figure 4.28 It's important to present and curate your pinboard listings as well as your pins.

Setting up a well-ordered pinboard display on your personal profile is easy. When visiting your own Pinterest profile, simply look for the small icon next to the Edit Profile button (see Figure 4.29). Clicking this icon allows you to drag your pinboards around the page to rearrange them in whichever order you would like.

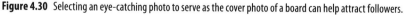

Figure 4.29 Click the Rearrange Boards icon next to the Edit Profile button to shuffle the order of your pinboards.

Rearranging your pinboards is an important part of curating your Pinterest presence over time. New boards show up at the bottom of your list by default, so if you're investing time in a new board, you'll want to shuffle the listings to make sure it's showing up more prominently.

It's also important to understand how images are assigned to represent your boards. By default, the most recent item pinned to a board will show up as the primary image for the pinboard. The smaller thumbnail size items under the primary images are also the most recent items added to the board.

To edit this, you'll need to scroll over the primary image of a pinboard listing and click the Edit Board Cover option (see Figure 4.30). This will display a widget that allows you to scroll through all the pinned images for that board until you find the one you'd like to set as the cover photo.

Figure 4.30 Selecting an eye-catching photo to serve as the cover photo of a board can help attract followers.

Friday: Start Pinning!

Now that you've got everything up and running, you can spend time just playing around on the site. Run a few searches. Look for topics that interest you or that you believe might interest your target audience. Search for brands and companies you're familiar with and explore the way they've set up their boards. Run some board-based searches and find new content to begin following.

Then jump into the mix and start pinning and repinning some content. We'll go more in-depth on the various ways to pin, repin, and even upload original content in the next chapter.

Week 2—Curating Content with Pinterest

Now that you've gotten yourself up and running with a Pinterest account, it's time to put it to use to start collecting ideas, links, and pictures. Remember, Pinterest is a powerful online filing system that gives you visual access to the content you might wish to use down the road. In the previous chapter, we talked about getting your account up and running. In this chapter, we'll be focused on the many ways to pin content to your account.

Chapter Contents
Monday: Repinning Content from Pinterest
Tuesday: Pinning New Content with the Pin It Button and Bookmarklet
Wednesday: Uploading Original Pins to Pinterest
Thursday: Pinning Products
Friday: Pinning Content Using a Smartphone

Monday: Repinning Content from Pinterest

Before you worry about pinning fresh content from your site and the sites you spend time reading, it's a good idea to understand how to repin content. A repin is the Pinterest equivalent of a Twitter retweet or a Facebook share. In other words, a repin is an endorsement of content someone else has already uploaded to the site.

How to Repin Content

Starting out on Pinterest by repinning content is the absolute simplest way to familiarize yourself with Pinterest and its many features.

To repin a piece of content, you hover your mouse over the Pinterest image you want to interact with. When you do, a set of three action icons will pop up. One allows you to repin the image, one allows you to "like" the image, and the last one allows you to comment on the image.

Clicking the Repin button will pop up an interface that allows you to assign the pin to one of your categories and to edit the description attached to the pin. Clicking the Pin It button then pushes the image into your own feed. The entire process takes less than 30 seconds (see Figure 5.1).

Figure 5.1 Repin content by clicking the Repin button, selecting a category and description in the pop-up box, and clicking the Pin It button.

Repinning Content from Your Friend's Feeds

The easiest way to find pins (and the way most people get started) is by looking through the feed produced for you by your friends' activity and repinning their pins. When you log into Pinterest, your friends' activity feed is the first thing that pops up (see Figure 5.2).

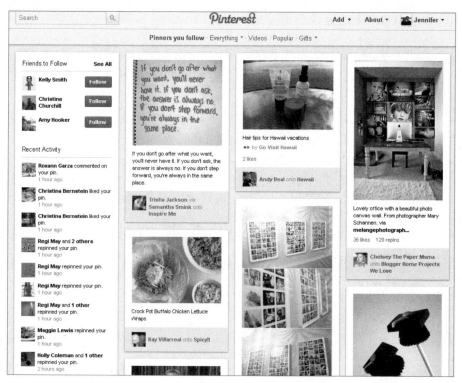

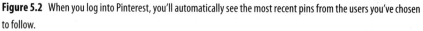

Figure 5.2 When you log into Pinterest, you'll automatically see the most recent pins from the users you've chosen to follow.

Scanning the list of pins from the people you've chosen to follow is a great way to familiarize yourself with the site. There's a high chance you share enough common interests with your friends that you'll be interested in repinning some content. You'll also have a chance to adjust your pinboards to reflect the content you actually find yourself pinning.

> **Note:** One of the interesting things about Pinterest is the sheer volume of "pass-along" that takes places. According to data released by RJMetrics (http://blog.rjmetrics.com/pinterest-data-analysis-an-inside-look/), over 80 percent of the pins on Pinterest are repins of content originally posted by other users. Compare this to Twitter, where Hubspot reports less than 1.5 percent of tweets are retweets.

Repinning Content from Category Feeds

Once you've spent some time scrolling through the pins listed in your Pinterest feed, you have two choices. You can either sit around and wait for your friends to pin more content, or you can head off into the category system of Pinterest to browse more content.

To visit the categories, you'll need to use the navigation options under the Pinterest logo at the top of the screen (see Figure 5.3). You'll have the option to choose from five options:

Pinners You Follow The feed created by compiling the pins of all the Pinterest users and pinboards you have chosen to follow.

Everything A drop-down box of the two dozen or so topical Pinterest categories. Select a category, or click Everything to see, well…everything.

Popular A collection of the most popular pins from all categories of Pinterest.

Gifts A collection of pins that feature a price tag associated with them.

Figure 5.3 Pinterest gives you five ways to browse the content on its site.

In the early days of your time on Pinterest, chances are good that your Pinterest feed will be filled with people who know one another, since most Pinterest users elect to follow their Facebook friends who have already signed up for the service. Visiting topical categories within Pinterest is a great way to introduce new content to your stream and to your followers.

Tuesday: Pinning New Content with the Pin It Button and Bookmarklet

Once you've had a chance to familiarize yourself with the different areas of Pinterest and have spent some time repinning content from the site, it's time to start exploring the idea of pinning new content. Pinning images and links you collect on your own travels through the Web is a great way to differentiate yourself as a Pinterest user.

With so much content being repinned to the site, original pins tend to stand out and the Pinterest users who post them can quickly gain credibility as a quality curator.

There are several ways to add new pins to Pinterest, so let's take some time today to walk through each of them.

Spotting the Pin It Button on Websites

The fastest and easiest way to pin content to Pinterest is using the Pin It button found on many websites. In most cases, this button will appear alongside other popular social sharing options from Facebook, Twitter, and Google+ (see Figure 5.4).

You found out you are pregnant. Never has it been more crucial to eat well. Not eating well during your pregnancy can increase your risk of complications.

Eating well has never been easier during pregnancy than it is now.

Figure 5.4 The Pin It button often shows up at the top of articles near other popular social sharing buttons.

In some cases, sites put a special emphasis on pinned content as part of their content strategy. These sites often feature multiple Pin It buttons paired up with prime images in their content. In these cases, you may notice the Pin It button showing up more often and/or showing up without other social sharing buttons (see Figure 5.5).

Figure 5.5 Some sites choose to place Pin It buttons next to prime images as a reminder to readers to share the content via Pinterest.

The Pin It button first popped up mostly on recipe, crafting, and home decorating sites, but it is quickly making its way onto more and more e-commerce sites (see Figure 5.6). Etsy has become one of the most pinned sites on the Internet, partly due to the extreme overlap in target audience with Pinterest, but also due to their early integration of the Pin It button.

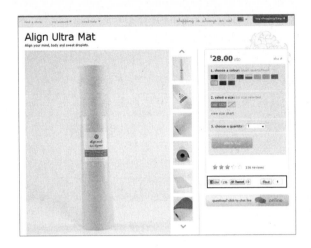

Figure 5.6 E-commerce sites targeting women, like Lululemon, have integrated the Pin it button alongside social sharing buttons for Facebook and Twitter to help capitalize on the increased exposure that comes with customers pinning products.

Installing and Using the Pinterest Bookmarklet

While more and more websites are adopting the Pin It button as part of their interface, the greatest majority of sites and blogs have yet to integrate it.

If part of your marketing plan includes curating unique content for your Pinterest account, lack of Pin It button integration could be a problem for you. This means the fastest and easiest way to add new content to Pinterest is by using the Pinterest bookmarklet.

You can install the Pinterest bookmarklet by visiting the Pinterest Goodies page (http://pinterest.com/about/goodies/). It's as simple as dragging a link from the screen to your bookmarks or favorites folder (see Figure 5.7).

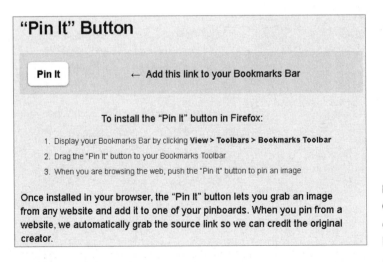

Figure 5.7 The Pinterest Goodies page gives drag-and-drop access to the Pinterest bookmarklet.

Installing it into the bookmarks folder that displays in your browser will give you easy one-click access to pin an image from any page on the Web (see Figure 5.8).

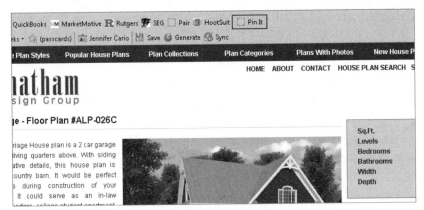

Figure 5.8 Click the Pin It bookmarklet while visiting any page featuring content you'd like to pin.

Clicking the bookmarklet will launch a small pop-up window that mimics the same interface attached to the Pin It button that shows up on integrated websites.

Using the Pin It Pop-Up Window

Whether you are using the Pin It bookmarklet or pinning content using an integrated Pin It button on a website or blog, the process is generally the same.

You'll be taken to either a new web page or a pop-up window asking you to select the image you'd like to represent the page in your pin. Once you've selected your image, you'll need to assign a category and write a brief description of the pin (see Figure 5.9).

Figure 5.9 To pin new content, simply select the image you'd like to pin, write a description, and choose a category.

You can also choose to publish your pin to Facebook or Twitter during this step.

Wednesday: Uploading Original Pins to Pinterest

Sometimes, you'll want to pin content that isn't already published to a website. Whether you are taking a picture with a camera phone and pinning it on the go, or you are creating a Pinterest-specific image you want to track the spread of, there are times you'll both need and want to upload an original pin directly into the Pinterest stream.

Why Upload an Original Pin?

There are many reasons a user might choose to upload an original Pin directly to the site. They might be using Pinterest as a place to host photos they've taken of their own recipes, of items they're thinking of using in a home remodel, or of places they've visited. Although Pinterest doesn't usually operate as a standard photo sharing site, plenty of people use it that way.

From the marketing perspective, there is a compelling reason to consider creating and uploading an original image that cannot be found elsewhere on your website.

Because Pinterest users are so enamored with DIY project ideas, step-by-step photo collages often spread very quickly. Many marketers choose to create a Pinterest-specific step-by-step photo collage that can be branded with the site name and entered directly into the stream. (We'll talk more about this approach in Chapter 7, "Week 4—Purposely Propagating Pins on Pinterest.")

Once you've created your image, uploading an original pin is quite simple. Visit the Pinterest website, log in, and click the Add + button located at the top of the page (see Figure 5.10).

Figure 5.10 Use the Add + button at the top of the screen to access the Upload A Pin feature.

Doing so will launch a pop-up window (see Figure 5.11), giving you the option to add a new pin, upload a new pin, or create a new board. When you select Upload A Pin, Pinterest will offer you a browser window to choose the file from your hard drive before taking you to the standard interface for choosing a category and writing a description.

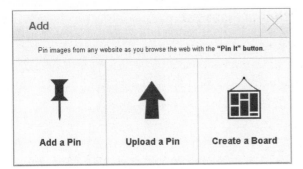

Figure 5.11 Click the Upload A Pin button to pin an image off your hard drive.

Mobile app users can also add pins using the Pinterest app for iOS or Android smartphones. Simply take a picture using the camera on your phone, or capture a screen shot of the web page or image you'd like to upload, and save it to your phone's photo album. Then look for the camera icon on the Pinterest app to start the upload process (see Figure 5.12).

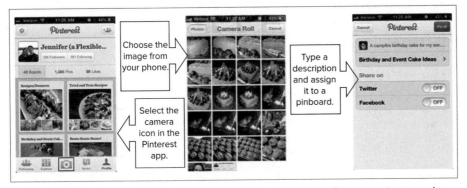

Figure 5.12 Selecting the camera icon from the Pinterest app allows you to take a new photo or access images saved to your phone's album in order to create a new pin.

Editing an Original Pin to Include a URL

The problem with uploading a new pin to Pinterest from your hard drive is there's no URL associated with it. For some reason, as of the publish date of this book, Pinterest has not seen fit to include a form field for the URL you'd like to attach the pin to.

That means you'll need to edit the URL associated with the pin if you want the pin to lead anywhere. In general, it's a good idea to understand how to edit the URL of a pin anyway. If you'd like to adjust the URL to include an affiliate code or a tracking code, you'll need to do this after you've added the pin to your account.

To edit the URL of an existing pin, simply hover your mouse over the pin and click the Edit button that appears next to the Repin button (see Figure 5.13).

Figure 5.13 To edit the URL of a pin, you must first click the Edit button that appears at the top of a pin. Doing so will launch a page where you can enter a new URL and save the pin to reflect the change.

This will take you to a page featuring the existing description, link, and board assignment of the pin. Simply edit the link (or add one if you've uploaded the pin from your hard drive) and click Save Pin.

Thursday: Pinning Products

While many sites eschew product postings and pretty much any e-commerce product promotion, Pinterest is very friendly in this regard.

How to Trigger a Product Listing

For users within the United States, adding a product listing to Pinterest is quite easy. You need to add a dollar figure, including the U.S. dollar symbol ($) to your description. Doing so will cause a small angled banner showing the price to appear over top of the image (see Figure 5.14).

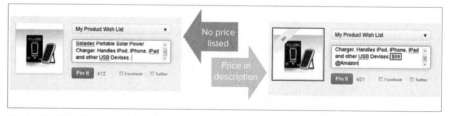

Figure 5.14 Uploading a pin without including a price in U.S. dollars will cause it to upload as a standard pin. Uploading a pin with a price in U.S. dollars will cause it to be tagged as a product.

As of this writing, Pinterest does not include support for non-U.S. currency. Given Pinterest's growing popularity overseas, it's a safe bet Pinterest will add this feature for other popular currencies in the near future.

How Pinterest Displays and Categorizes Products

All pins posted to Pinterest that include a price in U.S. dollars automatically get added

~~~ory~~ on the site. Pinterest divides product pins into six categories based

> use when keeping an eye out for birth-
> a great opportunity for repins as brows-
> them to boards they've set up for wish lists,
> ns serve to enter the product back into
> will be spotted and repinned yet again by

someone new.

An interesting thing about Pinterest's approach to product listings is the fact that product pins are not segregated from the general category topics and restricted to appearing only in the gift categories. In fact, products are the only pins that automatically show up in multiple categories without you needing to repin them into different boards.

Product pins will be tied to whatever category the board they are pinned to is associated with (see Figure 5.15). If your "camping wish list" is tied to the outdoors category, any product you pin to it will have a chance to enter the outdoors stream *and* the gift list stream.

Figure 5.15 Product pins will show up in the category stream associated with the board they are pinned to. This product pin of a bouquet shows up in both the gift stream and the gardening stream.

While Pinterest's Terms of Service specifically speak out against uploading your entire product catalog to the site, there are many creative ways to utilize this feature. Encouraging fans to curate seasonal or event-based boards that feature your product or even having your staff jointly curate a board featuring gifts within a specific price range can go a long way toward creatively including your products in your Pinterest stream and gaining them additional exposure.

We'll explore more ideas along these lines in Chapters 11, 12, and 13.

Friday: Pinning Content Using a Smartphone

Here's one of the great things about Pinterest; it's every bit as fun and entertaining to use Pinterest to browse eye candy and gather ideas via mobile apps as it is to use it on the computer. That makes Pinterest an ideal time killer for people waiting in line, for those who are stuck on the bus or train, or for those who simply feel like doing a little browsing without carting around a laptop.

Using the iPhone App

iPhone users who find themselves absolutely itching to find new ideas and inspiration when they're not near a computer can feed the addiction with the official Pinterest iPhone app (see Figure 5.16). The app allows users to run searches, explore category feeds, repin content, edit existing pins and boards, and connect with other users.

Figure 5.16 The official Pinterest app for iPhone gives users access to most of the standard onsite Pinterest tools and activities.

As mentioned earlier in this chapter, it even allows users to take and upload a photo from their phone as a pin. Unfortunately, pins uploaded from the iPhone app do not include URLs. In fact, users have to visit the actual Pinterest site and edit the pins they upload if they want to attach URLs to them.

This makes pinning from the iPhone app fairly pointless unless you are working to put together a simple gallery or collection for your own purposes.

Understanding this limitation is important as it can play a heavy role in scheduling your time on Pinterest as part of your overall marketing strategy. Pinterest users can focus on pinning new and original content from the computers and save repinning for times when using the mobile app or mobile site are more convenient.

Using the Mobile Version of Pinterest

After nearly a year of grumbling and more than a little pleading from the Android community, Pinterest finally released a native Android app in August of 2012. The app shares most of the same functionality of the native iPhone app.

For those who prefer not to download and use an app interface, Pinterest also offers a mobile friendly HTML5 version of the site (see Figure 5.17).

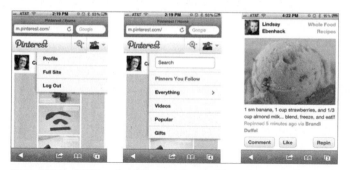

Figure 5.17 The HTML5 version of Pinterest is formatted for smaller mobile screens and includes the ability to browse pins, interact with users, and search or sort by category.

Although functionality of the HTML5 version of the site is strong, it does carry many of the same limitations the iPhone app does. The biggest is the difficulty in pinning new content.

Of course, not much new pinning tends to take place on the Pinterest website anyway, so the lack of this feature in the HTML5 and app versions of Pinterest are not completely surprising. The Pin It button that appears on many blogs and e-commerce sites will still work from a phone. The problem arises when you visit sites that do not have Pinterest integration.

The best workaround for this limitation is to install the Pin It bookmarklet to the bookmarks section of your phone's browser. This will allow you to pin new content from any website you can access with your mobile browser.

Getting your content into Pinterest is the single biggest battle you'll face when you first launch a Pinterest strategy. Figuring out how to enable your existing fan base to put content into Pinterest for you is the second. Once you have this down pat, it's time to start focusing on making connections and building followers. That's exactly what we're going to concentrate on coming up in the next chapter.

Week 3–Find and Attract Followers

While there's a lot about Pinterest that differentiates it from other social media channels, there's one way in which it is absolutely the same: the need to create a following. Much like Twitter, Facebook, LinkedIn, Tumblr, and the rest of the social media world, a Pinterest user without followers is an island unto themselves. The site stops functioning as a collective opportunity to explore the Web and starts operating solely as an image-based bookmarking website.

This week we'll take a look at the world of user-to-user interactions. You'll learn how to build a following and how to find people of value to follow. We'll also explore how your use of boards can play a strong role in building up your Pinterest presence.

6

Chapter Contents

Monday: Understand Followers and Following
Tuesday: Find People to Follow
Wednesday: Selectively Follow Users' Boards
Thursday: Understand Commenting and Liking
Friday: Recategorize Pins over Time

Monday: Understand Followers and Following

Most Pinterest users start off using Pinterest the same way they use Facebook. They connect with the people they are already friends with and spend time browsing and repinning content posted by their friends and family.

Although there's nothing wrong with this tactic, businesses and marketers who wish to use Pinterest to advance their clients will clearly need to put more time and effort into developing a following. Additionally, taking the time to find and follow other interesting posters can provide your Pinterest stream with an excellent boost in quality pins, making it even easier to find great content to repin.

For this reason, it's important to view your Pinterest interactions and relationships the way you might view Twitter. Each person you connect with or follow provides you with potential exposure to new people of interest. Additionally, each person who follows you provides your account with increased exposure to their friends.

Why Following Users Is Important

There are two primary ways to share content on the Pinterest network. You can either pin new content you discover as you make your way around the Web, or you can repin content that has been added by another user. Since roughly 80 percent of the content on Pinterest consists of repins, spending some time browsing existing pins and sharing them with your followers can be a fast and easy part of your content strategy for the site.

From this perspective, it quickly becomes clear why following more users is better than following just a few users. After all, the more people you follow, the more content you'll see flooding into your stream. That content can quickly and easily be repinned and shared with your own followers.

That said, if you are only following people you already know, chances are high there's going to be a lot of overlap in both Pinterest connections and repins. After all, many of the people you know probably also know each other. Repinning Courtney's content doesn't offer anything new to Melanie, Kara, or Kristine if each of them already follows Courtney's pins (see Figure 6.1). After all, who wants to see the same exact pin showing up over and over again?

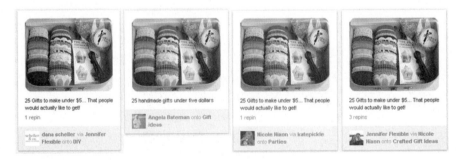

Figure 6.1 When all the Pinterest users you follow also follow each other, you're likely to see a lot of content overlap.

On the other hand, if you use Pinterest to "meet" Rachel, Leslie, Tammy, and Deanna and begin repinning their content, you'll likely be offering something new to the feeds of Melanie, Kara, and Kristine. This makes your stream more valuable.

In fact, for Pinterest users who don't have a lot of time to invest in finding and pinning new content, taking the time to follow unique Pinterest users can be an excellent tactic. The goal is to get original content in front of your followers. It doesn't always matter whether you do this by pinning new content or repinning content they've never seen before. If the pin is new to them, they're likely to find value in it.

Why Gaining Followers Is Important

In the world of social media, gaining followers is a key component of building a strong and successful presence. While Pinterest does allow for users with any number of followers to get original pins launched into category feeds, only a small portion of a user's pins can and will make it into the primary feeds.

This means you have limited opportunity to get pins into an area where they have open exposure to the general Pinterest population. You might make 14 pins in an afternoon, of which only one makes it into the Pinterest category stream. That means the other 13 pins are limited in exposure only to the people who have elected to follow your feed.

Having more followers is the key to increasing exposure of your pins because it provides a higher chance of getting repinned and gaining exposure to second- and third-tier audiences. The more people following and repinning your content, the better exposure your pin will receive.

Understanding the Exponential Reach of Pinterest

This is where the social sharing aspect of social media comes into play. It's what powers the amazing traffic potential behind social media channels like Facebook, Twitter, and Pinterest.

Consider a Pinterest user from a small interior design company. She's using Pinterest to create inspiration boards for clients as well as to build a following for her interior design blog. When she pins a new color palette to her account, that pin reaches the 153 users who have elected to follow her boards (see Figure 6.2).

Figure 6.2 When a Pinterest user pins an image, it broadcasts to the feeds of their followers.

What's important to realize is the reach doesn't stop there. If any of those users choose to repin the image, the broadcast opportunity starts back up again. A single repin suddenly gives you access to a whole new set of followers. Multiple repins cause that number to increase dramatically. Let's say 15 people from our previous example choose to repin the color palette. If those users have an average of 100 followers each, the pin has suddenly reached the original 153 people *plus* 1,500 new users (see Figure 6.3).

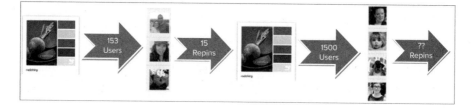

Figure 6.3 When Pinterest user followers choose to repin the content, the number of users exposed to the image can increase dramatically.

Take this process out to a third, fourth, or fifth degree and the numbers have a chance to multiply exponentially. It's this process that explains how a Pinterest user with a dozen or so followers is capable of having a pin rack up thousands of repins.

Tuesday: Find People to Follow

Now that we've explored why it's so important to follow a wide range of interesting pinners, it's time to invest a little time expanding our accounts and finding some new people to connect with.

There are several ways to expand the list of who you follow. You just need to make a plan to set aside 5 to 10 minutes a day for a few weeks. That will give you enough time to build a strong enough base that you can shift to adding people as you notice them over time.

The first thing you'll need to do, however, is make sure you've connected with the people you already know.

Finding People You Know

Pinterest does a great job of integrating your Pinterest account with your contacts from Facebook, Gmail, and Yahoo! Mail. You can use the system either to find friends who already use the service or to invite friends who might not have signed up yet. You'll find the connection options located under your username in the top-right corner of the Pinterest site (see Figure 6.4).

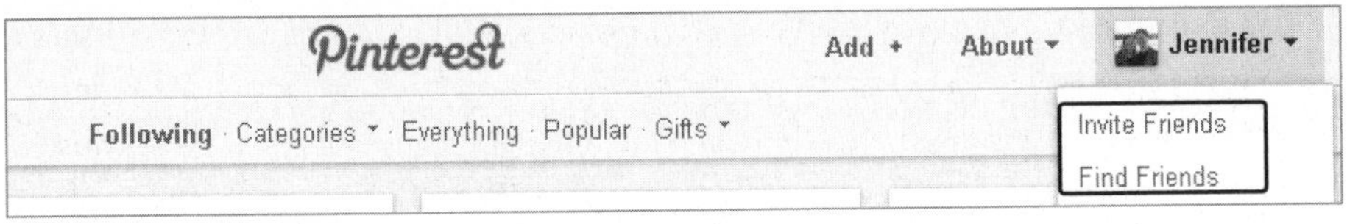

Figure 6.4 Clicking the down arrow next to your name will give you the option to connect with friends.

Doing so will take you to a page that allows you to choose the method you'd like to use to find contacts. Pinterest's registration process defaults to Facebook, which is generally the best option anyway as it guarantees you will be connecting with people you know. (Using Gmail or Yahoo! Mail will pull up anyone you've ever exchanged an email with.)

The Facebook connection screen will divide your Facebook friends into two areas (see Figure 6.5). The left side will feature your Facebook friends who do not yet have a Pinterest account along with an invitation button. The right side will feature any Facebook friend who has a Pinterest account that you are not already following.

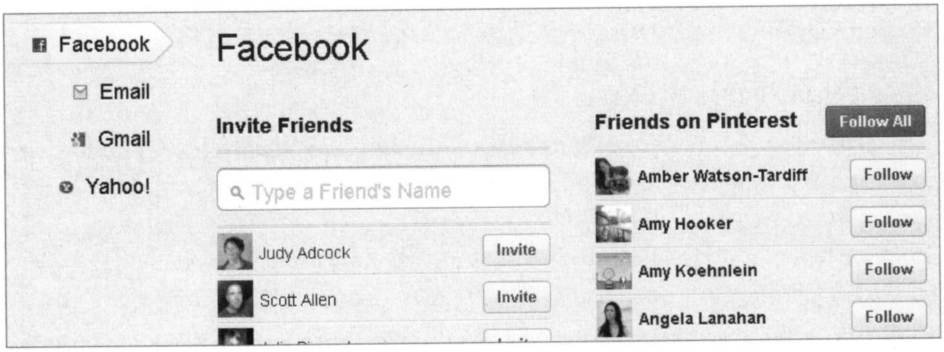

Figure 6.5 Pinterest allows you to invite Facebook friends to the service as well as connect with Facebook friends who already use the service.

Working your way through these options can be a great way to set up a starting point of connections on Pinterest. Since Pinterest users receive notification when someone follows them, it's also a great way to show up on the radar of your friends who may have joined the service before you.

People by Association

Another great way to find pinners is by following the repin trail. Let's say you see a pin come across your account that you like. Chances are high it's a repin. Taking a look at the listing will quickly show you who the friend of a friend was who pinned the content (see Figure 6.6).

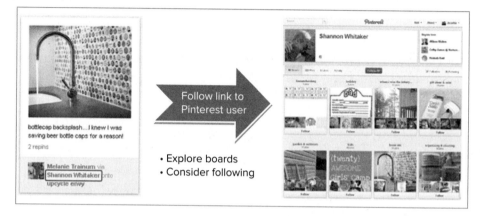

Figure 6.6 Pinterest repins include a link to the profile of the original pinner. Follow this link to explore new accounts you might wish to follow.

Clicking on that Pinterest user's name will take you to their personal profile, where you can review their board and decide if you'd like to follow them as well.

This tactic is an excellent way to explore new user accounts and connections. That said, it's important to remember that following a trail of users to expand the number of people you follow can have its limitations. After all, the entire purpose of following new people is to generate more original content for your own feed. That means the real value is in finding people your other contacts haven't heard of yet.

People by Category

Taking the time to research people who have pins landing in the various category streams can be an excellent way to expand your feed. In fact, it's pretty much the only way to connect with Pinterest users you don't already have a tie to.

Finding these users works much the same way as finding new followers from the repins showing up in your stream. The primary difference is you likely don't know any of the people showing up in the category stream (see Figure 6.7).

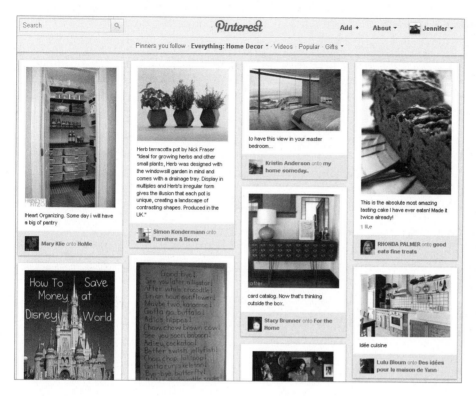

Figure 6.7 Chances are slim that you will recognize the names of any users showing up in the category feed. This makes for an ideal space to find new people to follow.

To find new people to follow, scan the category page for the pins that are a great fit for your Pinterest strategy. Then click the username of the Pinterest user who made the pin and take a look at their personal profile and pin history. If they consistently pin content you find interesting, start following them.

Wednesday: Selectively Follow Users' Boards

One of the biggest steps in going from new Pinterest user to skilled Pinterest user is understanding the value in following boards rather than users. After all, the chances are high that you won't enjoy all the same things a particular Pinterest user does. Why flood your stream with low-fat recipes and knitting patterns if you're only interested in creative tattoos and homesteading?

The Problem with Following a User

By this point, you should be pretty familiar with the concept of following Pinterest users. We've talked about how to find people you already know on Pinterest and how to daisy-chain connections via the repin option to find friends of friends. We've even talked about how to discover Pinterest accounts for people you've never heard of by spending time browsing the category feeds.

Unfortunately, the moment you start following all of these people, you're likely going to find your own Pinterest feed chock-full of content you couldn't care less about.

Say you follow a friend of yours simply because you are connected to him on Facebook. The next time you log in to Pinterest, you might find out this friend has created a board called "animals" where he pins random pictures of animals he finds to be funny (see Figure 6.8).

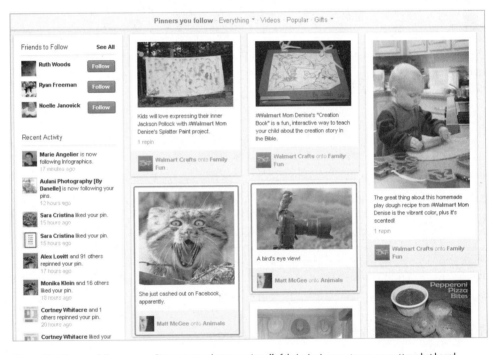

Figure 6.8 When you follow a user on Pinterest, you elect to receive *all* of their pins in your stream, no matter what board they are pinned to.

There's certainly nothing wrong with these pins—they're just not something you are interested in. The great thing about Pinterest is that you can easily remedy this problem. Unlike Facebook or Twitter, where you must follow all of a user's updates, Pinterest allows you to visit their profile and opt in or out of individual boards (see Figure 6.9). This gives you a solution for those pins you don't care about.

Figure 6.9 Visiting a user's profile page gives you the chance to unfollow any boards you might not be interested in. This lets you customize your Pinterest feed over time.

Taking the time to curate your Pinterest feed by unsubscribing to boards you don't find interesting can go a long way toward improving your Pinterest experience.

Follow One (or Many) Boards

Now that you understand how and why to unsubscribe from a Pinterest user's individual boards, you can begin to change the way you follow users.

For example, when you find yourself visiting the Pinterest profile of a user you've discovered via a repin connection or while browsing a category page, you can resist the urge to click the Follow All button and instead turn your focus to the individual boards they are curating.

Since Pinterest shows you five pins per board, it's fairly easy to tell at a glance what type of content a Pinterest user curates (see Figure 6.10).

Figure 6.10 While viewing the profile of a Pinterest user, you can quickly review five pins from each category to decide whether or not following that category makes sense.

Taking the time to browse through their boards to find the ones that are a good fit for your interests, or that match up well with your followers' interests, can be a great way to expand the number of pins showing up in your stream.

Refine Your Follow Strategy over Time

It's a good idea to occasionally revisit your stream from the perspective of what holds your attention and what provides valuable content for your own personal Pinterest strategy.

When you originally followed someone, you may have thought you'd be interested in the inspirational quotes they pin or the infographics they collect. As time passes, you may realize the content on those boards matches up with neither your own interests nor those of your followers.

In other words, if you find you aren't repinning content from a user's board, it's probably time to remove it from your stream.

It's also important to set aside time each month to go looking for new boards to follow. After all, there are always new users joining the service, and most users will continue to add boards over time as they discover new topics they're interested in pinning content to.

Building 15 or 20 minutes a month into pruning your Pinterest stream and finding new boards to follow can be a powerful investment toward maximizing the value of the repin portion of your Pinterest strategy.

Thursday: Understand Commenting and Liking

While pinning and repinning content are the primary ways people interact on Pinterest, the social side of the community goes beyond simply passing along content. Users also have the option of liking a pin or commenting on a pin.

Liking a Pin

Liking a pin is simple. Scroll your cursor over the image and look for the Like button. It shows up at the top of the image between the Repin and Comment buttons (see Figure 6.11).

Figure 6.11 The Like button shows up between the Repin and Comment buttons at the top of a pinned image.

Think of the Pinterest Like button as being similar to liking a Facebook status update or "favoriting" a tweet. It doesn't repin the content to your boards, but it does give you a way to express support for the pin or the pinner.

The images you choose to like on Pinterest are compiled in a "likes" listing that's available from your personal profile page. Simply look for the Likes link next to the Boards and Pins links (see Figure 6.12).

Figure 6.12 A Pinterest user's collection of "liked" pins can be found by visiting their personal profile.

Different users will have different strategies for using the Like button. Some users view it as a way to isolate the very best of their pins. They will both like and repin a piece of content so it will get saved in their boards but will also be accessible by browsing their like listings.

Other users view the Like button as a great alternative to the content they approve of but don't wish to repin to any of their boards. This is how I personally use the Pinterest Like button. My Likes board is full of content I found amusing or interesting but that I don't particularly care to keep archived anywhere (see Figure 6.13).

Figure 6.13 Liking content can be a great way to give a positive response to the original pinner without cluttering up your own Pinterest boards.

The Like button basically becomes my way of taking action on a pin without impacting my overall curation goals. It also gives me a chance to get my own username and account in front of the user who posted the content since Pinterest sends notifications of both repins and likes.

Commenting on a Pin

Another option for giving feedback to a pin you find interesting is to comment on it. The Comment button can be found at the top of a pinned image next to the Repin and Like buttons (see Figure 6.14).

Figure 6.14 The Comment button is located at the top of a pin with the Repin and Like buttons.

Commenting on a pin works much the same way that replying to a tweet, commenting on a Facebook status, or commenting on a blog post does. If you offer something valuable to the conversation, a portion of people will take the time to find out who you are and will consider following you as well.

A good commenting strategy is never as simple as just leaving a random comment on a bunch of pins. You'll want to watch for pins you can offer valuable input on as you do your regular Pinterest browsing. When the opportunity arises to add something that demonstrates your value, take it (see Figure 6.15).

Figure 6.15 Leaving a comment that adds something of real value to a pin is a great way to catch the eye of the original pinner and people who view the pin.

Another benefit of using the comment feature on Pinterest is that you can include URLs in your comments. These URLs will function as links on the site, giving the original pinner and any future viewers the chance to see and take action on the link you've included (see Figure 6.16).

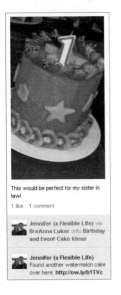

This would be perfect for my sister in law!
1 like   1 comment

Jennifer (a Flexible Life) via BreAnna Luker onto Birthday and Event Cake Ideas

Jennifer (a Flexible Life)
Found another watermelon cake over here: **http://ow.ly/b1TVc**

Figure 6.16 Users can add links as part of a comment on a pin.

One example of proper link usage would be to pin an image that inspired you to take action, perhaps a recipe or DIY project, and then link it to your own version in the comment section. Another might be to comment on a fan's pin that points to content on your site and to include a link to related or additional content elsewhere on your site. As with all instances of online linking, it's best to use links on Pinterest when it truly adds to the conversation and to only sparingly link to your own content.

> **Note:** While it's both possible and permissible to leave a link in the comment section of a pin, it's extremely important to use this tactic sparingly. As with any other form of self-promotion, make sure you carefully weigh whether the link will truly add value to the conversation.

It's also important to keep in mind that commenting on a pin that goes on to get thousands of repins also means getting lots of exposure for your comment and your username as the pin travels various Pinterest boards.

Friday: Recategorize Pins over Time

Well curated boards are an extremely important part of any ongoing Pinterest strategy. Since many users will quickly learn to follow specific pinboards rather than blindly following every pin shared by a specific user, it's essential to offer a combination of boards featuring high-quality content.

Without continual pruning, pinboards can quickly turn into an absolute mishmash of "this might be interesting" and "the picture was pretty, but I haven't clicked on it yet, so I didn't know the link was broken" pins. While this is rarely an issue with original pins, repinning content without first clicking through to view what's on the other side is a great way to clutter up your boards with oftentimes useless garbage.

Additionally, many Pinterest users find boards grow to overwhelming sizes as time goes on and find value in breaking these boards out into more specific pinboards over time. This approach allows other Pinterest users to fine-tune their own following approach to ensure the best content finds its way into their personal Pinterest stream.

Creating Multiple Boards for the Same Topic

Most Pinterest users will set up fairly broad pinboards when they first begin using the system. They'll have boards with names like "Home Improvement" or "Gardening" or "Recipes." While there's nothing wrong with this, the content that goes into these boards can cover a wide range of ideas. Someone looking for more information on organic vegetable gardening may not be interested in a more generalized gardening board that features pins about growing prize-winning roses or container gardening.

That's why the most effective Pinterest users learn to break their boards down into more targeted boards as they begin to compile a wide range of pins related to a specific subtopic.

A user with several hundred pins in a "Recipes" folder may decide to break those down to better target new followers. They might keep the general recipe folder as a catch-all while developing more targeted boards for vegetarians, party recipes, ice cream recipes, and even camping recipes (see Figure 6.17).

Figure 6.17 Savvy Pinterest users learn to expand their pinboards over time to deliver more targeted content to the Pinterest users they want to reach.

This approach works in nearly all verticals. There's no need to lump all infographics into one giant "Infographic" board. Break it down by topic so you can laser-target your followers. The same goes for the previously mentioned "Home Improvement" pinboard. There's no reason not to feature Home Improvement boards for bedrooms, bathrooms, porches, kitchens, dens, home offices, and so on.

There's no hard-and-fast rule that determines how many (or how few) boards are optimal. This makes your pinboard expansion entirely up to you. If there's enough content of a single subtopic to justify creating a new board, or if that new board gives you better targeting ability for followers, then it likely makes sense to create it.

The Value in Recategorizing

Recategorizing pins into more focused pinboards over time can be an excellent way to provide a well-curated set of pinboards that resonate with Pinterest users. It's important to realize that recategorization isn't just about creating new boards to divide up existing pins into more specific groupings.

Some of the most useful pinboards are the ones that give users input on the content being pinned. If we take our Home Improvement pinboards from the earlier example, we'll find ourselves facing content that is broken down by room. While this can be immensely valuable, many Pinterest users like to know the difference between what they can actually do on their own versus what requires a contractor versus what might simply be a "when I win the lottery" dream.

Pulling pins from some of these categories and recategorizing them into "DIY" or "Under $100 Makeovers" can be a great way to target the huge portion of the Pinterest population that is interested in DIY-style content.

Having a category for pins you've actually tried, and including some commentary on how they went, can also be a great way to build a highly respected board. For instance, I have several different recipe boards, but once I've actually used a recipe and it's proven itself worthy of repeat performances, it gets moved into my "Tried and True Recipes" pinboard (see Figure 6.18).

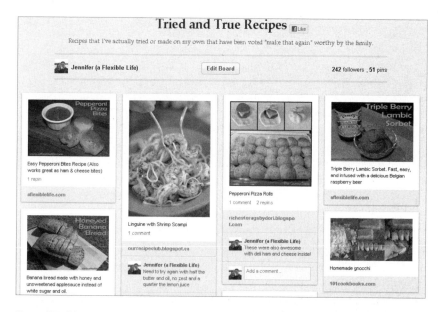

Figure 6.18 Moving pins into a new board once you've tried them and sharing your variation of the results can be a great way to offer proven content to your followers.

If you take the time to write a blog post sharing details of your experience with the pin, you've got a great opportunity to pin a link to your own content and drive some traffic to your site. If you choose to simply repin the original pin into your new category, you can add a comment sharing your thoughts, edits, or any relevant information about the pin.

Deleting Pins

Keeping your pins well curated isn't just about adding more pinboards or reassigning pins from one board to another. It's also about knowing when to prune down your pins and boards to make things more organized.

Many people who repin do it based solely on the image and description of the pin. This is especially true if they're taking a quick 5- or 10-minute break from work to scan through their Pinterest feed, or if they're browsing a category feed on their mobile device and repinning content as they come across it.

Although there's nothing wrong with repinning content this way, it often results in pinned content that features broken links, no links, or destination content that doesn't quite live up to the hype of the original pinned image.

This is where taking a little bit of time each month to prune your pins and delete the ones that aren't of value is a good idea. Did you try a recipe and didn't like the result? Make sure you either delete the pin or add a comment saying as much. Did you click through on a list of "50 Unique Ways to Save Money" only to find a veiled sales pitch for credit card services? Delete the pin. Click the image and get a broken link or find there's not even a link associated with it? Time to remove that pin as well.

A good rule of thumb is to set aside some time each week to double-check your repins. You can do this by clicking the drop-down arrow next to your name at the right side of the screen and selecting the Pins link (see Figure 6.19).

Figure 6.19 To see a list of recent pins, select the Pins option from the drop-down box next to your name on the profile page.

Doing so will bring up a list of your most recent pins (see Figure 6.20). Look through any of the repins that you added without first clicking through to read the content on the other side. Take some time to read through the content and decide if it's worth keeping. If not, delete it.

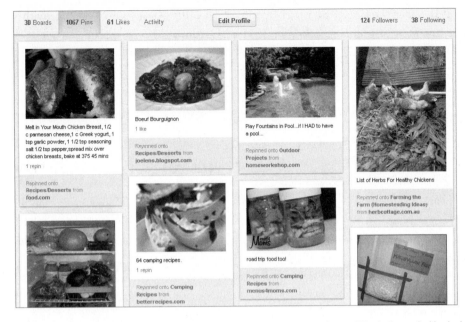

Figure 6.20 Pinterest makes it easy for you to see the list of your most recent pins and repins. Take the time to double-check them each week and delete any that aren't worth keeping.

Now that you're gaining a better understanding of how people use Pinterest to interact with your brand, you're ready to start learning how to track that interaction. Coming up in Chapter 7, "Week 4–Purposely Propagating Pins on Pinterest," we'll be exploring the metrics surrounding Pinterest usage and how to use that data to improve your campaign focus over time.

Week 4—Purposely Propagating Pins on Pinterest

While Pinterest is at heart an image-based social bookmarking service, it takes more than simply pinning random images if you want to generate any type of engagement or response from your account. The image you choose, the description you write, the time of day you post...each of these factors weighs heavily into whether or not your pin generates engagement.

This week, our focus is on learning how to increase the chances of having your pins propagate through the Pinterest community.

Chapter Contents

Monday: Getting Your Pins into the Stream
Tuesday: Building Momentum by Timing Pins
Wednesday: Controlling How Pins Are Posted
Thursday: Understanding the Impact of a Good Image
Friday: Creating Pinterest-Specific Image Collages

Monday: Getting Your Pins into the Stream

Although it's certainly possible to build a thriving Pinterest account without getting a single pin into the primary category streams, it's certainly not ideal. Think of the category streams as prime-time exposure for your pins. Getting your pins in these streams is your chance to reach outside the existing connections you've made to gather eyeballs and activity from the broader Pinterest community.

Because these are so visible, it's very important to learn how to increase the chances of your pins making it into the appropriate category streams. Unfortunately, like most areas of social media, the Pinterest algorithm is a constantly moving target.

In fact, this book had multiple rewrites and edits prior to going to print in an effort to present the most current and up-to-date insight into the Pinterest algorithm. Nonetheless, chances are high that by the time you read this chapter, the algorithm will have gone through several more revisions.

That's why it's essential to stop focusing on where the Pinterest algorithm is *right now* and to look at where it's likely to go *down the road*. Doing so will allow you to create a commonsense Pinterest approach that should be rewarded by future algorithmic changes rather than punished.

How Pins Enter the Topical Stream

As of this writing, two key factors determine whether a pin enters the category stream. One is a simple formatting issue that requires you to properly set up your pinboards. (We talked about that back in Chapter 4, "Week 1—Setting Up a Pinterest Account.") The other is the slightly more complicated algorithmic dance that Pinterest marketers will forever be trying to figure out.

Association with Category

When a user creates a pinboard, they have the option to associate that board with one of Pinterest's predefined topical categories. To have a chance of showing up in a category feed, a pin must be pinned to a board associated with the targeted category.

Time Passed Since Last Pin

When Pinterest originally launched, nearly every pin posted to the site made it to a category page. However, in an effort to combat spammers, Pinterest has reduced the number of pins a user can get into the category feeds. For a brief while, it was a fairly clear-cut rule of one pin per hour, per user. These days, it appears to be closer to a single pin per day.

For most users, that means the first pin of the day has a good chance of making it into the category stream, but most of their others do not. This is why it's important to make sure that first pin is a good one. In fact, some users may even wish to sit on a pin until the next day just to increase the likelihood of it getting picked up in the category stream.

Potential Changes

During the course of writing this book, I watched several changes take place with the Pinterest algorithm. Along with a limit to the number of pins each user can enter into the category stream each day, I also watched Pinterest briefly remove repins from the category stream. As of this writing, repins are back in the mix, but there's no guarantee they'll stay there.

For this reason, it's important to think about the Pinterest algorithm and the logical changes the Pinterest team might decide to implement. When you consider how search engine algorithms have changed over the years, it starts to get a little easier to anticipate future updates.

For example, each change made to the search engine algorithms is designed to place human-level values on content pages. Search engines have added new components to their algorithms over time to help judge the true quality and appeal of a website. They've looked at the words on a page, the age of a page, the number of links to a page, which pages those links come from, how much social sharing takes place around a page...the list goes on and on.

The key factor is that each of the things a search engine looks at creates a "value" that can also be judged by humans. This means you can make some assumptions about what might happen down the road with the Pinterest algorithm.

For instance, it would make sense for Pinterest to once again remove repins from the category stream. After all, by their very definition, repins do not add new and unique content to the stream. The Pinterest category pages are about helping people discover useful content about a certain topic. Limiting those listings to original pins would make sense.

Limiting the number of pins per day also makes sense as a way to combat spammers who might take advantage of the system. That said, it's also easy enough to judge the "value" of an individual user over time by looking at how many repins, likes, and comments their content receives. Users who curate pins that attract a lot of interest could easily be given extra posting privileges, and their content could be set to find its way into the stream more frequently.

Other factors—such as the number of followers, variety in URLs represented in a user's pins, and whether or not a piece of content has been previously pinned to the site—can and likely will be added to the equation over time.

How the algorithm will change over time isn't all that important for you to understand. Rather, just keep in mind that those changes will be designed to improve the quality of content appearing in category streams. So, the easiest way to ensure your content continues to find its way into the category feeds is to focus on building a strong Pinterest profile that pins unique and engaging content onto well-curated pinboards.

The "Popular" Stream

One of the most confusing aspects of the "Popular" category on Pinterest is just how pins find their way onto the page. Although marketers have been attempting to deconstruct the Pinterest algorithm since the day they first discovered the site, little if any consensus exists on exactly how images find their way onto the page.

In fact, the day I was writing this chapter, content was featured at the top of the Popular page that had been submitted to the site nearly 10 months prior (Figure 7.1).

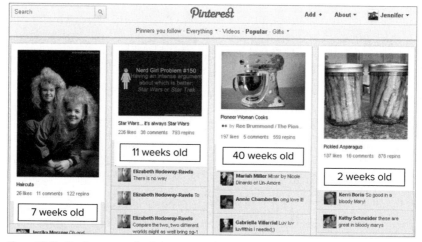

Figure 7.1 The Popular category often features content that is several months old.

Examination of submission dates; associated categories; and the number of likes, comments, and even repins reveal little in the way of similarities. The current Pinterest Popular category remains a mystery to most. That said, it's important to remember the service is still in the early stages of algorithmic development. Over the next year or two, they will likely settle into a better system designed to help feature fresh content of demonstrated interest to users.

For now, marketers will be best served by operating under the concept outlined in the previous section. Expect the algorithm to change in a manner that reflects the way human beings value content. Expect Pinterest to build a system that recognizes images that have previously been submitted and to limit the number of times they can hit the Popular page (or at a bare minimum, to increase the required activity around an image for subsequent visits to the Popular page).

Expect Pinterest to begin analyzing users to learn which ones contribute new and interesting content to the site and to weigh their submissions more strongly than users who only repin content onto their various pinboards. No matter how the algorithm changes with time, Pinterest users will be best served by pinning new and interesting content during peak hours and building a strong base of followers.

Getting into the Product Stream

We talked about how to upload product pins with prices attached back in Chapter 5, "Week 2—Curating Content with Pinterest." A portion of the product-tagged pins uploaded by users will find its way into the overall product stream just as a portion of pins will find their way onto category pages or even onto the Popular page.

Unlike the Popular category, the product stream is updated on a more real-time basis. In fact, it's possible for a Pinterest user to get multiple items listed in the product stream in a short amount of time (see Figure 7.2).

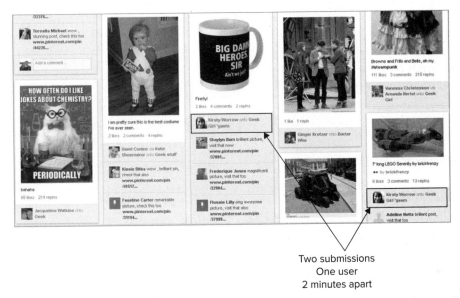

Two submissions
One user
2 minutes apart

Figure 7.2 User Kirsty Worrow has uploaded two pins within minutes of each other and had both appear on the appropriately priced product page.

However, since few companies will experience success by attempting to pin their own products, it's essential to take the time to make your e-commerce site Pinterest friendly. Your best chance at getting your products listed in the Pinterest product stream is to have your products pinned by visitors to your site.

That's why it's essential for companies to add the Pin It button to their product listings, blog posts, and other featured areas of pinnable content.

Tuesday: Building Momentum by Timing Pins

As with other popular social networks, Pinterest users tend to congregate on the site during certain times of day. That means companies can increase the potential for inter-action and engagement by timing pins to post during peak usage hours when their target audience is most likely to be browsing the site.

Testing the Impact of Pins by Time of Day

There's quite a bit of variation from studies and sources in terms of what the best time of day to pin is. Several news stories came out in early 2012 claiming peak hours for Pinterest activity were between 5 a.m. and 7 a.m. EST and between 6 p.m. and 8 p.m. EST.

However, those numbers are disputed by services like bitly and Pinerly, who released data suggesting higher rates of repins in the late afternoon and late evening.

The truth is, there's going to be variation in peak Pinterest usage that varies heavily depending on the type of content you are promoting. In my tests, I noticed that event planning and wedding content tends to gain more repins during the late evening hours between 8 p.m. and 10 p.m. EST. On the flip side, recipes and generalized handy tips for daily living did very well in the morning between 7 a.m. and 9 a.m. Infographics, studies, and work-related data performed well between lunch time and the early afternoon (noon to 3 p.m. EST).

This means it's essential to set up a system to track the impact of your own pins. (More on this in Chapter 8, "Week 5—Track and Monitor Pinterest Traffic.") As fewer pins find their way into the category feeds, and Pinterest users are forced to rely heavily on the followers they attract to their individual pinboards, personalized testing becomes increasingly important.

Give some thought to the content you are trying to promote, and use a little common sense to think about when the target audience of that content is most likely to be online. A busy working mom looking for party ideas is likely to use Pinterest at a different time of day than the young professional marketer seeking out infographics for an upcoming business presentation.

Keeping tabs on when different types of content perform best can help you set up a Pinterest content strategy that maximizes the reach and exposure of your pins.

Giving Pins a Boost

As with Twitter, Facebook, and the rest of the social media landscape, getting an influential Pinterest user to repin your content at a specific time of day can go a long way toward helping boost the activity around it.

Just as the time of day can have a heavy impact on the reception of a pin you upload to the site, the time of day that content is eventually repinned can also cause an engagement boost if the repin comes from the right user.

Building a relationship with other respected pinners works much like building a relationship with an influencer on any other social network. Taking the time to establish these relationships often means you can contact a pinner directly and ask them to consider repinning your item at a specific time of day. Don't count on this tactic working outside of your most solid and mutually beneficial relationships, but a properly timed repin can help get the ball rolling again for a pin that's dying off.

The Cycle of Popular Pins

Because there are several ways a pin can capture the attention of users, there's generally a pretty constant cycle in terms of repin activity. Pins that find their way into the category feed often experience a rapid burst of repins as category browsers spot the new listing and add it to their own boards.

After a short amount of time passes, this burst in activity tapers off as the pin moves further down and eventually disappears from the category page. Of course, while category-related pin activity is going on, there's also the potential of the pin being spotted by Pinterest users who follow your boards. These Pinterest users might not spot the pin for hours or even a few days after it's been posted. A single repin by these users can spike activity again as the repin displays to their followers and has the potential to once again find its way into the category boards.

I've seen this happen over and over again with pins. Oftentimes, the pin activity spikes twice. The first spike happens when the initial pin is made and enters the category stream. The second pin generally happens when it either reenters the category stream for a second time or gets pinned or repinned by a highly influential user (see Figure 7.3).

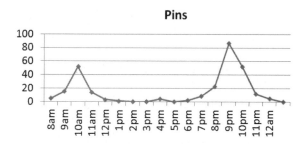
Pins

Figure 7.3 Some pins will see an initial spike in activity when they are first pinned, followed by a higher spike after they are repinned by a highly influential user.

Wednesday: Controlling How Pins Are Posted

The truth is, any business that believes they have control over how their content is shared to Pinterest is sadly mistaken. While it's true that you can block Pinterest users from pinning content directly from your site (more on this later), there's no guaranteed way to keep the content you create from being submitted to Pinterest.

Given that, there are things you can do to increase the potential of a good initial pin.

Influencing the Images a Pinner Shares

One thing many site owners wonder about is whether they can dictate which images are available for pinning. In the case of blog posts, product listings, and other content-heavy pages, certain images can deliver a more enticing Pinterest experience and increase the potential of driving traffic from a pinned image.

There's an ever-growing number of plug-ins and third-party tools aiming to give site owners more control over which images are pinned. For example, the "Pin It On

Pinterest" WordPress plug-in (`http://wordpress.org/extend/plugins/pin-it-on-pinterest/`) allows site owners to predefine which image will get pinned rather than popping up the standard selection box launched by Pinterest's own Pin It button.

Some site owners will even integrate a Pin It button alongside the images they most wish to see pinned as a way to influence user actions. Although these tactics can certainly play a role in influencing Pinterest users to share the strongest images from a page, there is no surefire way to exercise absolute control over which images a pinner can select.

Note: Several widgets and plug-ins are designed to give you specific control over which images get pinned from your site, but it's important to realize that ultimately, you do not have control over the images a user selects. Regular Pinterest users who wish to pin an image other than the one you've assigned using your own internal Pin It button will likely just use the Pinterest bookmarklet to enable their selection of a specific image.

Along with image control, many website owners also wish to influence the description that accompanies a pin. Since the description of a pin holds the potential to motivate a user to click through to the associated content, it's also essential to properly format your site to increase the chances of good content in the description field for each pin.

Influencing the Description of a Pin

Pinterest looks to one of two areas for the default text when an image is pinned. Pinterest will first look to the alt attribute assigned to the image in the HTML code of your website. The alt tag will automatically populate the description field in the Pin It pop-up window (Figure 7.4). While many users will edit this content to suit their own purposes, a good portion of Pinterest users pin content using the default description, especially if it's a good one.

Figure 7.4 Pinterest automatically looks to the alt tag in the image code on a website to populate the description of a pin.

When the alt tag is left empty in the code, Pinterest looks to the title tag of the web page to populate the description field (Figure 7.5). Although this tag can still produce a fairly accurate description, it gives you as the website owner less control over the text surrounding a specific image. Consider a blog post featuring half a dozen images and ask yourself whether a single title tag can accurately describe each image.

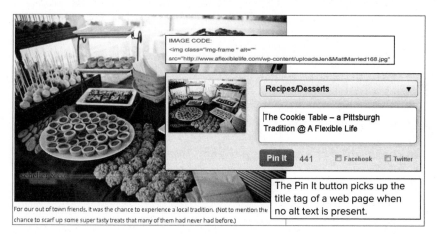

Figure 7.5 When no text is present in the alt tag, Pinterest looks to the title tag of the web page for a default description.

This is why taking the time to write accurate and enticing content for the alt tag of each image on your site becomes extremely important as part of a Pinterest marketing strategy.

Again, it's important to realize that many Pinterest users will end up editing the description. That said, you can at least take steps to ensure a stronger pin for those relying on the default description.

Additionally, as Pinterest continues to refine their internal search algorithm, these descriptions should factor more heavily into the search results. Writing conversion-friendly, keyword-rich descriptions now could go a long way toward helping you gain more visibility down the road.

Disallowing Pinning from Your Site

If for some reason you do not wish to allow users to pin content from your website, you'll need to add a snippet of code to any page featuring content you do not want pinned.

Simply add the following line of code to the header of the pages you wish to block:

```
<meta name="pinterest" content="nopin" />
```

This code can be assigned to a single page or to every page, giving site owners better control over how and when users pin their content.

 Note: It's important to realize that while Pinterest provides code to allow site owners to block direct pinning from any of their web pages, the code will not stop determined pinners from adding images to the service. Users can download images directly to their hard drive and then upload them to the system. Pins that are uploaded in this way will not include attribution or links back to the original site.

If you do not wish to have your content shared on Pinterest, or if you come across your images being used without proper attribution or credit, Pinterest does provide a copyright infringement notification form on its website at `http://pinterest.com/about/copyright/dmca/`.

Thursday: Understanding the Impact of a Good Image

Half a dozen or so years ago, content marketing was all about writing an intriguing headline that motivated the reader to click through to visit your site and the rest of your content. These days, it's all about selecting a compelling image to help drive the click.

Pinterest can be a massive traffic driver for websites, often driving as much (or more) traffic than Twitter and Facebook. For companies that understand the impact of a good image, Pinterest can drive server crushing loads of traffic to a web site.

Pins vs. Repins: The Difference Is in the Drive

When it comes to pinning new content to the site, the average Pinterest user doesn't always give much thought to the specific images they pin. These users are often using Pinterest as a personal inspiration board or as a resource to store links to information and ideas they want to revisit later.

These users will likely pin their favorite image from the page they are visiting and leave it at that. For step-by-step posts, this is often an image of the finished product. For the pinner, the image is related to content they have already digested and they feel strongly enough about the value of this content that they want to pin it. In other words, the conversion has already happened when they decide to pin—you've already got them hooked on that particular piece of content.

Driving repins is slightly different. Repins tend to come from Pinterest users who are scrolling through the pins in their own feeds and in the category feeds looking for ideas. In these instances, the repin action is often an impulse reaction to an image that catches their eye. Users don't always visit the content before making the choice to repin. They simply scan listings, pausing on the ones that are visually appealing and then quickly scan the description before deciding whether to repin (see Figure 7.6).

As users scan pins, they repin impulsively as an image catches their eye.

Figure 7.6 For many Pinterest users, repins are an instant activity, driving by impulse as users scan through images in their feeds.

This is part of why having great images that clearly have a story behind them or that require further explanation is a key component of a good Pinterest strategy. Your site's image is your chance to capture the impulse click of someone on a repinning mission.

Types of Images That Capture Interest

Considering that the majority of active Pinterest users are women, it should come as no surprise that things like cute animals, delicious food, and do-it-yourself tutorials are among the most repinned topics on the site.

For the most part, popular pins can be broken down into six key areas:

Adorable Animals   Whether it's a baby bunny nose to nose with a puppy or a cat stuffed into a clear glass bowl, Pinterest users absolutely love pictures of cute, funny, or otherwise adorable animals. Add a creative caption to the mix and the repins shoot even higher.

Quotable Quotes   Taking the idea of "pictures are better than words" to an ironic extreme, graphical images of catchy, pithy, or romantic quotes tend to spread like wildfire.

Dream Big   Whether it's a three-story wall of books in someone's personal library, a $67,000 wedding dress, or a breathtaking photo of a crystal-clear lagoon off the coast of Italy, beautiful images of things that are out of financial reach for 99.9 percent of the world play extremely well on the site.

Gorgeous Food   Forget the calorie count—the more extravagant and decadent the recipe, the further it will spread on Pinterest. (Don't let that discourage you too much; beautiful pictures of healthy recipes also do well...but let's be honest, the brownies stuffed with cookie dough and topped with Reese Peanut Butter Cups are going to catch anyone's eye!)

Why Didn't I Think of That?   Simple everyday solutions to common problems, creative upcycling, and low-cost ways to reproduce high-cost items or experiences play extremely well on the site. Think innovation and originality and then find a way to represent the concept in a single image.

Instructographics   An entirely new form of image, these cousins of infographics provide step-by-step instructions with photographs mixed into a single long-run vertical image. These images run on websites in place of a blog post and when pinned to Pinterest give a hint of the content, but are often too small to be read on the site, causing users to click through to the original source.

Why Teaser Images Work So Well

The problem with many of the images mentioned so far is that there's often no reason to click through to the original site. If a user simply wants to laugh and smile at the picture of the cute cat stuffed into a mason jar, they can repin it to their cute animal category and go on their merry way.

From the marketing perspective, these images are a helpful way to gain attention for your Pinterest account and potentially boost followers, but from a business conversion perspective, they are nearly worthless. After all, a total of 15,000 repins does little for your site if it doesn't produce traffic, engagement, and ultimately, conversions.

That's why "teaser" images are such an important part of any Pinterest marketer's arsenal. While giving away the full content within the image may garner more repins, it will result in far fewer click-throughs. Teaser images are designed to catch the eye and drive impulse repins, but they also require the user to click through to the site to reap the full benefit of the content (see Figure 7.7).

Figure 7.7 While the image on the left could garner more pins and repins, it doesn't carry anywhere near the traffic potential of the image on the right.

The general idea is to showcase the final product or a portion of the final product in such a way that users want to find out how to replicate it, where it came from, how it works, or what to do with it. These are the images that drive traffic from Pinterest to your website.

The Question of Watermarks

One of the biggest concerns many content marketers and site owners have about using Pinterest is fear of image theft. It's not unusual to see pinned images show up on blogs or forums with no mention or link to the original source. In addition, many Pinterest users simply skim through pinned images without ever clicking through to the associated website.

A solution to both branding issues and potential image theft is the use of a watermark on images created for Pinterest or included in content likely to be pinned. A noninvasive watermark will not take away from the value of the image, but it will provide some level of protection to keep the image from being lifted and reused by another content provider.

Additionally, a well-placed watermark can help boost your Pinterest efforts. A watermark is viewable on the image as people scroll through pins, and it reinforces the destination site each time they view or pin the image (see Figure 7.8).

Figure 7.8 While the image on the left is visually appealing, its lack of watermark gives it no association with the site or company that created it. The image on the right bears a subtle watermark associating the image with the blog that created it.

Friday: Creating Pinterest-Specific Image Collages

When it comes to using Pinterest to market your business or brand, it's absolutely essential to have a plan in place to drive traffic back to your site. After all, your website is the place where you can get visitors to purchase products, register for newsletters, subscribe to your feed on other social media channels, and take whatever other steps are considered valuable to your bottom-line business goals.

For many companies, that means taking the time to create images specifically for Pinterest. Although high-quality images are clearly important, it's essential to look past the eye candy and to make sure you are creating images that drive traffic as well as repins.

Using Step-by-Step Collages

Earlier in the chapter I mentioned the ever-growing popularity of "instructographics." These images are designed to convey step-by-step instructions for doing something. Done improperly, they run the risk of giving away all the information within the image, leading to high numbers of repins and low numbers of click-throughs.

Done properly, they create an enticing image that's ripe for impulse repins as well as eventually driving traffic to the site when people are ready to dig deeper into the process. There are a few key ways to go about doing this (see Figure 7.9).

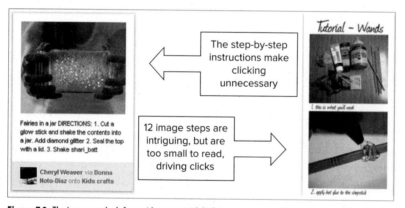

Figure 7.9 The image on the left provides users with little to no reason to click. The image on the right is part of a long instructographic and will drive more traffic.

First, you need to consider the size of your image and the impact it has on a user's ability to interact with the pin. The repin, like, and comment buttons only appear at the top of a pin. Make your image too long and users will have to scroll too far to digest the content of a pin to see the buttons anymore. They'll be forced to scroll back up to interact with the image. This extra step will decrease the amount of engagement around a pin.

As of this writing, any image longer than 5,000 pixels will cause the average Pinterest user to have to scroll far enough down the page that the repin, like, and comment buttons will vanish. For this reason, I highly recommend that you design your images to be less than 5,000 pixels tall.

Second, you need to understand how and when Pinterest resizes an image and the impact resizing can have on readability. Pinterest will only show images of a certain display size on an individual pin page. This means images larger than the Pinterest limit will automatically be shrunken down to an acceptable size.

As of this writing, Pinterest will shrink down any image longer than 2,500 pixels. As long as you are not using a massive font, an image of this size should be mostly unreadable by the average Pinterest user. This provides them with a taste of the content while still requiring them to click through to your site in order to fully digest it.

Using Before-and-After Images

While step-by-step instructographics offer a powerful way to attract repins and drive traffic, they're not appropriate in all circumstances. A project may have too many steps, or the time required to create the graphic may be out of reach. Additionally, infographics work well because they make up a small portion of the pins on Pinterest. It's essential to test different approaches to Pinterest images and to include several strategies in your campaigns.

One of the simplest and most effective forms of image marketing on Pinterest is the before-and-after picture. These images are small and easy to digest, and they can show a dramatic enough transportation to inspire people to click through to learn more (see Figure 7.10).

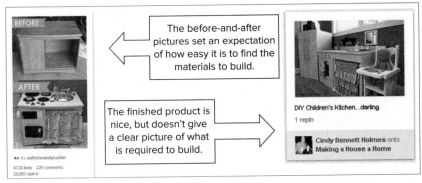

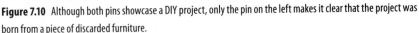

Figure 7.10 Although both pins showcase a DIY project, only the pin on the left makes it clear that the project was born from a piece of discarded furniture.

Using a Magazine-Style Captioned Image

One of the dangers of Pinterest is the description field. Because users can edit descriptions, or even rewrite them entirely, your images are at the mercy of Pinterest users. This means your picture is every bit as likely to end up with a description like "sweet!" as it is to end up with a description that actually describes the content.

One way to protect against this problem is to create Pinterest-specific images that include a description of the content on your site (see Figure 7.11).

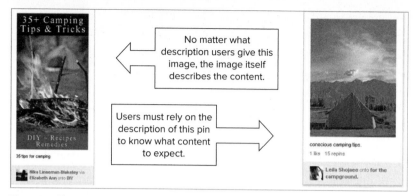

Figure 7.11 The image on the left includes a description of the content associated with the pin. The image on the right relies solely on the description assigned by the pinner to help Pinterest users know what to expect.

It's important to remember that any image from your website or blog can be pinned. Adding captions to an image, creating a before-and-after picture, and/or building instructographics allow you some measure of control when launching the content yourself, but there's no guarantee your readers will select those images when pinning your content.

For some site owners, that means making the primary image on the post one that is formatted or tweaked for Pinterest (see Figure 7.12). Adding a caption to the

Figure 7.12 This site adds captions to all recipe images to ensure the proper description accompanies them on Pinterest.

photo or featuring a before-and-after collage right next to the Pin It button can go a long way to helping desirable images get fed into the Pinterest stream by your visitors.

Overall, getting the right images into the Pinterest streams is about finding balance. You need to remember that pins can be launched by your internal marketing team, by the influencers you build a relationship with, and by the Pinterest users who find your content on their own. This is why testing, tracking, and experimenting to see what works best is an essential part of building any Pinterest strategy, a topic we'll talk more about in Chapter 8.

Week 5–Track and Monitor Pinterest Traffic

As with all other areas of social media, there's not much sense in investing time and effort in Pinterest if you have no way to know whether or not your efforts are paying off. That's why, before we dig too deeply into brand building and leveraging Pinterest as a traffic generator, it's essential to take a look at some of the metrics and measurements behind a good Pinterest campaign.

Chapter Contents

Monday: Finding Out What Content Has Been Pinned from Your Site

The single most important question you can ask regarding your efforts on Pinterest is what content is actually being pinned (and repinned) from your website. What people choose to pin, where they pin it, and who is doing the pinning can provide amazing value for your brand in terms of market research and marketing activity. (We'll dive deeper into how to refine your campaigns based on your findings in Chapter 14, "Week 11— Measure and Refine Your Strategy.")

Searching Pinterest for Pins from a Specific Website

One of the very nice things about Pinterest from a marketer's perspective is just how easy it is to compile a list of pinned images from any website. In fact, as long as you know the URL of the site, Pinterest will show you the most recently pinned images associated with it.

Simply type `www.pinterest.com/source/domainname.com` (replacing *domainname .com* with the domain URL of your choice) into the address bar of your browser to generate search results from Pinterest (see Figure 8.1).

Figure 8.1 By placing the URL for The Matador Network in the Pinterest string I gave you, you can easily see what images have been pinned by members of the Pinterest community.

For companies working to build an active Pinterest presence, it's a very good idea to conduct this search on a regular basis for all of the reasons I've mentioned. Well-trafficked sites will likely see enough Pinterest activity to necessitate daily checks. For less trafficked websites, you might only need to check in on a weekly or biweekly basis until activity levels increase.

No matter how often you choose to check, keep in mind that Pinterest will show you only the most recent images pinned from a domain. This is why many companies are turning to third-party tools like Curalate to help them better track pin activity for their domains. We'll talk about Curalate later on in this chapter.

Keep in mind that proper Pinterest research and analysis goes well beyond simply looking at your own listings on the site. Keeping tabs on your competitors to find out what pieces of content are being pinned from their site can help provide you with valuable insight that could impact your own content marketing strategy.

Quick-Click Access to Other Pinned Images

Although it's easy enough to check the pinned images for a website you are already aware of, Pinterest also provides a wonderful opportunity to discover new sites.

Perhaps you've noticed the same image passing through your Pinterest feed time and time again. In early 2012, it was all about the piñata cookie, zucchini tots, and crockpot chicken teriyaki. Even now, as you're reading this book, chances are high you've seen the same image pop up over and over again. If that image is a good fit for your target audience, it might be worthwhile to see where it originated and to figure out what other content is being pinned from the site.

To do so, you'll simply need to do a little clicking around. Start with the pin you've seen popping up over and over and click on it. This will cause it to expand to the full width of your Pinterest screen (see Figure 8.2).

Figure 8.2 Once you've clicked on a pin, it will expand in size and give you several additional pieces of information.

Most people simply use this page to click through to the website the pin originated from, but if you take the time to scroll to the bottom of the listing, you'll also find several excellent research options (see Figure 8.3).

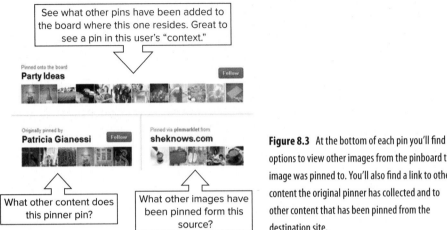

Figure 8.3 At the bottom of each pin you'll find options to view other images from the pinboard the image was pinned to. You'll also find a link to other content the original pinner has collected and to other content that has been pinned from the destination site.

Above all, take note of the bottom-right link on each pin-specific page, the one allowing you to see all other pins from the website it came from (see Figure 8.4). This link is a great way to find out what other pieces of content are being produced from the site responsible for uber-popular pins.

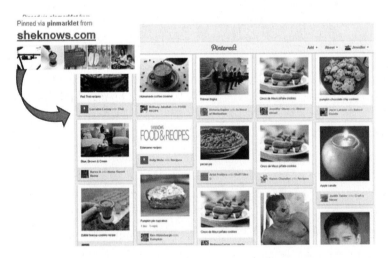

Figure 8.4 Clicking the domain name in the "pinned from" section of a pin will take you to a full listing of all other pinned content from that domain.

What to Look for in the Listings

As with most information, it's not just about finding it; it's about understanding what to do with it. When analyzing the content being pinned from your website (or from your competitors' sites), you'll want to start by looking at several factors:

Organic vs. Brand-Driven Pins One of the most important things to consider is whether the pins on Pinterest are coming from your marketing team or from your readers. There's a distinct set of value to both, but most established sites will (and should) have a much higher organic pin rate than brand-driven pin rate.

Telling the difference between these types of pins is easy. All pins show who pinned (or repinned) them, so just look for your brand name or team members' names to isolate your brand-driven pins from organic pins (see Figure 8.5).

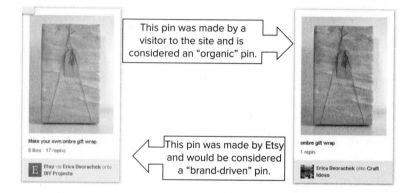

Figure 8.5 The image on the left shows a brand-driven pin; the image on the right shows a consumer-driven organic pin.

Image Selection Another key piece of information available by looking at the pin activity for your content is the choice of images tied to the actual pin. For e-commerce sites, taking the time to understand which product images get pinned and repinned the most can provide amazing consumer insight. In Chapter 14, we'll explore how some companies are using Pinterest research to reshape their product pages.

Topical Selection At its most basic level, Pinterest provides brands with an incredible visual overview of the topics on their site that most capture the attention of the Pinterest community. By scanning the list of images pinned from their site, brands can quickly observe patterns in pins and adjust their content marketing plans accordingly.

Brand Evangelists We'll explore the idea of evaluating click-through and traffic rates to help value evangelists later on in this chapter.

Pins vs. Repins The final thing you will want to look at is whether your content is being pinned by a wide range of sources or is being powered by a small number of influencers who attract a large number of repins. We'll dig more deeply into the difference between pins and repins from a marketing and measurement stance in the next section.

Tuesday: Understanding the Value of Pins vs. Repins

Back in Chapter 5, "Week 2—Curating Content with Pinterest," we talked about the difference between a pin and a repin. As a quick reminder, to "pin" an image means to add an image to Pinterest after you've run across it on a website. To "repin" an image means to take someone else's pin *from* Pinterest and add it to your own Pinterest collection.

Think of a pin as a "discovery" and a repin as someone else passing that discovery along. One of the primary things you'll need to understand about how people are using your content on Pinterest is whether you're being pinned or repinned.

What Does a High Number of Pins Mean?

Some websites have an extraordinary number of pins present on Pinterest. Running a search for pinned content from their domain can result in what seems to be a never-ending scroll of images being pinned by users. In some cases, you'll have to scroll through pages of listings before you see a single repin (see Figure 8.6).

Figure 8.6 Exploring the content on Pinterest from popular recipe site SkinnyTaste.com turns up a seemingly never-ending list of pinned content without a single repin on the list.

There are two primary reasons for a listing to look like this.

The first is that a small number of people are pinning a large amount of content and no one really cares about it enough to repin it. You can often identify this problem by seeing the same small number of pinners popping up over and over in the listings. Oftentimes, this type of pin activity is reflective of a brand or website that either has created multiple accounts for the purpose of promoting their own content or has hired people to repin the content. The lack of repins in this case generally means that either the pins are not reaching an interested audience or the content of the pins isn't appealing to the people seeing it.

The second reason you might see a pin profile like this for a site is due to sheer volume of activity for the domain. Highly popular content sites generally have such a high volume of traffic they can literally flood the Pinterest stream with unique pins being made by their many visitors. In this instance, it's not that the content isn't being repinned, it's simply that so many site users are pinning content directly from the site that the repins get buried in domain searches. Sites with this "problem" are fairly easy to identify because they have such high volume of pin activity showing up in their domain searches.

What Do Pins Mean for Your Marketing Efforts?

In many ways, a high volume of pins is incredibly desirable to a marketer. As long as the pins are coming from a wide range of Pinterest users, pins mean people are visiting your site of their own volition and are choosing to push your content into their Pinterest feeds.

These original pins make it clear to you that Pinterest users appreciate the content you are creating on your site. It means the people who find their way to your site via other channels enjoy it enough they want to archive and share it via their Pinterest accounts.

Consider a high volume of pins to be confirmation of your content marketing efforts. Use your observation of this pin activity to further refine your content or to reach out to users who pin a large number of images from your site.

On the other hand, if you're seeing a lot of pin activity and very little repin activity, you might want to ask yourself why other Pinterest users are not repinning the content. If you are a well-established site with extremely high traffic, you likely have nothing to worry about. However, if your traffic levels are lower, you need to give some thought to how you can make your future content more repinnable so all that pin activity from your regular visitors can attract new sources of traffic.

What Does a High Number of Repins Mean?

Sometimes you'll look at the Pinterest profile for your domain (or for a competitor's domain) and you'll find a lower number of pins that each have some repin activity for them (see Figure 8.7).

Figure 8.7: Double Durango Farm, a goat farm in Loganville, Georgia, doesn't have a high volume of pins, but most pins listed have repin activity associated with them.

There are two primary reasons for having a high amount of repin activity for images from a specific domain. The first is that the content is of high interest to a specific niche present on Pinterest. In the case of Double Durango Farm, the community of Pinterest users interested in raising goats is well connected to each other. That means that whenever a member of the community finds and pins content from a new resource, that content quickly gets repinned by other aficionados who plan to visit the site to gather more information at a later date.

Another reason a site's content might have a high volume of repin activity is because it innately appeals to other Pinterest users. This often happens with sites that consistently produce high-quality original content and that create images specifically for Pinterest marketing. This content is naturally repinnable and does an excellent job of capturing users' attention.

What Do Repins Mean to Your Marketing Efforts?

Although it may sound like I'm talking (er...writing) out of both sides of my mouth, a high volume of repin activity is also incredibly desirable to a marketer. Repin activity tells you something about how your content is being received within the Pinterest community, or at least within subsets of it.

Repins either mean you've created such a compelling image and idea that people can't help but stash it away for later, or that your content has been shared by the type of people who are already connected with your target audience.

While pins make it clear that your content appeals to the people who visit your site, repins make it clear that your content is playing well with an audience that probably was not already visiting your site. Repins mean exposure to new users and the potential to drive new visitors to your website for the first time.

This means you'll need to make sure your site is conversion friendly. Double-check your analytics goals and make sure you have created (and are tracking) several conversion points. Take a look at your site visually and make sure it's quick and easy for new visitors to subscribe to your site via email, RSS, Facebook, Twitter, Pinterest, and so on.

You'll also want to maximize the potential for additional pin activity from these new visitors. Many Pinterest users will spend time browsing through the site they discover on Pinterest, pinning new content as they stumble across it. Installing a widget or program that points visitors to similar content at the end of your posts can be a great way to draw them deeper into the site, generating more pins and increasing the potential they'll subscribe to one of your feeds to get ongoing access to your content.

Coming up in tomorrow's section, we'll talk a bit about how to dig into your analytics to get a better understanding of what traffic from Pinterest is doing once it arrives at your site.

Wednesday: Tracking the Traffic Generated by Pins

All the work you do to build and implement a Pinterest strategy won't mean much if you do not have the ability to track the traffic those efforts generate. A simple and free analytics tool like Google Analytics will allow you to track the traffic coming in from Pinterest. With a little customizing, you can even do some segmentation to learn more about how your Pinterest traffic is interacting with your site.

Checking Your Analytics for Traffic Increases

Assuming you already have some type of analytics program up and running for your site, your first step is as simple as logging in to your dashboard. From there, you'll need to take the steps required in your software to view the traffic sources to your site.

For the purposes of this chapter, we'll be working in Google Analytics to look at the data from a small blog that uses Pinterest to reach its target audience. During the month of March, shortly after the site began leveraging Pinterest, their overall traffic numbers were just over 900 visitors (see Figure 8.8).

929 people visited this site			
■ 31.97% Search Traffic 297 Visits			
■ 45.32% Referral Traffic 421 Visits			
■ 22.71% Direct Traffic 211 Visits			

Search Traffic	Source	Visits	% Visits
Keyword	1. pinterest.com	126	29.93%
Matched Search Query	2. google.com	59	14.01%
Source	3. thelactivist.blogspot.com	57	13.54%
Referral Traffic	4. bento-logy.blogspot.com	55	13.06%
Source	5. facebook.com	38	9.03%
Direct Traffic	6. m.facebook.com	28	6.65%
Landing Page	7. m.pinterest.com	25	5.94%

Figure 8.8 This site receives just over 900 visitors per month. Pinterest is its most popular source of referral traffic, sending just under 30 percent of the total referral traffic for the month.

Roughly 45 percent of the traffic to the site comes from referral traffic. When we look at the breakdown of those referral sources, we see that Pinterest clearly leads the way, providing nearly 30 percent of the site's link-based traffic. For most sites with strong content, Pinterest is probably showing up as a top 25 referrer, even if you aren't actively leveraging it yet.

If Pinterest isn't showing up near the top of your list, take the time to scroll through your referrer sources looking for the Pinterest URL. Keep in mind that Pinterest.com and mobile Pinterest traffic will show as two separate listings. (In fact, if we add the two Pinterest sources together, we find Pinterest is actually responsible for over 35 percent of the referrer traffic flowing into the site.)

Measuring Pinterest Traffic

When it comes to measuring the traffic from Pinterest, there are several things you want to look for. Most obviously, you'll want to consider the overall impact on traffic. How much traffic is Pinterest sending and are those numbers rising or falling?

You'll also want to look at things like their bounce rate, length of visit, and number of pages visited. This data is also easily accessible in a program like Google Analytics (see Figure 8.9).

	Source	Visits ↓	Pages / Visit	Avg. Visit Duration	% New Visits	Bounce Rate
☐	1. pinterest.com	126	1.27	00:00:33	92.86%	8.73%
☐	2. google.com	59	1.63	00:00:45	93.22%	32.20%
☐	3. thelactivist.blogspot.com	57	4.77	00:03:56	70.18%	24.66%
☐	4. bento-logy.blogspot.com	55	5.76	00:22:56	81.82%	5.45%
☐	5. facebook.com	38	1.82	00:01:56	47.37%	10.53%
☐	6. m.facebook.com	28	1.18	00:00:54	82.14%	14.29%
☐	7. m.pinterest.com	25	1.12	00:02:22	84.00%	48.00%

Figure 8.9 This chart shows the difference in page views per visit, visit duration, and bounce rates of traffic from Pinterest vs. other referral sources.

Keep in mind, sometimes there will be a difference between how visitors from web-based Pinterest and visitors from the mobile version of Pinterest will interact with your site. For the site shown in Figure 8.9, mobile traffic spends more than six times longer on the site but visits fewer pages and bounces at a higher rate. This means that when a mobile user does find a piece of content that resonates with them, they spend a fair amount of time digesting it once they reach the site.

By setting up an advanced segment that only includes traffic from Pinterest, you can quickly narrow your data to look only at Pinterest traffic (see Figure 8.10).

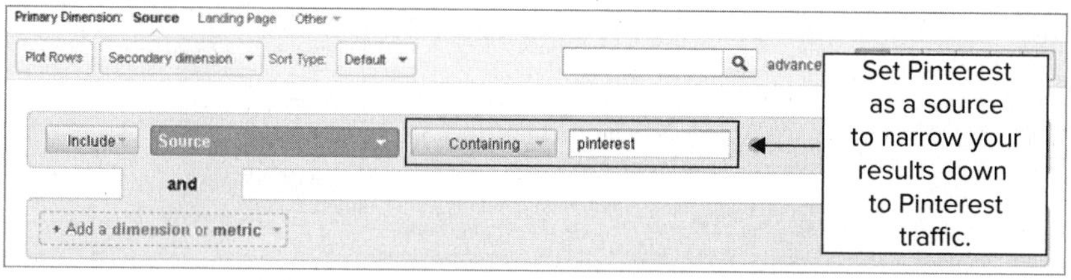

Figure 8.10 Adding an advanced segment for Pinterest traffic is simple. Just choose the advanced option from the referrals page and type "Pinterest" into the box.

At this point you can take a look at any goals you've set up for tracking within Google analytics and compare how Pinterest stacks up against your overall averages for the site (see Figure 8.11).

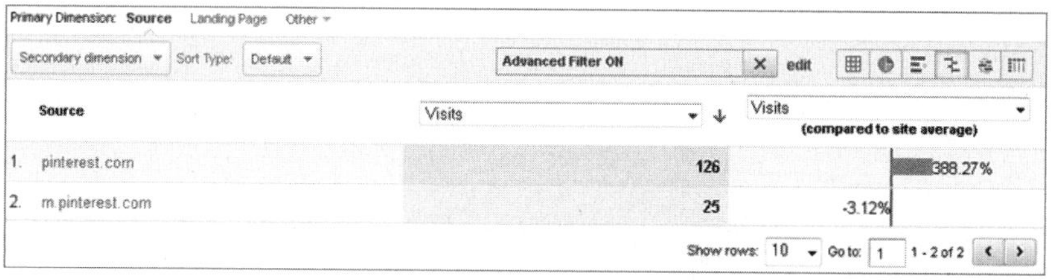

Figure 8.11 In this instance, traffic from the Pinterest website performs 388 percent better than the average website visitor, demonstrating how Pinterest is an extremely effective means for driving new social media followers and subscribers.

Think about the goals you've established for your site. Whether it's a certain level of user engagement, the sale of products, the creation of a lead, the choice to subscribe to a social media channel, or some other action, it's important to take the time to understand how traffic from Pinterest measures up.

Identifying Traffic from Individual Pins

Another great thing about the way Pinterest sends traffic is that each and every pin has its own unique ID in the referral string (see Figure 8.12). This means you can actually measure (and value) traffic from an individual pin to determine which pinners create the most value for your marketing campaign.

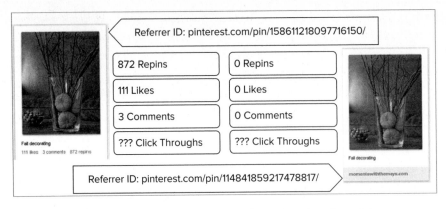

Figure 8.12 Though pins and repins may look the same, your analytics software knows better. As long as you properly set up your tracking, you can easily tell how much traffic came from each pin.

To dive more deeply into the traffic being produced by Pinterest, you'll need to create a custom report that shows the full referrer. (There are plenty of walk-throughs on the Web showing how to set up this type of report, so we won't go into that here.) Once you've created this report, you'll be able to dive down deep enough to see how individual pins are meeting the goals you've established for the site (see Figure 8.13).

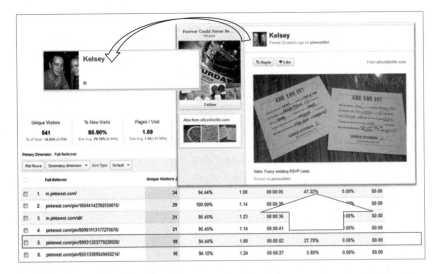

Figure 8.13 By examining your Pinterest referral data by individual pin ID, you can track the activity back to the original pin and the pinner who made it. This can be a great way to research influencers and evangelists as part of a Pinterest outreach plan.

Which Pins Create the Most Value

The true benefit of being able to look at traffic, engagement, and conversions from pins is the information and value it provides for your marketing team.

Imagine knowing which of your product shots when pinned to Pinterest result in the highest traffic and conversion rates. You could then apply that knowledge to your choice of which image to use in a Facebook ad or in an email newsletter, or even as the default image on the product page of your site.

Even when the image on several pins is exactly the same, the person who did the pinning can have a heavy impact on how much exposure the pin receives and how much value it drives to your site (see Figure 8.14).

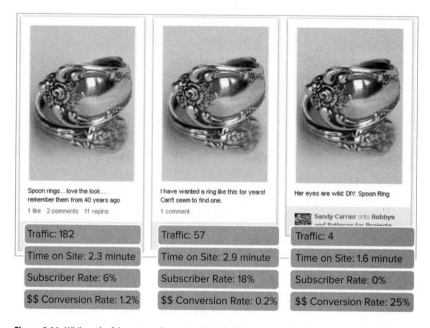

Figure 8.14 While each of these pinned images are identical, it's quite possible for one to send far more traffic than the others. It all depends on who pinned it, where they pinned it, whether it made a category feed, and who follows them.

This is why it's essential to know your goals for your Pinterest campaign. Although there's clearly value in traffic, sometimes strong sales are not associated with high-volume click-through rates. Figure out how you want to value the Pinterest activity for your website and have a plan for putting that knowledge into action. (We'll talk more about how companies are using this knowledge in Chapter 14.)

Thursday: Understanding Why Pinterest Traffic Arrives over Time

One of the most frustrating and wonderful things about Pinterest traffic is that it doesn't always show up the way you expect it to. By its very nature, Pinterest is not a "here it is, now it's gone" type of site. The high rate of repin activity means content will get reintroduced and recycled on a regular basis. It also means traffic ebbs and flows over time as the content is rediscovered and shared with a new round of users.

This can be a beneficial process for site owners on several fronts. Most important, it means traffic is more likely to stream in as waves over an extended period of time rather than crashing up against your server in a crushing blow that leaves your site down and you frantically calling your host.

The Pinterest Wave

When looking at a chart of the traffic produced by a popular piece of content on Pinterest, a "wave" pattern quickly becomes visible (see Figure 8.15).

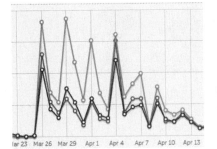

Figure 8.15 The Pinterest Wave describes the common pattern of traffic driven to a site by a popular pin. Traffic levels spike repeatedly as new communities of users find and repin the original piece of content.

This is because a popular piece of content will get introduced to Pinterest and cause a nice surge in traffic as people click through to explore it. The traffic will then taper off as the exposure wears off—that is, until one of the repinned images gets spotted and shared by a new user, triggering another round of activity and traffic buildup.

A single piece of content can create a wave-shaped traffic pattern for weeks, months, or even a year. A big part of this is also due to the commonality of impulse pins.

Impulse Pins and Latent Click-Throughs

To understand why traffic from the site runs in waves, it's important to understand user patterns of behavior on the site. For many Pinterest users, the site is a place of discovery. They visit the site in short bursts, gathering information to review at a later date.

This means it's not even remotely uncommon for a pinner to repin dozens of images without ever clicking through to view the content on the other end. At some later point in time, they might check back in to the pinboard where they've collected all this content so they can invest the time in clicking through to the associated website to read the full scope of the content (see Figure 8.16).

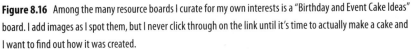

Figure 8.16 Among the many resource boards I curate for my own interests is a "Birthday and Event Cake Ideas" board. I add images as I spot them, but I never click through on the link until it's time to actually make a cake and I want to find out how it was created.

At this point in time, one of several things usually happens. The most common thing is for the user to click through to the site, digest the content, and either act on it or decide they aren't interested and delete the pin. These actions will produce traffic for you but won't do much else.

Another option is for the user to click through to your site, really like the content, and start exploring other pages of your site. When this happens, it's not even remotely uncommon for the user to pin additional content from your site, causing a secondary uptick in exposure. The great news on this front is that the new pinning activity often results in several pins, increasing the chance of exposure to the pinner's followers as well as increasing the chance one of your pins might find its way into the category stream. This is the ideal scenario for latent click-throughs.

Either way, it's important to understand that unlike standard social sharing activity, Pinterest content often produces its traffic days or even weeks after the content was originally shared, which leads to my next point.

Why Traffic Doesn't Always Match Pin Numbers

A great piece of targeted content launched to Pinterest at just the right time and finding itself showing up in the category pages can result in hundreds or even thousands of repins. You might even notice your notification system getting slammed with these repin notices.

If you hadn't already read the previous section on latent click-throughs, you might even rush over to Google Analytics to watch the traffic flooding in. As those of you reading this book know, there's a good chance you'd end up disappointed.

That said, there are a few other things to consider regarding the pin-to-traffic ratio. Sometimes, people do click through to view the destination page before repinning the content. If they don't like what they find when they arrive, they're not going to hit the Repin button when they return to the Pinterest interface. Of course there's also the chance you've made the mistake of promoting a "no-reason-to-click" image.

You may recall back in Chapter 7, "Week 4—Purposely Propagating Pins on Pinterest," when we walked through the various types of images that tend to perform well on Pinterest. Among them were two key types that often result in a high number of repins and an almost nonexistent amount of traffic: quotes and overly detailed instructions (see Figure 8.17).

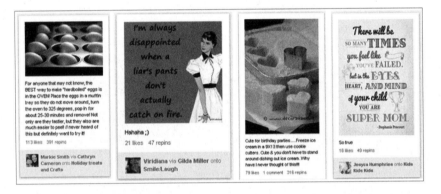

Figure 8.17 Each of these images has received a decent number of repins, but it's highly unlikely any of them have created significant traffic for their host sites.

The two quote images shown in Figure 8.17 carry the entire message within the image and the two food pictures explain the entire process in the description. None of them gives any motivation to click through to the site. In fact, these images could rack up literally thousands of pins and repins over their lifetime and probably wouldn't present much in the way of traffic at all.

This is why it's important to understand that repins should not always be the primary goal of your Pinterest content.

Friday: Using Third-Party Tools for Pinterest Analytics

Throughout this chapter, we've explored the various ways to gather data about the Pinterest activity related to your website. We've talked about the need to explore pinning versus repinning. We've even looked at some ways to use Google Analytics to dig a little deeper into how Pinterest is impacting your site traffic.

While Pinterest has yet to release a public API, companies are already springing up to offer additional insights and services to help Pinterest marketers. Keep in mind that until an API is released and can be programmed around, some of these services technically violate Pinterest's Terms of Service. Use them at your own discretion.

PinAlerts

Because Pinterest has not yet created any type of analytics dashboard, it's tough to gather data from within the site. Currently, the site will send you a notification if another user repins, likes, or comments on content you've submitted to the site, but it has no way to notify you when people pin content from your domain.

This is where PinAlerts (www.pinalerts.com) steps in. This free service allows you to set up an account and specify the domains and frequency with which you wish to track and receive notification by email detailing the pins posted from your domains to Pinterest (see Figure 8.18).

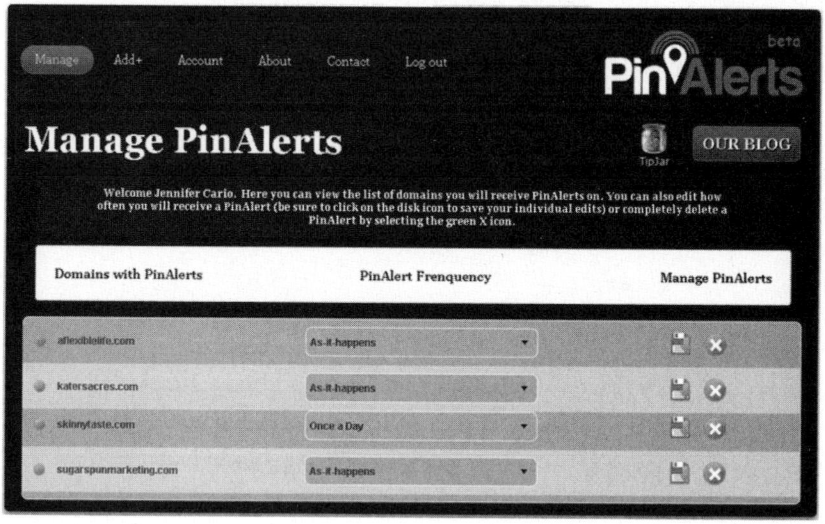

Figure 8.18 PinAlerts allows users to set up multiple domains and manage the alert frequency for them individually. This allows you to set instant notifications for smaller domains or timely campaigns and daily or weekly archives for more active domains.

Once you've set up your tracking and notification parameters, PinAlerts will shoot you scheduled emails containing the data you've requested (see Figure 8.19).

Figure 8.19 A sample email from PinAlerts

It's important to note that while PinAlerts will let you set up notifications for domains you don't own, there are some restricted domains based on sheer volume of content being pinned from those sites. Don't expect to be able to track activity from sites like eBay, Yahoo!, or Flickr.

Curalate

One of the most impressive Pinterest-related analytics tools I've seen so far is the subscription-based option from Curalate. Many of the Pinterest-based analytics tools that come up frequently in conversation are aimed at tracking how the pins you post on the site perform. While there's most definitely value in this information, it only provides a small glimpse of the reality of your brand on Pinterest.

What Curalate looks to do is gather together *all* of the activity for the content from your site, including the times your images are pinned without even linking back to your domain. They do this using software that scans and maps the images on your site and then seeks out those same images on the Pinterest site.

Curalate then breaks this information down by pin to show you how many visits each piece of content is actually producing (see Figure 8.20).

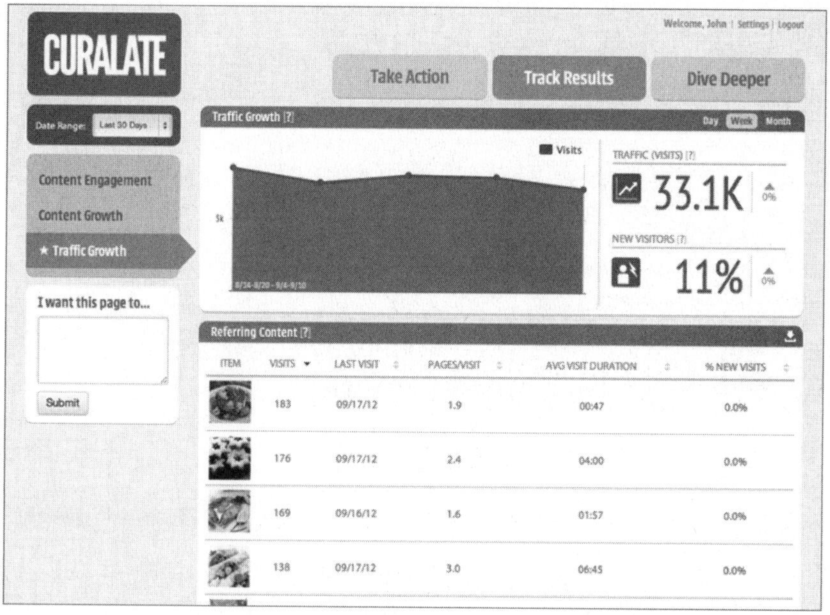

Figure 8.20 This screenshot from Curalate shows overall traffic growth as well as a breakdown of traffic by individual pin.

Curalate does an impressive job of segmenting out the content being shared by your brand and the content being shared by visitors to your site. This can give you a great overview of how well your organic presence is faring on Pinterest as well as how successful (or not) your Pinterest marketing campaigns are.

The tool will even break down individual pinner profiles to help you identify the most active pinners for your brand, making it a useful tool for companies who wish to reach out to pinners.

As of this writing, Curalate services range from $19 to $99 per month based on the levels of tracking and services you desire.

Repinly

Most of the tools I've mentioned so far have been aimed at helping you understand more about how people are reacting to the content you post to Pinterest or exploring what content people are pinning from your site. Repinly is all about providing you with a snapshot of what's going on with the Pinterest community as a whole.

Want to know what's trending right now as the most popular pins for the month in the DIY and Crafts category? Repinly has you covered (see Figure 8.21).

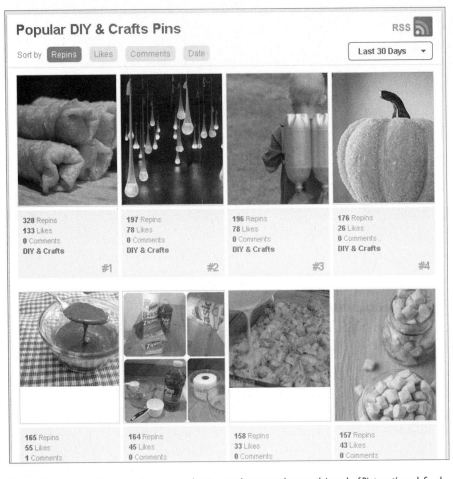

Figure 8.21 Repinly will show you the most popular pins over the past week or month in each of Pinterest's predefined categories.

This can be a great way to understand what's trending. There was a period of time in 2012 where any recipe with the word "cake batter" in the mix shot to instant popularity. Spotting this trend using Repinly could have helped influence the editorial calendars of sites to address this trend and attract more interest.

Repinly also supplies marketers with an overall view of how people are using the site. Whether it's the current stats on repinning, liking, and commenting, or simply a breakdown of which categories are the best performers, Repinly has the data (see Figure 8.22).

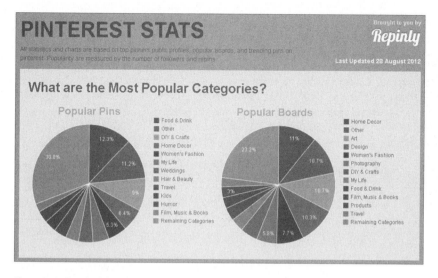

Figure 8.22 Repinly continually updates the activity data for each of Pinterest's predefined categories.

Now that you've got some of the basics of Pinterest analytics and measurement, it's time for us to move on to developing and launching a strategic Pinterest marketing plan. We'll dive into this topic coming up in Chapter 9, "Week 6—Developing a Successful Pinterest Strategy."

Week 6—Developing a Successful Pinterest Strategy

Up to this point, we've built a solid foundation of understanding regarding what Pinterest is, how and why people use it, and what you need to do in order to get your business up and running on it. Now it's time to start exploring the strategy behind Pinterest.

Chapter Contents

Monday: Learning How Your Target Market Uses Pinterest
Tuesday: Discovering Patterns in Topical Pins
Wednesday: Recruiting Evangelists and Fans for the Effort
Thursday: Finding Tie-ins to Other Social Media Channels
Friday: Understanding Your Staffing Availability

Monday: Learning How Your Target Market Uses Pinterest

As with most social media channels, one of the best ways to get rolling with strategic planning on Pinterest is to invest some time and effort into consumer research. After all, if you want to attract the attention of Pinterest users with both the content on your site and your own pinboards, you must develop a strong understanding of how and why they use Pinterest. You'll need to be able to identify the types of content they'll be most interested in, and you'll have to make appropriate adjustments to your content marketing plan.

Keep in mind that a great Pinterest strategy requires a two-pronged approach. You'll need to work on curating pinboards that will attract followers as well as creating pinnable content that will perform well once it's made available to Pinterest users.

Mining Pinterest Search for Consumer Insight

Much like the world of search engine optimization, a great place to start is with a little keyword research. It's important to spend some time identifying the topics your target audience is interested in and what related topics might make it easier to expand your outreach efforts to bring in new customers.

By taking the time to brainstorm topics related to the target audience you want to reach, you can build a list to work from while researching Pinterest activity among your potential customers.

If you've already got strong social media efforts in place, chances are high you can dig into analytics to understand which topics on your existing social media presence best attract traffic and engagement. Putting together a list of related topics can do wonders toward helping you run searches and research activity on Pinterest (see Figure 9.1).

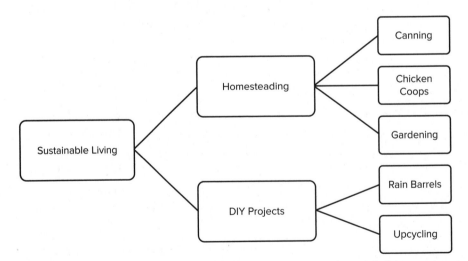

Figure 9.1 As with search engine optimization and content planning, Pinterest research goes easier if you map out your topical approach.

Running Pinterest Searches for Individual Pins

Once you've created your brainstorming list, there are two primary routes your research can take. First, you can run searches for pins using the keyword from your list. This will help you find out what types of images and content perform well on those topics (see Figure 9.2).

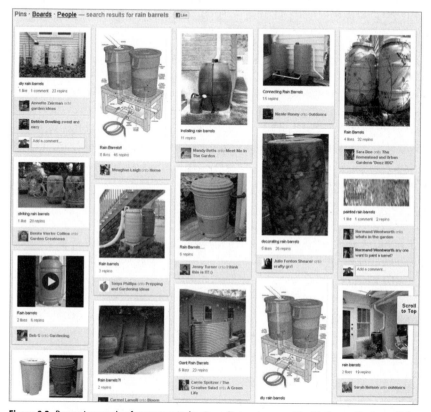

Figure 9.2 By running searches for your targeted topics on Pinterest, you can identify the specific pieces of information and ideas Pinterest users are looking for.

Consider the images shown in Figure 9.2. With the exception of a set of schematics, the rest of the images are not high-quality studio shots. These pictures, while well photographed, were taken of rain barrels in place in a yard. Scrolling further through the search results confirms this pattern. This is good news for the site that writes about or even sells rain barrels. There's likely little need to invest in super-expensive photography for the purposes of Pinterest. However, a few common patterns are worth noting:

Dual Rain Barrels   In both the selected screenshot and upon further exploration of the search results, nearly all of the pinned images feature more than one rain barrel. Clicking through to any of the images quickly makes it clear the second barrel is an overflow barrel used to maximize storage capacity. This could be useful information regarding the best approach to writing about or even selling rain barrels. It demonstrates an easy opportunity to upsell more product by focusing on the benefits of having multiple barrels.

Barrels Made from Reclaimed Materials The greatest majority of rain barrels featured in pinned images are upcycled products. Whether it's a used food-grade 55-gallon drum or a large plastic trash can, most rain barrels featured on Pinterest were made, not purchased. That also provides useful information to site owners. Perhaps companies that sell rain barrels might want to consider selling an upcycle kit for transforming a trash can into a rain barrel as a way to capture some revenue from DIY types.

Pretty Rain Barrels Perhaps the biggest surprise to me personally as I ran through these results was the number of pins showing hand-painted rain barrels. The entire search result listing was simply full of them. This is a great example of Pinterest offering an extra peek inside the dreams and wishes of consumers. Why have ugly gray rain barrels when you could have one painted to blend into your garden? This opens the door for tutorials, contests, and sponsored giveaways.

Running Pinterest Searches for Boards

While it makes sense to start off with searches for individual pins in order to see which pins show up repeatedly and gather a lot of repeat activity, it's also essential to spend time searching for Pinterest boards.

That said, it's important to remember that when it comes to boards, it's sometimes necessary to work your way back up to the higher levels of your keyword tree. Consider our original keyword tree from earlier in this section. If we ran a search for "chicken coops" and selected board search, we would receive dozens of listings for topically focused boards (see Figure 9.3).

Figure 9.3 Running a keyword search for Pinterest boards gives you quick and easy access to dozens of topically curated boards.

A narrowly curated board topic can be a great way to dig deep into a specific area of interest, but it can also cause you to miss out on higher-level topics you might not know are drawing interest from your customer base.

It's easy enough to find pins of rain barrels or boards featuring chicken coops, yet that content is also often found in higher-level boards like "Homesteading" and "Sustainable Living" (see Figure 9.4).

Figure 9.4 By searching for boards using "parent topic" keywords, you open yourself up to discovering related topics you might not be aware of.

Once you've identified these boards, you have several research options. For one-off topical research, your best bet is to take the time to click into each of them to view the content that has been collected. You can look for patterns in terms of both the type of content and the type of image that gets repinned as well as click through the listing to the related web page to see what type of content has garnered the pin.

If the research is part of a longer-term Pinterest plan (say, for instance, you work in-house as a marketer or you have a focused account to keep tabs on a specific client's target audience), you can seek out the boards that have a high number of pins and a strong number of followers. These two qualities will help you recognize well-curated boards.

By following these boards, you'll open up your Pinterest account to a steady stream of pinned content from your target audience. Finding and following a reasonable number of boards of interest to your target audience can be a great way to feed yourself a steady stream of trending pins. This can help you identify new trends or topics that may pop up in the future as well.

Identifying Potentially Influential Pinners

A great thing about running searches and spending time in targeted pins and pinboards is the chance to conduct some research on individual pinners as well. Keep in mind that on Pinterest, the person who pins or repins your content can be nearly as important as the quality of the content itself.

There are three primary traits you want to look for in a pinner as you are exploring listings (see Figure 9.5):

Figure 9.5 When looking for potential influencers, check boards for the number of followers, the number of pins that have been repinned, and the ratio of pins to repins.

Number of Board Followers   As of this writing, Pinterest's search did not seem to factor number of followers or repin activity into their search algorithm. This means you'll need to click through to each board to check out the number of followers it has. Boards with higher numbers of followers equate to more exposure for the pins placed within them. If a board is extremely targeted to your audience, connecting with the pinner could be a great way to help get your content into their feed down the road.

Number of Pins That Have Been Repinned   The final concern you should have when scoping out potential influencers is the amount of activity around their pins. When it comes to finding the most influential users for your topic, simply having a lot of followers and cranking out a lot of content isn't the ultimate goal. Those traits will help create an environment where content is more likely to go viral and be repinned, but they don't guarantee it. Scan through the listings in their boards to see if people react to the content they share. A user with a high percentage of pins being repinned most definitely qualifies as a highly influential pinner.

Ratio of Pins to Repins   Another thing to look at when exploring boards is the percentage of pinned content to repinned content. The greatest majority of Pinterest activity is made up of repins. A board that features a high percentage (over half) of pinned content denotes a Pinterest user who invests time in finding and adding new content to the stream. These users are prime candidates for helping to launch and spread new content and will earn a more loyal following because of their tendency to introduce brand-new content. Unfortunately, you'll have to take the time to manually review the pins on a pinboard to determine this ratio as it is not a number tallied or shared by Pinterest itself.

Tuesday: Discovering Patterns in Topical Pins

Yesterday, we explored the need to get into Pinterest search to start digging around and gathering data. Today we're going to build on that foundation by digging a little bit deeper and being even more observant about what we find.

There's a wealth of insight available about your target audience on Pinterest, and the best part about it is they offer the information for free. Everything from which images are selected to what descriptions are used to what boards they pin the content to takes part in painting the picture of what interests your audience.

In Chapter 7, "Week 4—Purposely Propagating Pins on Pinterest," we talked about what types of images tend to capture Pinterest users' attention, but the focus there was on overall Pinterest usage. Yesterday we discussed getting an idea of what particulars of a topic or idea capture the attention of our target audience on Pinterest. Today, we're going to focus on three key areas of observation that can help you better understand what appeals to your target audience and how they are using the content they are collecting.

What Concepts or Ideas Are Pinned Repeatedly

Although it's valuable to know that fashion collages, cute animals, and gorgeous shots of bucket list vacation ideas play well with the overall Pinterest crowd, it's extremely important to keep tabs on the specific interests within your Pinterest community.

Moms who spend time perusing birthday party boards know that Angry Birds, Lego, and Obstacle Course parties are big hits for boys right now and spa parties, cupcake parties, and Just Dance parties are big hits for girls. Cosmetics companies that patrol fashion boards will find thousands of pins showing step-by-step guides for eye makeup or high-art nail designs. Sports and fitness sites will soon recognize that text-based graphics outlining quick exercise sessions spread like wildfire.

The point is, if you don't spend time on the boards your audience frequents, you'll miss seeing what they care about at any point in time. Not only does taking note of highly pinned content provide you with insight for your own Pinterest strategy, it also gives you valuable insight for your overall content strategy.

If you run a fitness blog and Pinterest shows you that quick workouts and inspirational quotes do well, generate that type of content and include it as part of your blog, Twitter, and Facebook strategy.

What Images Are Being Selected

Many marketers confuse the idea of examining selected images with examining the content of images. These are two very different things. When we look at images to examine the concepts, we're talking about the end result of the pin: What does the pin lead someone to, or what does it try to communicate?

When we look at the image being selected for the pin, we're talking about *how* the concept or idea is portrayed in the image, not what the concept is. We're talking about showing a finished product vs. step-by-step instructions or favoring one particular angle over another.

Because Pinterest allows us to see a list of all the pins made from a particular URL, we have the ability to dig in to do a side-by-side comparison of which images get pulled from a particular post or web page. Taking the time to count which images from the post get the most Pinterest activity can provide some excellent insight into how your content is received. Think of Pinterest as a chance to fine-tune your image approach by allowing Pinterest users to show you which images they favor (see Figure 9.6).

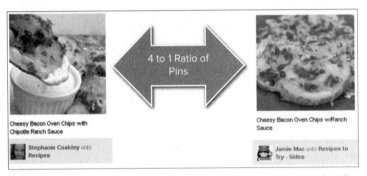

Figure 9.6 The image on the left has been pinned four times more than the image on the right, even though both are from the same blog post.

Of course there are a few qualifiers you have to take into account when considering the images showing up in the listings. The first image in a blog post is more likely to be selected as the pinned image simply due to its location. (That means you should give even more credence to a lot of pin activity for an image showing toward the bottom of the post.)

It's also important to keep tabs on pins vs. repins. Repins will not necessarily reflect the same image insight as original pins because the repinner wasn't faced with the same choice when it came to selecting an image to represent the content.

Special calls to action, image collages created specifically for Pinterest, and the location of the Pin It button also factor heavily into the equation. For most marketers, there's no need to track these factors in heavy detail—an occasional visual scan of the results will be enough to provide the necessary insight.

What Are the Board Names Being Used for Pins?

One last factor—which is often overlooked but that can weigh heavily in terms of understanding how Pinterest users are digesting your content—is the names of the pinboards they pin content to.

Early on in my days of experimenting and testing on Pinterest, I created a site that featured DIY wedding tips and ideas culled from my own outdoor farm wedding. One project in particular garnered a fair amount of attention on Pinterest. We had built a fake prop wall featuring large picture frames that perfectly fit holes cut in the wall. This allowed people to stand behind the frames to have a picture taken for our guest book.

The pin received hundreds of repins in a matter of a day or so. What struck me, however, was that the pins and repins weren't necessarily coming exclusively from brides planning parties. A common theme began to show up, making it clear that my wedding idea was being co-opted for other uses (see Figure 9.7).

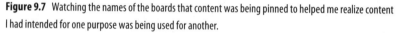

Figure 9.7 Watching the names of the boards that content was being pinned to helped me realize content I had intended for one purpose was being used for another.

Along with brides-to-be and photographers pinning the content into boards titled things like "our wedding" and "photo booths," I was also seeing pinboard titles like "party ideas," "2012 Prom," and "Joanie's birthday." It was a great reminder that I may have been targeting my content too narrowly. It would have been easy enough to take a new set of photos with the booth that weren't wedding related and to put up a new blog post talking about the various ways a photo booth could be utilized.

Regularly checking the Pinterest activity for your content and keeping an eye on the names of the pinboards being used can be a great way to stay ahead of the curve with your content planning.

Wednesday: Recruiting Evangelists and Fans for the Effort

One of the great things about Pinterest that isn't present on most other social media channels is the ability to gather together a group of people to jointly curate content. Outside of blogs there are very few areas of social media that give companies and organizations the opportunity to pool resources together to create stronger content.

This is an especially important concept for small businesses and nonprofits to understand. Using group-oriented techniques to build your Pinterest presence can be a highly effective way to overcome staffing issues. It can also be a way to boost attention to a growing board or organization by piggybacking off the reputations of a wider range of existing Pinterest users.

Letting Influencers and Evangelists Curate Your Boards

When considering using Pinterest's group board option, it's important to clarify that I don't simply mean giving third-party users access to pin to the site using your login. I'm talking about the freedom to gather together multiple users to contribute to a single board created by your business or organization. This can be a great way to foster community and to gain credibility within a niche on Pinterest.

The Benefits of Group Curation

There are quite a few reasons why creating group pinboards can benefit your organization. First and foremost, it gives you the chance to foster community and to bring people together to contribute to a common cause. In much the same way bloggers use blog carnivals or other forms of group contribution to a single topic, Pinterest group boards allow multiple people to contribute pins they find interesting to a single, collaborative board.

Second, building a group pinboard can be a great way to build credibility for your organization within a community of related bloggers. Acting as a central hub that brings people together in a way that can benefit all of them is generally very good for your reputation and relationships.

Third, bringing in a group of trusted influencers to pin as part of your brand can provide a huge boost to the quality of your content and to the way you are received by potential customers.

Fourth, group curation can be an amazingly effective way to reduce your workload in the social media space. As long as someone is investing the time into properly vetting potential contributors and moderating the pinned content, group boards can allow multiple people from outside your company to generate content that benefits your company.

Inviting Pinners to Curate Your Pinboard

Inviting other Pinterest users to post to your boards is easy. Simply visit the Edit Board page for the pinboard you are looking to expand and type in the names of the Pinterest users you wish to invite (see Figure 9.8). It's important to note you must already be following a Pinterest user in order to invite them to participate on your boards.

Figure 9.8 You may invite other Pinterest users to post to you boards by adding them from the Edit Board page for the board in question.

Once you've sent the invitations, they'll receive an email telling them they have been invited to join your board and linking them to the board for their review (see Figure 9.9).

Figure 9.9 Pinterest will automatically send an email to any Pinterest user you invite to your boards so they can review the board before responding.

If the Pinterest user is considering joining your board, they can click the link to take a look at the existing board. It will show them what content has already been pinned there, who the other contributors to the board are, and how many followers the board has. It will also include a call to action to both accept the invite and join the board or to decline (see Figure 9.10).

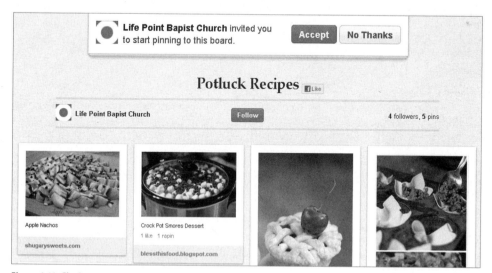

Figure 9.10 The Pinterest users you invite to co-curate your pinboard will have a chance to preview the board before accepting your offer.

When to Open up Curation

Because users get a chance to preview your boards, it's extremely important to make sure your boards are in a state that will help encourage other Pinterest users to join in. Take the time to curate relevant images, write good descriptions, and build a following. If you plan to approach influencers to help curate your boards, plan your timing carefully.

If you have a great relationship with an influencer, there's a good chance you might be able to approach them to help you launch a pinboard. If you're trying to reach out to influencers, however, it's probably a good idea to build your jointly curated pinboard up a bit with more approachable pinners first (see Figure 9.11).

Figure 9.11 The Pinterest users you approach to join your pinboard can see which pinners are already part of the group. Building credibility through your choice of pinners can help attract more popular Pinterest users.

Of course it's also essential to maintain daily moderation of any pinboard you've opened up access for. These pinners represent your business or your organization, and potential customers and followers will view their actions as a reflection on your company. This is why it's wise to grow group curation boards carefully.

A Warning Regarding Group Boards

Although there are many potential benefits to putting together a plan to bring contributors into your pinboards, it's extremely important to also be aware of the pitfalls.

Invited pinners may or may not share the same values, beliefs, and judgment as your company. This means there's always a chance they will post something that offends some of your customer base. Even worse, there's always the potential of an invited pinner using your board to upload unrelated content in an effort to spam the board (see Figure 9.12).

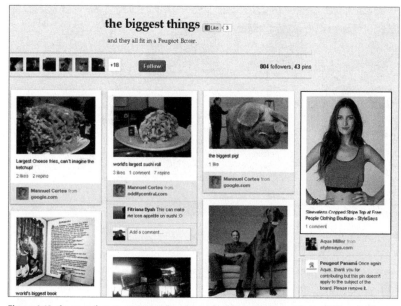

Figure 9.12 One contributor to a group pinboard set up by Peugeot Panama added multiple spam pins to the board.

Over time, Pinterest has refined the administrative controls for group pinboards to help alleviate these issues. Board owners can remove pinners from their boards if problems or irrelevant pins or spam attempts occur. (Unfortunately, Pinterest has not yet offered a way for the creators of group pinboards to remove pins added by invited curators.) For this reason, it is extremely important to carefully screen new pinners before adding them to a group board.

Pinning and Featuring Fan Content

Mining Pinterest content for pins to include on your own boards can be an equally effective way to leverage the activity of other Pinterest users to build your own presence. While we've explored the idea of finding good Pinterest users to follow in order to help provide insight and even aid in new pin discovery, it's also important to consider how collecting content on Pinterest can help sell your brand.

One company that does this extremely well is Chobani. They've created pinboards that feature fan-created recipes using Chobani yogurt as an ingredient. They scour both Pinterest and the Web for these recipes and highlight them on a pinboard titled "Chobanic Creations" (see Figure 9.13).

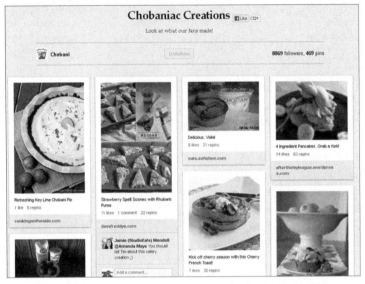

Figure 9.13 Chobani created a pinboard that features fan recipes found around the Web.

Companies can also encourage users to tag them in pins that feature their products or related items. This allows fans to get content in front of brands and makes it easier for brands to find the content to pin or repin to the proper boards.

Thursday: Finding Tie-ins to Other Social Media Channels

Pinterest is an extremely popular and growing social media channel on its own, but it works best when paired up with other social media channels to drive traffic to and from different types of engagement with your brand. For companies that are new to building a presence on Pinterest, it's even more important to leverage your existing connections on sites like Twitter and Facebook to draw attention to your newly created Pinterest account.

Promoting Involvement on Facebook

Of all the existing social media channels, Facebook probably carries the highest level of overlap in users with Pinterest. In fact, many Pinterest users discovered the site by watching friends' notifications of Pinterest posts show up in their streams (see Figure 9.14).

Figure 9.14 When users connect Pinterest to their Facebook accounts, Pinterest activity can show up in their newsfeed.

Companies can also choose to integrate their Pinterest activity by adding Pinterest as one of the apps on their Facebook Page's Timeline (see Figure 9.15). This allows Facebook users to become aware of a company's participation in Pinterest while visiting the Page's Timeline.

Figure 9.15 Pinterest can be integrated into the app section of a Facebook Page's Timeline.

This integration can be achieved using iFrames and will even allow Facebook users to view and interact with a brand's Pinterest profile and pinboards from within Facebook itself (see Figure 9.16). This can be a great way to build awareness and attract new followers since users can follow boards without ever leaving Facebook.

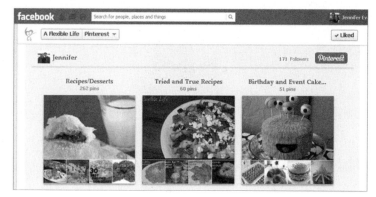

Figure 9.16 By using iFrames, marketers can fully integrate their Pinterest boards and profile into the Facebook environment.

The most direct approach is to utilize your Facebook news stream to invite followers to join you in the world of Pinterest. Many brands use Facebook to announce contests or to recruit contributors for group boards. Still others choose to publish some of their favorite pins directly to their Facebook newsfeed in an attempt to entice Facebook users into joining them on the other site.

The Twitter Connection

While Twitter can be utilized in some of the same ways Facebook can, there are some limitations in terms of getting your messaging in front of users. The Facebook news-feed is a naturally image-heavy environment, whereas Twitter requires users to expand image-based tweets to see the related picture.

This means marketers will need to rely on text-based persuasion to convince users to come and visit them on Pinterest or to link directly into new pinboards.

Video Sites (YouTube and Vimeo)

As of this writing, there was not an integrated relationship between Pinterest and YouTube or Vimeo, at least not the same way there is between Pinterest and Facebook or Twitter. Pinterest will support videos that have been pinned from the two popular video sites, but that's where the "integration" ends.

Users have to rely on the Pinterest bookmarklet to pin content from the site as neither one has integrated the Pin It button alongside videos. That said, the growth of videos on Pinterest since marketers first took notice of the site in early 2012 has been impressive.

When it comes to promoting your video content through Pinterest, there are a few key things you need to consider. Because high-quality images and beautiful pho-tography play so well on Pinterest, videos that rely on randomized screen captures or that feature nonprofessional videography might not perform as well as those featuring customized video thumbnails (see Figure 9.17).

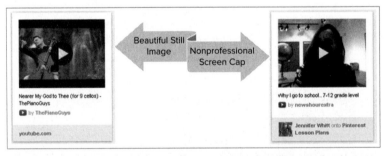

Figure 9.17 The video on the left features a professional still image that is likely to perform better on Pinterest than the screen capture of the consumer-generated video on the right.

It's also important to understand that shorter videos are more likely to perform well on Pinterest than longer videos. Keep in mind that Pinterest is a gateway site, a place where people go to find links and images that either offer an instant solution or impact or that link them off to a site that features more information on the relevant topic. While it's possible that some pinners will be open to digesting longer videos by coming back to watch them later, most Pinterest-based video activity revolves around shorter, immediately digestible video clips.

Friday: Understanding Your Staffing Availability

As with other social media channels, it's absolutely essential to develop a Pinterest strategy that takes into account your social media staffing and the hours they have available to devote to Pinterest activity. It's also essential to have some type of business-related goals and metrics in place for Pinterest so you can place a value on your activities there over time.

Determining Staff Needs

For the most part, even large brands can get away with fairly minimal staffing when it comes to Pinterest. Most brands don't pin more than a few pieces of content per day, and it's not unusual for a brand to pin only a few times per week. Because users are able to follow only the boards that apply to them, many users scroll through content when they log in and are able to see pins that were made even a few days prior.

Your staffing needs will depend heavily on how you plan to use Pinterest. If you are simply interested in putting together some boards designed to appeal to your target audience to position yourself as a resource, a single person squeezing in some Pinterest time here and there will likely get the job done for you.

On the other hand, if you are planning to use Pinterest for consumer insight and research or to conduct extensive testing on which images and pieces of content receive the best response from your target audience, you may wish to dedicate more hours or even a team of people to the cause.

How Much Time to Spend on Pinterest

Another key question you'll need to examine is how much time to devote to Pinterest and when to devote it. Most big-brand Pinterest accounts pin either daily or a few times per week. Much of your Pinterest time also depends heavily on whether you plan to repin or to pin original content.

If you plan to pin original content, the good news is you can install the Pinterest bookmarklet to your browser and take a few extra seconds to pin worthwhile content as you run across it. This is one of the strongest reasons for adding multiple people within your organization to your Pinterest account. A team of like-minded individuals pinning relevant content as they go can create a pretty strong presence with very little extra time.

On the other hand, if you plan to spend time repinning content and or running searches for pinned content that is relevant to your brand, you'll likely need to carve out some time each day for these activities. Since you will ideally be seeking out highly relevant boards and following them to create a strong Pinterest feed, repinning shouldn't take much effort. Scheduling 10 to 15 minutes to scan existing pins or run some searches each morning will cover the needs of most businesses. Larger brands or highly pinned brands may want to double or triple their time investment.

Regular Hours or Scattered Hours

There are distinct pros and cons to scheduling your hours or working via scattered hours. Pinning content during peak hours (early morning before work and early evening after dinner) can result in higher interaction from Pinterest users but also opens you up to higher competition for attention from other pinners.

Users who are seeking to repin content are also better able to repin batches of content from their personal Pinterest feed or search results in single concentrated sessions. Original pins are harder to make in concentrated batches because they require more time investment spent searching for quality content.

On some fronts, scattered pinning of original content creates a natural pattern. It allows users to add new content as they run across it during everyday Internet browsing. That said, there are some problems with this approach. As Pinterest continues to adjust their category feed algorithm, there's the ongoing potential that the length of time that has passed since your last pin might have an impact on whether or not your pin gets promoted to the category feed.

For that reason, some Pinterest users may wish to hold off on pinning a particularly juicy piece of content until some time has passed since their last pin. This can make pinning original content a bit of a challenge—it becomes necessary to schedule time to revisit the piece of content and to pin it at a later hour or date.

Week 7—Leveraging Boards for Better Reach

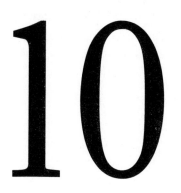

As *with real life, first impressions via social media are extremely important. In the world of Pinterest, your profile page and your board structure are what people scrutinize when trying to decide whether to follow you. Additionally, since Pinterest users can elect to pick which of your boards they wish to follow, the order and display of your boards can make or break the expansion of your presence.*

This week, we'll tackle board structure. We'll look at how and when to rearrange the order, how to organize the boards themselves, how to leverage evangelists and marketing teams for better board content, and how to make use of seasonal and situational boards for short-term marketing efforts.

Chapter Contents

Monday: Creating a Strategic Pinboard Structure

Users can discover your brand on Pinterest in multiple ways, but there's only one way they can see the full line-up of pinboards you curate and choose to follow a handpicked selection of your stream. They'll need to visit your brand's Pinterest page and choose which pinboards to follow. This means you must put thought, time, and even a little testing into your pinboard structure to increase the likelihood of people following your boards.

What Are Your Goals for Pinterest?

Before you start working on a list of pinboards you think your target audience will be interested in, or start shuffling around the order of your boards to increase exposure and conversion rates, you need to ask yourself one very important question:

Why is your brand on Pinterest?

Note: As with all other forms of social media, Pinterest has the potential to become a serious time sink for your business or your marketing team. Distractions abound and it's easy to get sucked into the journey of discovery. More so than with almost any other social media channel, it's absolutely essential to build a focused Pinterest strategy that clearly defines your goals and how your time will be justified. Otherwise, you run the risk of losing hours and hours of marketing effort with little to show for it beyond an adorable collection of baby animals and a gazillion upcycling ideas.

The answer will play a huge role in defining not only how you end up using Pinterest, but also how you will determine which pinboards to build, how to feature them, and how and when to add new ones to the mix. As with many forms of online marketing, the primary goals of Pinterest tend to fall into one of four categories. More than likely, you'll be using Pinterest to drive traffic, build your brand, foster community, motivate sales, or for a combination of several of these goals.

Using Boards to Drive Traffic

One of the biggest draws to Pinterest, especially for content-focused websites, is the potential boost in traffic. Since the online marketing community discovered the potential of Pinterest in early 2012, case studies, stories, and data collectors have touted the amazing traffic potential of the site. In fact, data aggregator Shareaholic shows Pinterest referral traffic outperforming Twitter in multiple months during the first half of 2012 (Figure 10.1).

The outperformance of Twitter is especially impressive considering Twitter has roughly 500 million active users to Pinterest's estimated 15–20 million. This demonstrates not only the depth of Pinterest's use by consumers as a gateway to ideas and

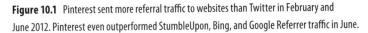

January - May 2012 All Traffic Sources Report

Source	Share of Visits - January	Share of Visits - February	Share of Visits - March	Share of Visits - April	Share of Visits - May	Share of Visits - June
Google (Organic)	48.9%	48.81%	48.48%	48.88%	47.68%	46.80%
Direct	19.44%	18.20%	18.32%	18.44%	18.63%	19.57%
Facebook	6.92%	6.38%	6.08%	6.10%	6.32%	5.65%
Yahoo	1.60%	1.61%	1.67%	1.67%	1.69%	1.63%
Bing	1.24%	1.21%	1.27%	1.29%	1.27%	1.18%
StumbleUpon	1.30%	1.29%	1.05%	1.13%	.93%	.96%
Google (Referral)	.68%	0.91%	.99%	1.05%	1.05%	1.09%
Twitter	.88%	.82%	.85%	.85%	.88%	.92%
Pinterest	.85%	1.05%	.80%	.74%	.83%	1.19%

Presented by: **shareaholic**

Figure 10.1 Pinterest sent more referral traffic to websites than Twitter in February and June 2012. Pinterest even outperformed StumbleUpon, Bing, and Google Referrer traffic in June.

resources, but also the absolutely immense traffic potential of the site as its user base continues to expand.

If your primary goal for using Pinterest is to increase the traffic that clicks through to your website, you'll need to focus on a pinboard structure that either mimics or supports the content and category breakdown users have come to expect from your website. This allows existing fans who connect with you on Pinterest to see continuity of content across both platforms while also serving as an introduction to your site's focus for new fans who discover you via Pinterest.

Consider the content site ApartmentTherapy.com, one of the Internet's most popular destinations for tips, ideas, and makeovers for people who live in small spaces. Since the site is flush with beautiful photographs and serves as inspiration to legions of city dwellers, it should come as no surprise that they joined Pinterest fairly early in the game (see Figure 10.2).

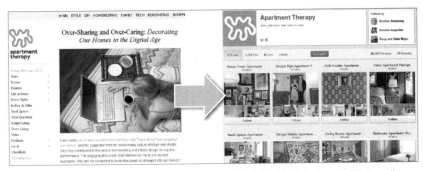

Figure 10.2 ApartmentTherapy.com uses Pinterest to share beautiful and inspiring images of life in small spaces.

ApartmentTherapy.com is a site perfectly suited for leveraging Pinterest to drive traffic. Pinterest's key demographics have a strong overlap with ApartmentTherapy .com's target audience, and the site has long featured the exact type of content Pinterest users are looking for. Unfortunately, they are missing the boat on several fronts, primarily in their board structure.

The ApartmentTherapy.com website focuses on a few key areas: tours of people's homes, room-by-room inspirational posts, a wide range of DIY projects for the home, and a breakdown of décor styles. Unfortunately, this is not reflected in their pinboards. As of this writing, the site featured only 10 boards. In terms of content matching, they share a pinboard focused on tours, one with design tips, one with style guides, one focused on colors, and a handful focused on a specific room of the house.

This lack of continuity with their website fails to capitalize on the thing that makes Pinterest so valuable: the ability to segment content for your audience. ApartmentTherapy.com forces its long-term readers to select from extremely broad pinboard categories, despite the fact that the website allows them to quickly narrow the content to their specific area of interest. Additionally, there's no pinboard for the DIY-style project posts that perform so well on the site.

Additionally, the site pins only content from its own website. This completely misses the point of Pinterest and could actually be keeping the site from gaining the maximum traffic potential from its Pinterest account. A simple shift to a Pinterest presence that not only mimics the navigational structure of the site via their pinboards but also incorporates third-party content and product links to provide more context and resources to their readers would likely increase followers, maximize exposure within Pinterest via repins, and ultimately generate far more traffic.

Using Boards to Build Brand

Companies that rely heavily on brand-based emotions and imagery can also be well served by setting up a support pinboard structure. Companies like Nike, Red Bull, and Starbucks curate boards that shore up the associated concepts they've tied to their brands over the years. Nike features scores of inspirational photos and quotes for athletes; Starbucks shares "Inspiring Spaces" and photos of "Coffee Moments."

Despite a more generalized focus on the Pinterest rarity—young men—Red Bull has invested time and effort into building a Pinterest presence that perfectly matches up with the brand of their demographic (see Figure 10.3).

It's important to keep in mind that because pinboards can be individually followed, Pinterest fosters the opportunity to connect with all the subsets of your brand without isolating or overwhelming your audience. In the case of Red Bull, their board structure manages to do this quite effectively.

Figure 10.3 Red Bull's Pinterest page is full of pinboards that evoke the emotions and inspiration so common to the Red Bull brand: wings, extreme sports, summer, and youth.

Boards like "Festibull" and "Festival Fashion" catch the eye of female fans and fashion fans who wonder what styles and looks were big at Red Bull–sponsored Coachella. Boards like "#Redbull" and "Holy Sh!t" provide adrenaline-pumping photos that play to the young male adrenaline-junkie side of the brand.

Pinterest gives businesses the ability to boost the emotional and topical ties they have worked to associate with their brands by allowing brands to curate boards related to those topics. If your goal is to solidify, support, or define your brand's imagery, Pinterest may provide you with a platform to accomplish this.

Ask yourself what topics or ideas you want people to associate with your company. If you are in investments, it may be things like "bucket lists" and travel destinations. If you're peddling sustainability and solar-powered systems, it might be boards about homesteading, off-grid living, and creative power conservation. A moving company might curate boards focused on organization and space-saving techniques (see Figure 10.4).

Figure 10.4 The moving company PODS curates a wide range of boards covering topics that support their overall brand.

Keep in mind the content you pin will show up in followers' streams with your name attached to it. Your pinboards and your content provide the ideal chance to cement your brand's association with the ideas, inspiration, and photos you pin.

Using Boards to Foster Community

For some companies, setting up shop on Pinterest is about being able to connect with their fans and consumers. It's about identifying potential (and active) evangelists and encouraging their activity by showcasing the results. It's about encouraging community involvement.

These brands will need to focus on incorporating pinboards that support this goal and/or rewarding online consumers who participate. That might mean creating group-curated pinboards that bring brand evangelists together to generate your content, it might mean featuring ongoing contest focused boards that encourage consumers to connect with your brand, or it may simply mean featuring and highlighting the content that's already being uploaded about your brand.

One company that has done this extremely well with their pinboards is Chobani. They feature the typical brand-building categories you might expect like "Nothing but Good" quotes and Fitness and Nutrition pinboards. They also do an excellent job of building, fostering, and rewarding the community by featuring Chobani-focused recipes culled from food bloggers (see Figure 10.5).

Figure 10.5 Chobani features pinboards that showcase the many ways to integrate their product into healthy recipes as well as highlighting fan content featuring Chobani in recipes from blogs and other websites.

Highlighting existing fan content can be a strong way to build up your brand's follower base. It gives exposure to the people who are already promoting your content, which motivates more people to share content. It also demonstrates the extent to which your fans believe in and value your products.

Highlighting product-related posts isn't the only way to build community via Pinterest. We'll talk more about the use of contests in Chapter 13, "Week 10—Pinterest Marketing Through Contests," and more about inviting Pinterest users to help curate your brand's pinboards later in this chapter.

Using Boards to Motivate Sales

Since Pinterest caught the eye of online marketers in early 2012, retail outlets and results-based social media marketers have sought to explore any direct connection between traffic referred from Pinterest and ultimate e-commerce purchases. Shopify, a web-based e-commerce platform, released data in mid-2012 that painted a fairly positive picture of Pinterest's direct sales potential. (See `www.shopify.com/blog/6058268-how-pinterest-drives-ecommerce-sales`.)

The study showed that when traffic from Pinterest results in sales, those sales figures typically are higher than those from Google or Amazon traffic, and roughly twice as high as similar referral traffic from Facebook. Additionally, Pinterest's share of social media–referred e-commerce buyers has risen steadily over the past year. While Pinterest accounted for only about 1 percent of overall social media–driven sales in 2011, it accounted for nearly 17 percent of social media–driven sales for the first half of 2012.

Powered by Pinterest and Zombies?

Positec Tool Group was featured in a *Forbes* article, "How Positec Uses Pinterest (And Zombies) to Sell Power Tools," in June 2012. The article highlighted the company's use of Pinterest to push its WORX brand products to consumers. With expected boards like "Father's Day Gift Guide" and the tongue-in-cheek "Zombie Defense Guide," the WORX team has targeted Pinterest users to drive new interest in their products. The impact on WORX's sales has been strong, with Loftlon Worth, the Digital Global Director of Positec, claiming the average buyer from Pinterest spends $129 (as compared to $64 from their average Facebook customer). When asked why he believes such a dramatic difference exists, Worth told *Forbes*: "Facebook is interaction and visiting—not going out and saying 'Go try this.' But enabling Pinterest on the site has enabled us to let our customers be evangelists. Because the products are visually appealing, it's the product that takes charge."

Creative companies are finding unique ways to feature their products on Pinterest without moving into the realm of blatant sales pitches and obnoxious purchase pleas. Whether it's a fashion company featuring stylized looks with links back to purchase pages or a food brand pushing recipes that utilize their ingredients, Pinterest provides an ideal showcase.

One of the most creative examples of a company leveraging their pinboards to build brand awareness while also indirectly pushing sales of their products is Peugeot

Panama. By creatively leveraging the layout of Pinterest's boards, Peugeot Panama was able to create a mini-commercial for each of the vehicles in their fleet while still playing to the collection and curator nature of Pinterest users (see Figure 10.6).

Figure 10.6 Peugeot Panama has taken advantage of the pinboard order to effectively create mini-commercials that tout the selling factors of their products.

Whether it's touting the massive cargo space in its new van by showcasing pictures of "the World's Biggest Things," or the eco-friendly nature of its smaller sedans by curating photos of the cute animals your eco-friendly purchase will save, Peugeot has done a marvelous job of tapping Pinterest's branding and sales potential.

Tuesday: Categorizing Boards

Once you have a solid idea of what you are looking to accomplish with the pinboards you create, you're ready to start diving a little deeper with your Pinterest strategy. Deciding when and why to create new pinboards is a major part of this strategy. The right board launched at the right time can be a great way to draw attention to seasonal offerings or a current marketing strategy.

When it comes to building pinboards, it's important to understand that it's not just about what you launch and when you launch it—it's also about what you call it. The names you use to describe your pinboards can play a significant role in attracting new followers.

When to Add New Boards

The key to determining when to add a new board to your Pinterest account is pretty simple: Add it when you need it. Of course, the less smart-alecky and more useful approach is to consider the two key times that adding a new pinboard make the most sense.

When You Plan to Begin Curating a New Topic

The easiest answer regarding when to add a new pinboard is when you either decide to curate a new topic, or you discover a piece of content you wish to pin and you don't have a board appropriate to place it in.

This might come about because you've decided to start pinning a new topic related to your business, because you've decided to start curating pins that fit the lifestyle or brand image of your business, or because it's time to launch a seasonal or contest-related board.

Content-focused companies and websites often add new pinboards to match up with current features or trending news topics. That said, it's often retail-based companies that do the best job of creatively adding new categories to showcase creative ideas that might lead people to purchase their products. The popular paint brand Benjamin Moore has created some excellent pinboards along these lines (see Figure 10.7).

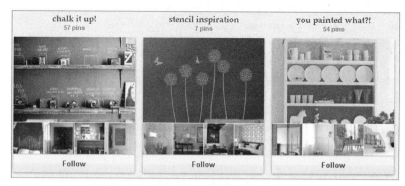

Figure 10.7 Paint brand Benjamin Moore often adds new pinboards featuring specific ideas or concepts that are trending on Pinterest and home design blogs.

Companies like Party City tend to launch and prioritize seasonal pinboards to help attract attention to new focuses in curation (see Figure 10.8).

Figure 10.8 During the month of July 2012, Party City launched and highlighted boards like "4th of July Party Ideas" and "Summer Party Ideas" at the very top of their Pinterest profile page.

Launching and naming boards to take advantage of trending topics, and relocating these topics to the top of your company's profile when they are most relevant, can help drive new followers to your pinboards.

When an Existing Pinboard Is Ready to Be Subdivided

When most individuals and brands begin pinning, they tend to build very generalized categories. Over time, these pinboards fill up with hundreds of pins and can become a bit overwhelming for new followers to visit and sort through.

This overload of pins on a specific topic opens up the door for a category to be subdivided and for one pinboard to morph into several. For example, what starts as an overall recipes board can eventually be divided up into type of recipe (such as entrees, appetizers, or desserts), style of food (such as Mexican, Italian, or Asian) or even specialized diet (such as diabetes-friendly, low-carb, or gluten-free).

This expansion of pinboards allows followers to pick the pinboards featuring the topics they are most interested in and showcases the variety of valuable content your brand is offering on the site.

A good rule of thumb is to start thinking about subdividing your pinboards when they reach 200 or more pins. At that point, there will almost always be a few common themes that are worth separating out into their own unique pinboards.

Determining Board Names

Another key consideration for brands as they build their Pinterest strategy is what to name their boards. As with most things marketing related, it's essential to balance conversion potential with search impact.

That's part of why it's important to understand the various ways a Pinterest user can find or run across your pinboards. The manner they are using to find your pinboards can be heavily influenced by the naming choices you use.

Spotting a Pinboard on a Pinterest Profile

As of this writing, the only way you could follow a Pinterest account or any of their pinboards was to first visit their Pinterest profile. When users visit your profile, they're faced with the task of scanning your existing pinboards to see which ones capture their attention.

Generally, this means scanning the pictures that are showing up for each board and reading the titles of the boards to determine what's in them. In some cases, it also includes clicking through to take a look at the content of the board, but typically, people make an instant decision based on the board name and the pictures being displayed.

This ability to quickly scan through board listings means the titles you choose for your pinboards can be an important part of getting the conversion. This is why descriptive yet motivating titles can do very well (see Figure 10.9).

Figure 10.9 Fitness site Fit Sugar offers up both inspirationally and descriptively titled boards designed to appeal to female fitness fans.

While no data or studies have been released by Pinterest to confirm as much, usage patterns of Pinterest users suggest viewing and choosing to follow a pinboard from your brand or company's profile page is likely the most common way to gain new followers.

Spotting a Pinboard in the Pinterest Stream

Another common way for Pinterest users to spot boards is by seeing a pin that strikes their fancy while searching a category page. (This doesn't hold true for their Pinterest stream as only pins from boards they already follow will show up there.)

A crafter looking through the DIY category might spot some great ideas and notice they have been pinned to seasonal boards like "Halloween" or "Easter" and decide to begin following those boards to get the specific content. An urban chicken owner might spot a pin made to "Urban Chickens" or "Backyard Chickens" in the outdoors category and click through to subscribe to the feed.

This is why specific pinboards that feature well-curated content can play very well on Pinterest. Although there's always going to be interest in more generally tiled categories like "travel," "recipes," "crafting," and "DIY," many people are comfortable searching Pinterest's top-level categories for these topics. This is why niche-focused pinboards like "Ways to show your spouse you love them" or "250cc Scooters" or "Ohio Day Trips" can be a powerful way to catch the eyes of Pinterest users and convince them to add your well-curated content to their own feeds.

Finding a Pinboard as Part of a Board Search

The last way Pinterest users have to find your boards is by running a Pinterest search and narrowing the results to show only boards. These searches are a great way for users to help increase the specialty topics in their streams based on their personal interests or needs. These searches also give individual Pinterest users and companies the chance to get their pinboards in front of potential followers.

Unfortunately for companies looking to brand themselves and build their presence on Pinterest, the Pinterest search algorithm runs contrary to some of the best naming practices employed by brands on their profile pages. As of this writing, the Pinterest algorithm resembled early organic search engines. In other words, the more times a word shows up in the title, the more likely it is to rank for that keyword.

This means board searches tend to be flooded with boards that have the exact same title (see Figure 10.10).

Figure 10.10 Because Pinterest's search algorithm is still new, the pinboards that dominate the results tend to simply repeat keywords over and over in the title.

There can certainly be some strategy toward naming boards in a way that lands them at the top of search results, but there's clearly a need to balance search potential with properly naming your pinboards.

Wednesday: Organizing and Reorganizing Boards

Pinterest boards are a fairly fluid form of content. Seasonal boards may come and go; topical boards may capture your attention, then get deleted down the road; and areas of special interest may eventually need to be divided into completely new pinboards. For this reason, it's important to occasionally take a look at your Pinterest profile page through the eyes of a consumer and do a bit of shuffling.

That might mean moving pins around from board to board or changing the order in which pinboards appear on your profile. Either way, keeping things fresh and relevant means being open to making changes in the way your Pinterest content displays.

Moving and Removing Pins Over Time

Many Pinterest users spend their time collecting pins and repins without many repeated visits, but the most useful Pinterest boards are the ones that are fine-tuned and refined over time. This might mean relocating pins to more topically appropriate boards, duplicating them onto several boards, or even deleting them from existence completely.

Whatever your reason for moving or removing pins from your site, taking the time to review the pins in your pinboards and do a little tidying up can make a big difference in the value you offer your followers. Here are some key scenarios that typically warrant revisiting your pin.

When You've Launched a New Board

One of the primary reasons to relocate pins and repins is because you've created a new pinboard to more narrowly focus your content. In yesterday's section, we talked about the reasons to subdivide your boards. Once you've done this, you'll need to take the time to browse through existing boards so you can relocate any content better suited to the new pinboard (see Figure 10.11).

Each of these pins can be relocated to "Kid Friendly Recipes"

Figure 10.11 When you've broken existing pinboards down into more specific pinboards, you'll need to take the time to browse the original boards to locate pins that will need to be moved.

Unfortunately, as of this writing, there was no way to move pins in a batch. You'll need to search through your boards and click the Edit Pin button on each pin you wish to move, choosing the new pinboard name from the drop-down window and saving the pin to its new location (see Figure 10.12).

Edit Pin · Delete Pin

Description: Simple School Snack Solutions

Link: http://www.parents.com/recipes/cooking/kid-

Board: Recipes/Desserts ▼

Save Pin

Simple School Snack Solutions

Hopefully, Pinterest will eventually introduce editing options that will allow for the bulk transfer of multiple pins to new or existing pinboards.

When It's Worth Duplicating

Sometimes, a pin is worth listing on more than one pinboard. This can be especially true if you have created some specialized boards to target customer bases and there's some content from one of those boards that is also a great fit on a broader board.

Let's say you have a recipe site that features pinboards dedicated to specific meals of the day as well as breaking meals down by season and even by special dietary restrictions. You might find a recipe that fits in both a vegetarian and an entrée pinboard or that fits into entrée, summer dishes, and gluten-free pinboards (see Figure 10.13).

Figure 10.13 Adding a pin to multiple pinboards can help ensure exposure to the targeted audiences that have chosen to follow only some of your boards.

As you continue to fine-tune your boards over time and seek to create well-curated pinboards on specific topics, don't forget to ask yourself if there's room for your pins in more than one category. If the answer is yes, make sure you repin your own pins into the appropriate boards.

When Pins Do Not Hold Value

Because a great deal of pinning activity revolves around repinning pieces of content as a user browses through their Pinterest feeds, it's not uncommon for people to repin content without ever clicking through to the site it links to.

It's not uncommon to revisit those pins later only to realize the links are broken, the content is inaccurate, or the pin isn't what it was presented as. In such cases, deleting pins is essential. Otherwise, you are sharing irrelevant, or worse, spam-related content with future followers.

It's also possible that upon further reading or review of the content, you may decide to remove the pin. A fitness board focused on collecting 10-minute workout ideas might get cleaned out a few times a year to remove content that's too close in focus to other content. An interior designer may remove items from an inspiration board as she or the client decides they aren't a good fit for the project.

The reasons for deleting a pin are endless. The point to be made here is, whatever your reasons, pins that offer no value to your followers need to be deleted from your pinboards.

The Value of Reordering Board Displays

There are three primary reasons to shuffle the order of your pinboard displays on your Pinterest profile page: to promote seasonal content, to promote a contest, and to draw attention to or boost a specific board. Each has its benefits, but it's important to consider these changes in the overall context of your Pinterest marketing goals.

By default, new pinboards tend to show up toward the bottom of your profile page. Depending on your reasons for creating the new board, chances are high you'll need to shuffle your display order. (We talked about how to reorder your pinboards in Chapter 4, "Week 1—Setting Up a Pinterest Account.")

Not taking into account the relocation of brand-new pinboards once you've created them, let's explore several reasons why you might want to shift some pinboards to the top of your profile page.

To Promote Seasonal Content

The most obvious reason to shuffle your board display is to draw attention to seasonal content when it's most likely to drive conversions. Shifting Valentine's Day–themed gift lists or crafts to the top of your feed in early January makes perfect sense (as does placing Christmas- and New Year's Eve–related content toward the bottom of your profile as those seasons draw to a close).

Jewelry store Ice.com shifts seasonal boards like "Summer Style" and "Red Hot Rubies – July Birthstones" to the top of their profile for the month of July while allowing boards like "Mother's Day Gift Ideas" and "Valentine's Day Ideas" to settle to the bottom (see Figure 10.14).

Figure 10.14 Ice.com promotes seasonal content and drives sales by highlighting birthstone-related jewelry and jewelry-friendly holidays like Mother's Day and Valentine's Day.

Billboard Music features pinboards like "Coachella" and "BBMA 2012: Behind the Scenes" during the lead-up and wind-down from those events.

The ability to bump these boards when the time is right is exactly why it can be so valuable to find and build up content on seasonal pinboards when it's off season. Taking some time during the January retail slowdown to build and prepare a Father's Day gift guide that gets hidden away at the bottom of your profile and then bumped to the top and featured on your blog or Facebook Page in late May makes perfect sense.

To Promote a Contest

Another great reason to shuffle your boards is to move a pinboard focused on a current contest or promotion to the top of the list. Perhaps you are highlighting pinned content featuring your product and inviting likes as a form of voting for them, or you're show-casing content pinned by a "fan of the month." Either way, moving these pinboards front and center when they are in their prime can be an excellent way to draw attention to them when people are checking out your Pinterest presence.

To Draw Attention to or Boost Specific Boards

Another reason to consider shuffling your board order is to boost interest in an under-performing pinboard or to maximize the exposure of a surprise performer. Keeping in mind the various Pinterest analytics options we covered in Chapter 8, "Week 5—Track and Monitor Pinterest Traffic," it's important to consider testing varied layouts of your pinboards.

You may discover one of the boards at the base of your profile page is getting a strong number of followers in comparison to its location. This might be due to people running searches for boards, or it may mean people are scrolling down the page to follow that specific board. This is why it's a good idea to keep a tally on follower rates and repin rates for each of your boards (see Figure 10.15).

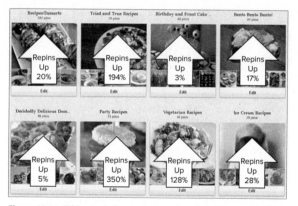

Figure 10.15 Taking stock of your current pinboards and the associated stats is a great way to understand which boards are underperforming and which are overperforming. This can help you decide whether to increase focus, delete a board, or shift its location to garner more activity.

Either way, it might be worth relocating it further up the page to see if it captures even more interest. You can always move it back down the page at a later point if you wish.

Thursday: Creating Boards with Multiple Curators

Back in Chapter 6, "Week 3—Find and Attract Followers," we talked about the idea of recruiting fans and evangelists to help curate your boards. Now that you have an understanding of how to go about creating these group pinboards, let's dig a little deeper into the marketing potential of this tactic.

The Value of Multiple Curators

The single biggest value to your brand or business on Pinterest when it comes to group curation is the potential increase in amount and diversity of content. No two people will find every single pin engaging, so why would you believe a single pinner adding content to your stream would capture the interest of every single follower you've gained?

Some runners are inspired by pushing themselves physically, some are inspired by the chance to get in shape, and some enjoy the Zen-like focus that can come with running. One person might have a hard time pinning content that appeals to each of those audiences. A group board made up of runners from a wide range of backgrounds might be appealing to all.

A variety of curators also helps provide more content without increasing the workload for you or your Pinterest team. We'll talk more about the various ways to leverage these new curators in Chapter 12, "Week 9—Using Pinterest to Engage with Fans."

Finding and Adding Curators

There are a few key ways to go about finding potential contributors to your Pinterest boards. The first is to recruit them from among your existing social media fan base. Opening up an invitation via your Facebook page, your Twitter account, your blog, your email newsletter, and your Pinterest account itself could attract plenty of applicants. From there, it's simply a matter of screening them to see who might be a great fit for your account.

The second is to spend some time researching on Pinterest. Think of the topics you'd like to find someone to pin content for, and then run searches for those topics on Pinterest. Consider narrowing your search to boards to find people who are already focused on curating the content you are seeking (see Figure 10.16).

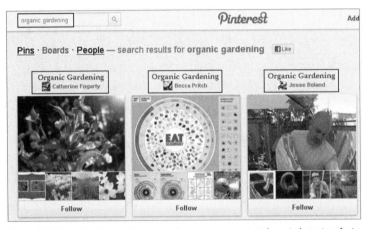

Figure 10.16 Searching for topical boards can be a great way to review the topical curation of existing Pinterest members while seeking people to approach about group curation.

Once you've researched the boards of these pinners and found a few you'd like to approach about contributing to your boards, ask yourself a few questions:

1. How many followers do they already have?   Group curation can be an excellent way for Pinterest users to gain more followers and exposure. However, that means Pinterest users who already have thousands or tens of thousands of followers may not need or be looking for the boost that could come from contributing to a group board.

2. How often do they pin content?   Understanding a Pinterest user's current habits can help you gauge how active they might be for your boards. That said, you can also use this knowledge to set the tone for them in your approach, outlining the need you may have for them to post more or less than they are now.

3. Are they already contributing to other boards?   The amount of commitment a Pinterest user has to other group boards may impact their openness to curating for your board. Too many group boards might mean they are spread too thin; no group boards may mean they're not open to the idea. Don't let this sway you from approaching them; simply take it into consideration.

4. What benefit will they gain from curating for you?   As with all social media–based pitches, this is the key question you need to be ready to answer when you approach a Pinterest user about joining your group board. What's in it for them? Can you offer exposure? Links? Compensation of some sort? Be prepared to explain how working with your company might benefit *them*.

Although the idea of finding and adding new pinners to your team can seem daunting, the truth is it's more work to vet them than it is to find them. After all, Pinterest is chock-full of people pinning content. You want to make sure they're pinning content that is a good fit for your followers.

This is why no matter how you find them, it's a very good idea to observe the pins they add to their own account for a while before you invite them to contribute to your own pinboards. This will give you a chance to offer some feedback on the types of pins you would like them to share and to point out the types of pins you would rather they not contribute to your pinboard.

Friday: Creating Short-Term Boards for Marketing Purposes

Sometimes the pinboards you create will have a life span. They may be to promote a specific event or news item, they might be inspired by a marketing campaign or contest you're running, or they may be seasonal in focus. Whatever the reason for these boards' creations, they hold the focus of your marketing team and your audience only for a limited time.

Seasonal Boards

The most obvious type of short-term board is the seasonal board. While these boards are most easily equated to the standard four seasons and their impact on everything from food choices to exercise choices to the best vacation destinations, there are plenty of other seasonal options.

Fashion sites tend to focus on seasonal boards to highlight the current fashion trends. Event companies might focus on popular wedding months, and florists and spas might feature special Mother's Day pinboards. Understanding the seasonal impact of your sales and marketing cycle can go a long way toward helping you develop new boards.

Ask yourself what marketing features you have coming up over the next several months, and then ask yourself what recurring features you have each year. If you sell lawn equipment, you'll likely want to consider boards for holidays like Father's Day. You'll also probably want to feature spring gardening and landscaping tips and perhaps another board for tackling fall lawn maintenance.

The great thing about seasonal boards is they can be revamped and reused each year with no need to delete them. These boards can be relocated to the bottom of your profile page while you quietly add content to them as you run across it (see Figure 10.17).

They can then be relocated to the top of the page and plugged via your other social media efforts as part of the lead-in to the season the following year.

Figure 10.17 During the off season, Home Depot relocates pinboards like "Valentine's Day" and "Mother's Day" to the bottom of their profile page.

Event-Driven Boards

Another popular reason to create a short-term or temporary board is to tie in with an event your brand is hosting or taking part in. Maybe you're sponsoring an event and you want to help promote both the event and your involvement in it by setting up a temporary board. Perhaps you are throwing the event and you want to use the new board as a gathering place for event coverage from other sites (see Figure 10.18).

Figure 10.18 *Better Homes and Gardens* magazine curated a "Chill and Grill 2012" pinboard featuring photos, recipes, and highlights from the BH&G-sponsored festival.

Consider using them not only to highlight your own event participation, but to piggyback off other popular events and trends. A fashion site could easily launch an "Affordable Oscar Knock-offs" pinboard to showcase lower-cost articles of clothing and accessories that duplicate popular red carpet looks. A fitness site could launch an "Olympic Dreams" pinboard to highlight inspirational quotes and stories from high school and college-age Olympic hopefuls.

Whatever your reasons for launching them, event-specific boards can not only gain traction in terms of building new followers, but also do an excellent job of showcasing your involvement with events and your target audience's community.

Campaign-Driven Boards

The final reason to create a board that might have a limited life span is for the sake of pushing a new marketing campaign, contest, or other feature. These are the boards that are created for cross-channel marketing with your other social media presences.

When Peugeot Panama launched their Pinterest jigsaw puzzle campaign, they were able to use it to cross promote their website, their Facebook Page, and their Pinterest account (see Figure 10.19).

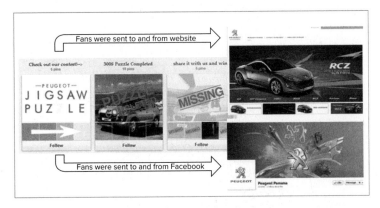

Figure 10.19 Peugeot Panama ran a Pinterest-based contest that required entrants to find and pin images from both their Facebook Page and the Peugeot Panama website.

The boards for this campaign were a great way to bridge the gap between multiple social media channels and to increase engagement with fans on each channel.

Of course, these types of boards can also have a limited life span. Unless it's a specialized board for a recurring event like an annual conference or a yearly special feature, it's a good idea to delete these boards after a few months of inactivity so they don't clutter up your profile page.

Take the time to consider each of the social media marketing initiatives you have coming up over the next six months to a year and ask yourself if there's a legitimate Pinterest tie-in. If so, consider adding a new board and highlighting it at the top of your profile and via your other social media channels.

Above all else, keep in mind that until Pinterest offers up brand accounts and official business pages, your company's profile is the closest thing you have to a "business page" on Pinterest. The pinboards you create, the structure you use to organize them, and the reasons you launch them will not only determine the success or failure of your Pinterest campaign, but could heavily impact your overall social media success as well.

Week 8–Using Pinterest to Attract Traffic

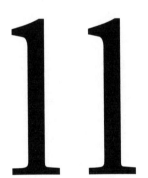

This week we'll be diving into some of the specific tactics brands and organizations are using to leverage Pinterest for traffic and brand building. After all, it's not just about creating the right content or attracting the most followers. It's also about the reasons you join the site and the types of content you aim to share while you're there.

To that end, it's time to start learning about the nuances of creating content for the Pinterest audience, walking the line between self-promotion and creating value and understanding the best ways to leverage the time and team you have.

Chapter Contents

Monday: Promoting Your Own Content
Tuesday: Creating Pinterest-Focused Content
Wednesday: Leverage Your Team
Thursday: Developing a Resource Board
Friday: Pinterest Best Practices

Monday: Promoting Your Own Content

As with all forms of social media, one of the most difficult balancing acts you'll face while building your Pinterest strategy is figuring out when, how, and why to pin your own content. Find a good balance and maintain it consistently, and you could find yourself on the winning end of a very positive Pinterest traffic boost.

When to Pin Your Own Content

The super simple answer to the question of when to pin your own content is this: Pin your own content when it benefits your audience. Unfortunately, the phrase "when it benefits" is a tad bit subjective. As with all of social media, companies oftentimes have difficulty being realistic about what they *want* people to care about versus what people actually *do* care about.

Unlike many social media channels, Pinterest actually encourages users to pin their own material to the site; they simply ask users to self-police their activity and to carefully consider what is best for the community. Of course, even with Pinterest's self-policing mentality, there's still a lot of room for interpretation.

Consider ApartmentTherapy.com's use of Pinterest. They have nearly 50,000 followers and they use the site to pin images from their blog posts and articles. Apartment Therapy pins *only* their own content. Their Pinterest profile basically serves as a Pinterest-powered feed of the ApartmentTherapy.com website (see Figure 11.1).

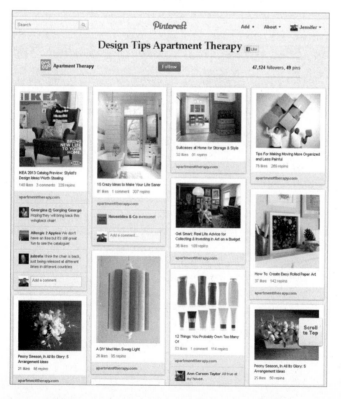

Figure 11.1 Apartment Therapy pins only content from their own site, dividing it up among pinboards designed to mimic the content areas of their website.

Though this strategy can work for brands, it does have some downfalls. First, it fails to embrace the attitude that makes social media work so well for brands: Everyone offering something of value gets to play. Second, it delivers no unique content. The only value in following the brand on Pinterest is in getting their content fed to your Pinterest feed and cherry-picking which content you visit from there rather than continuing to visit the website. (Unfortunately, this is how a very large portion of content-driven brands operate on Pinterest.)

Clean Eating magazine breaks from the trend and separates itself from the competition by sharing pins from third-party sites as well as its own. While it does curate boards like "Classics Made Clean" and "20 Minutes or Less" that feature recipes from the magazine's website, it also features boards like "CLEAN ME" that showcase recipes from around the Web (see Figure 11.2).

Figure 11.2 *Clean Eating* magazine finds balance between showcasing its own content and curating worthwhile content from other websites.

The key here is to understand the need for balance. Using Pinterest as a pure content feed from your website adds very little value to Pinterest users. That said, it also doesn't make sense to invest in a social media channel without also promoting your own content. That's why building a Pinterest strategy that balances at least a one-to-one (though ideally a one-to-three or one-to-four) ratio of your content to other people's content is crucial. The more value you add by curating solid content from other sites, the more leeway you will have to promote your own content as well.

Joining or Creating a Cooperative

The challenge of Pinterest is similar to the challenge on other social news and social bookmarking services. Attracting enough attention to get the ball rolling on your content can be difficult, especially in the early days when you're working to build a following.

This is where pinning cooperatives can come in handy. Just as multiple marketers will band together to help submit and promote each other's content on social news and social networking sites, marketers and site owners alike are building connections with other Pinterest users to help feed content into the stream (see Figure 11.3).

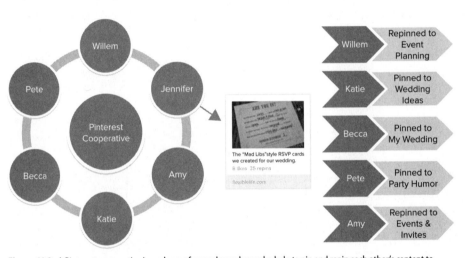

Figure 11.3 A Pinterest cooperative is made up of several members who help to pin and repin each other's content to provide additional exposure on Pinterest.

This can be especially handy if you've been able to do enough testing to understand what time of day or what day of the week you receive the highest level of repins. Having a second (or third, or even eighth) Pinterest user submit your content at peak hour can help get your pin back into the category stream as well as gain fresh exposure to whoever follows the person who pinned your content.

As of this writing, working together with other Pinterest users was not a violation of Pinterest's Terms of Service. That means banding together with other users in a "you scratch my back, I'll scratch yours" scenario can be a good way to drive visibility of your pins.

Tuesday: Creating Pinterest-Focused Content

While it's fine and dandy to tout the standard social media and search engine marketing tagline "content is king," anyone in the marketing world knows that creating awesome content is simply a stepping-stone. You have to lay the foundation to enable social sharing of that content, and occasionally, you've got to understand the nuances of presenting that content to a particular social media audience.

There are two primary approaches you need to consider when working to understand what types of pins perform best. You can approach it by topic or you can approach it by presentation style. In other words, you need to consider which *topics* receive the most attention as well as understand what *style* of content receives the most attention.

The Most Popular Topics on Pinterest

Back in Chapter 1, "Understanding Pinterest," we talked about the demographic make-up of Pinterest. We know that women from the heartland of the United States make up the strongest portion of Pinterest's demographics. Thanks to data compiled by companies like RJMetrics, we also know which topics they spend most of their time exploring on the site (see Figure 11.4).

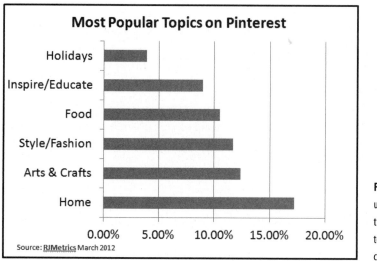

Figure 11.4 Pinterest's users invest most of their time on the site exploring topics related to homes, crafting, fashion, and food.

It's important to note that more than 60 percent of pinboards fall into the top 4 categories. That leaves 40 percent of the content spread out over the other 27 categories. Of course, the stronger interest in home, crafting, recipes, and fashion should come as no surprise given Pinterest's purpose and user base. Nonetheless, it's important to keep an eye on these figures as more and more men join the network and tilt the balance of interest.

It's also important to note that RJMetrics pegs food-related pins as the most viral in nature, with food pins accounting for almost double the number of repins as the next highest topic.

The Most Popular Types of Pins on Pinterest

Whereas the topic of a pin can weigh heavily on whether or not the pin gets popular, the type of pin can also go a long way toward determining its lifespan and traffic potential. Next to no studies have been released as of this writing that show what types of images perform best in terms of repins and traffic. Anecdotal data and good marketing sense pave the way for the testing of several techniques.

The Before-and-After Shot

Before-and-after shots always have been and probably always will be one of the most compelling market tactics around. People see a solid example of what something was versus what it has become, and they want to know how the transformation happened (see Figure 11.5).

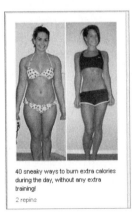

40 sneaky ways to burn extra calories during the day, without any extra training!

2 repins

Figure 11.5 A good before-and-after shot does an excellent job of showing the impact that can be made by the tips being offered.

Leverage this image type for your best transformation posts. Whether it's turning a discarded pile of pallets into a beautiful porch swing or showcasing a mom who dropped 45 pounds after her fourth baby in five years, let your picture spark wonder at the transformation that's taken place.

The Instructographic

One of the top reasons people go to Pinterest is to gather ideas and inspiration on how to do things in new and different ways. Images that show the step-by-step process for an idea and link through to the full tutorial tend to perform very well on the site (see Figure 11.6).

Figure 11.6 Showcasing the steps taken to complete a DIY task can help convince Pinterest users of their own ability to complete the task.

Leverage this by featuring only the photos, so there's a reason to click through to your site. Alternately, make sure you use a graphic size that is large enough (approximately 2,500–3,000 pixels high) that Pinterest will shrink it small enough it won't be readable. This will also require users to click through to your site for the full content.

The Infographic

It's no news that infographics perform extremely well on social networks. Link builders and content marketers have been using them with great success for years, and their popularity on Pinterest comes as no surprise (see Figure 11.7).

Figure 11.7 Showcasing facts, data, and information in a graphical format has been a popular content marketing strategy for years.

Leveraging infographics on Pinterest is about giving your audience useful information in a size and scope that is digestible to the Pinterest audience. Alternately, infographics can be chopped to display only part of the data with a call to action to visit the site for the full graphic. Keep in mind, however, that many Pinterest users will simply choose to pin the full infographic instead once they've seen it.

 Note: It's essential to remember that while each of these techniques can (and often does) perform extremely well, they can also quickly become overused and lose their impact. The greatest majority of pins from your website will likely come from individual users who choose to pin content as they run across it on your site.

The good news is that many of these pin types are images that can be created and incorporated into the content piece on your website. The stylized text overlay, the collected image collage, and the before-and-after shot are natural fits to serve as the primary image for your content piece. If you've integrated a Pin It button into your content, it should show up right next to the lead image, helping to encourage your visitors to push these supercharged images to Pinterest as well.

The Stylized Text Overlay

Sometimes the image you are working with doesn't do enough to communicate exactly what a user will find when they click through to your site. Overlaying a stylized text description can protect the integrity of your pin even if users begin rewriting the description as they pin or repin it (see Figure 11.8).

Figure 11.8 Adding stylized text to an image can help ensure that Pinterest users know exactly what it leads to.

Leverage this idea when the picture is not 100 percent self-explanatory. Otherwise, your 100-calorie double-chocolate fudge cake might get passed over by the person who sees only a picture and assumes it's as calorie laden as it looks.

The "How'd They Do That?" Shot

For DIY posts and ideas, a finished product shot showcasing something impressive, while still appearing to be "doable" by the average person, can make for a compelling pin (see Figure 11.9).

Figure 11.9 Crafting ideas and simple or ingenious "how-to" posts can attract clicks and repins from users who want to visit the full post to find out whether or not they can truly make what's pictured.

Leverage this idea by selecting your best image of the finished product and including a description that explains the selling point of the idea (low cost, upcyled, quick to make, etc.).

The Inspirational Quote/Image

Though they cannot always be counted on to deliver traffic to your site due to the fact that most of the value is contained within the image itself, inspirational quotes and pictures tend to do extremely well in terms of driving likes and repins (see Figure 11.10).

Figure 11.10 The key to marketing via inspirational quotes or images on Pinterest is to include a watermark of your brand or to integrate the URL of your website.

Leverage this idea by choosing a consistent image style and sticking to it over time. This will help make your quotes recognizable and can boost brand awareness as long as you've watermarked the images.

The Collected Ideas Collage

A popular way to draw traffic from Pinterest is to invest the time in creating a compilation post that shares a variety of takes on a single topic. Whether that's 120 recipes using Oreo cookies to celebrate Oreo's birthday or its 60 things you never knew you could do with a pocket knife, these posts allow your pin to serve as a resource (see Figure 11.11).

Figure 11.11 Compilation posts that feature a collage of images can be a great way to catch the eye of people who pin resources.

Leverage this idea when you've got a stronger ability to research than to create. The content required to support these pins is labor intensive but can rack up the pins as people bookmark the resource for later reference.

The pin types I've outlined here are primarily for when you've created extraordinary content that you want to purposely push on Pinterest for your brand or for a client. Take the time to test these approaches against standard images and photographs from your site to see which pins perform the best.

Wednesday: Leverage Your Team

As with most social media channels, creating and showcasing a personality for your brand either through a collective persona or by letting individual team members shine can be a powerful way to connect with the Pinterest audience.

That's why it's essential to take stock of the team you have on hand, determine how much time can be invested toward Pinterest, and consider how your team's interests can best play to your target audience.

Taking Stock of Team Interests

One of the first things to consider when putting together your Pinterest strategy is which members of your team have the time and ability to invest in Pinterest.

One benefit of Pinterest over many other social media platforms, however, is the limited time required to curate a strong presence. Because Pinterest is more about the content being shared than the conversation taking place about the content, there's often far less time required to build and maintain a quality presence than on more time-intensive channels like Twitter, Facebook, and YouTube.

This means that even smaller companies can sometimes afford to allow multiple team members to participate in building a Pinterest presence. Larger companies can decide whether to have one team member focus on building a strong presence or whether to have multiple members of the team collaborate.

No matter how many people you plan to have participate in your Pinterest strategy, it's a good idea to sit down and take stock of both time and interest. Examine how many minutes per day each team member can realistically expect to spend on Pinterest, keeping in mind that team members who are already spending time surfing the Web for ideas and inspiration may not need much additional time to pin key pieces of content as they run across it during their standard web usage (see Figure 11.12).

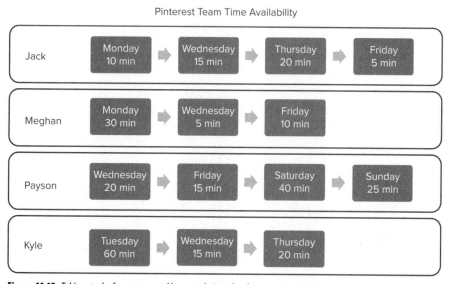

Pinterest Team Time Availability

Figure 11.12 Taking stock of your team and how much time they have to put toward curating pins will help in your planning process.

You'll also want to explore the topics and concepts each of your team members shares an interest level in. This will help you consider the topics that will be easiest for your team to cover. Let's consider a sports apparel brand that looks to appeal to runners. They'll need to figure out which topics their Pinterest staff is already interested in and committed to (see Figure 11.13).

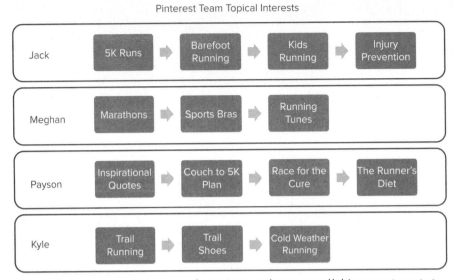

Figure 11.13 Considering the existing interests of your team can go a long way toward helping you create a content strategy.

This strategy provides a starting point for putting together a Pinterest content plan. Having an idea of where your Pinterest team's natural interests lie will also help you look for the natural extensions that will lead your team from what they know to what your customers are interested in. Reshaping each team member's topical focus to meet the needs and interests of your customer base allows you to maximize the time they spend on Pinterest (see Figure 11.14).

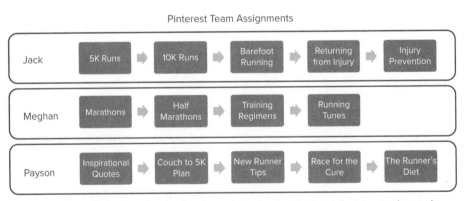

Figure 11.14 By creating curation assignments based on a combination of existing knowledge/interest and targeted topics, companies can leverage existing interests to build their Pinterest presence.

Focused vs. General Staff Involvement

Although many companies will choose to have individual staff members focus on specific topics as part of their joint Pinterest efforts, there are also some benefits to allowing your team to work as a collective. Because of the overlap in interests that often exists, it can make sense to have multiple team members contributing their perspective to the same topics.

Your goal is to appeal to a wide range of Pinterest users. After all, your Pinterest audience is not made up of a single person with a single take on a specific issue. Since it's unreasonable to expect any one Pinterest user to value each and every pin your team posts to the site, it might also be unreasonable to expect any one pinner to be able to meet the needs and interests of your entire target audience.

The only way to know for certain which method will work best for your company is to analyze the activity around your Pinterest stream and make adjustments accordingly. If pins made by specific team members to specific topics are severely underperforming, it may not be worth their time to continue searching for and pinning content to that category.

One Account or Multiple Accounts?

The decision of how many people to have contributing to your accounts and what their topical focus needs to be are just two of the things you need to consider when you build your Pinterest strategy. You'll also need to decide whether you want to have everyone contribute via a single corporate login or via their own accounts using group pinboards.

In Chapter 10, "Week 7—Leveraging Boards for Better Reach," we discussed the idea of having multiple curators serving as individual contributors to one collective board. Not only do companies need to decide whether or not to use this tactic as a way to recruit third-party contributors, they also need to decide whether it's an appropriate fit for their internal contributors.

Cases for One Account

In most instances of social media, having a collective brand-based presence that is responsible for all levels of engagement on social media is the standard choice. It allows for a cohesive presence that is easily identifiable and that can both build on and borrow from the strength of the brand.

A single account also makes it easy for fans to find and connect with the business or brand on Pinterest. There's no need to search out the various contributors and spend time looking through their pinboards to determine whether they represent the parts of the brand you're most interested in.

A single account also simplifies metrics and measurement, making it easy to track the long-term activity and results of the company's Pinterest efforts.

The downside of running a single account is the inability to allow individuals to represent the various focuses and interests of your target audience. For a brand like Nike that appeals to runners, fitness enthusiasts, basketball players, and so on, a single account can be forced to focus on multiple topics. Allowing individuals from within the company to each focus on their own areas of expertise can result in more focused pinboards that better appeal to specific target audiences.

Cases for Multiple Accounts

In many cases, a diversified approach serves a company more effectively than having a single account. Multiple accounts contributing to branded boards can equal greater overall exposure as individual users attract followers who are then driven to the brand's collective boards (see Figure 11.15).

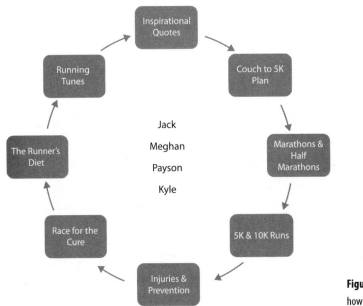

Figure 11.15 Test some ideas on how this collective flow works.

The downside of the multiple-account strategy is the potential loss of exposure when Pinterest users follow an individual contributor instead of the brand or the brand's specific pinboards. This can fracture the brand's collective Pinterest activity and weaken its ability to draw both followers and repin activity.

This is why it's important to understand how Pinterest users are already engaging with your brand and your competitors' brands on Pinterest. If your company is well branded and is able to attract followers via name recognition and by promoting your Pinterest activity via other social media channels, chances are high you'll be best served by having all of your activity take place under the banner of the corporate Pinterest account.

If your company is not well known and has had difficulty gaining followers, you may be better served by a collective approach. Setting up group pinboards under your brand allows you to set up a Pinterest strategy that continues to boost your brand by associating the boards with it, but also builds up interest and followers by letting your team divide and conquer with their individual accounts as well.

The Unique Situation of Pinterest

In the early days of Pinterest, there was no questioning the value of keeping all activity housed under a single branded account. It made a brand easy to find and kept the focus on the brand, rather than on individual team members.

That all changed when Pinterest began limiting the number of pins from any individual Pinterest account that could be featured on the category pages each day. Additional Pinterest accounts equal additional opportunities for category page exposure. In a world where a single pin can generate hundreds of thousands of visits to a website, the additional opportunities for exposure can be hard to overlook.

For that reason alone, it's difficult to ignore the benefits of a multicontributor approach. Each and every account presents additional opportunities for content to be included in the category stream, dramatically upping the chances a piece of content will be liked, repinned, or visited. As long as team members are set up as contributors to pinboards under the primary brand's account, a multiuser approach can be highly effective.

When Your Team Consists of a Single Person

At this point, those of you who work for extremely small businesses or who are solopreneurs are wondering how in the world you can compete against the large companies that can afford to task multiple people with contributing toward their company's Pinterest efforts.

The bad news is that in many ways, you will operate at a disadvantage over companies with larger staffs. The good news is you're probably already used to that, which means you're also used to coming up with creative ways to compete anyway.

Whether your Pinterest team consists of 24 dedicated individuals or a single multitasking person, building a great Pinterest strategy is about taking the time to understand what your target audience is looking for and then finding a way to deliver that content within the limitations of your company. There are dozens of individual Pinterest users who have amassed millions of followers all on their own. There's absolutely no reason why you as an individual pinner cannot also be successful.

The biggest disadvantages you will face are time, familiarity with a subject, and the singularity of your account. Though time limitations and limited knowledge of a specific subject might require a little extra work to get past, even an individual user can open and manage multiple accounts. Associating additional Pinterest accounts with a wide range of Twitter accounts can open the door to a nearly endless number of Pinterest account opportunities.

That said, it's important to understand that as of this writing, the Pinterest API had not yet been released and no third-party tools were available for the management of multiple Pinterest accounts. This means moving forward with a multiple-account strategy as an individual will require continue logging in and out of Pinterest and a dedication to detailed tracking to determine whether a multiple-account strategy is worthwhile.

Thursday: Developing a Resource Board

Many e-commerce brands and content brands work to leverage Pinterest as a way to drive traffic and boost sales, but there's another compelling reason to build a Pinterest profile that holds special interest to nonprofits, educational organizations, and even some brands and content networks: to act as a resource.

Creating this type of Pinterest presence takes a slightly different mind-set than working to directly market your products and services. It requires a strong understanding of your target audience and careful consideration of what you want to teach them or how you want to inspire them.

Pinning Content That Educates Your Audience

For many brands, Pinterest presents an opportunity to build credibility by helping to educate a target audience on topics that matter to them. We might see this in a brand like Patagonia supporting a program like Common Threads to help encourage the repair, recycling, and reselling of clothing. A medical facility like Nationwide Children's Hospital in Columbus, Ohio might focus on educating parents about how best to talk to their children about tough topics (see Figure 11.16).

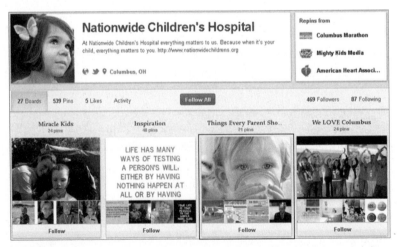

Figure 11.16 Nationwide Children's Hospital curates several educational boards on Pinterest, including one aimed at helping parents talk to their children about tough issues.

With this strategy, the goal is to leverage what you know about Pinterest (it's a place people go for ideas and inspiration) with what you know about your target audience (parents who are concerned about their children's health and well-being) and to combine those pieces of knowledge to create a new board. For Nationwide Children's Hospital, this meant a board full of well-curated tips, ideas, and approaches for talking to your kids about everything from drug abuse to bullying to the nightly news (see Figure 11.17).

Figure 11.17 Nationwide Children's Hospital's pinboard for parents links to tips, resources, and articles on a wide range of online parenting sites

The key here is to understand what your customer base cares about and to identify which of those topics are a natural fit for your company. From there, it's simply a matter of investing the time in finding good-quality resources on that topic and offering them to your audience.

Pinning Content That Inspires Your Audience

Sometimes it's not just about education. Sometimes it's about motivation and inspiration. Maybe you're a financial investment advisor and you want to inspire your customers to dream of beautiful retirement homes and extended tours of Europe. Maybe you sell running shoes and athletic gear and you want to help motivate your customers to get up off the couch and get moving.

In these instances, it's more about sharing quotes, pictures, and stories than it is about sharing information. Consider lululemon athletica's pinboards. They have a wide range of boards sharing information and education about yoga, running, and their various product lines. They also curate several pinboards aimed at motivating customers in their wellness efforts and inspiring them to keep their bodies moving (see Figure 11.18).

Figure 11.18 Fitnessware company lululemon athletica curates boards like "yoga | inspiration" and "run | motivation" that are filled with pinned quotes, inspirational images, and reasons to keep moving.

It's important to remember that this style of pinboard is all about evoking emotion. That might mean making people smile, helping them feel determined, or even getting them fired up and angry over a shared cause. Emotional reaction is one of the strongest drivers of social sharing. Learn how to leverage it to your advantage to push your content toward more pins and repins.

Pinning Content That Supports Your Brand

For some brands, it's not so much about evoking emotion or educating the mind. It's about building an association between your brand and some concept or idea you want to have associated with your brand. If you run a pet store, you want people to think of cute and adorable animals. If you own a secondhand clothing store, you want people to think of vintage couture and creative accessorizing.

Ask yourself what defines your brand. (If you don't know, it's time to put this book down and invest some time connecting with your customer base and analyzing how they view your company or organization.) The next question to ask yourself is how you would *like* to define your brand. Your efforts on Pinterest, and the way you carry those efforts over into other social media channels, can help you steer things in that direction.

Moving and storage company PODS curates boards focused on small spaces, home organization, and room layouts. Southwest Airlines curates a board that features plane crafts and aviation-themed decoration ideas.

In some cases, the connection is even more obvious. Kitchenware company Williams-Sonoma curates more than a dozen recipe-related boards (see Figure 11.19).

Figure 11.19 The Williams-Sonoma Pinterest account is full of pinboards featuring beautiful, healthy, and unique recipes and entertaining ideas—a perfect match for the Williams-Sonoma brand.

While the pins included on these boards do not directly feature Williams-Sonoma products, they are directly tied to how customers use Williams-Sonoma products. This strategy continues to build a positive association between the brand and the consumer and allows Williams-Sonoma to leverage Pinterest to attract the attention of foodies on Pinterest.

Pinning Content That Displays Your Brand in Use

The most obvious and also the most perilous way to leverage Pinterest is to directly feature your products on your pinboards. Of course, as with all things marketing related, there's a right way and a wrong way to do this.

First things first. Pinterest is not an online catalog. It is not a place to go, create pinboards for each of your product categories, and then begin filling them up with pinned images from your e-commerce site. Not only does using Pinterest in this manner violate the Pinterest terms of service, it also makes you an irresponsible social media user. (In other words, Pinterest + posting all your products = nobody likes you.)

What *does* work extremely well on Pinterest is building brand support by showcasing your products being used in interesting and creative ways. Fashion brands do an incredible job of highlighting their offerings in this manner, as do many home retailers. That's because those industries have a long-established history of integrating their products into fashion shoots for magazines and television shows. Pinterest simply gives them a new place to showcase their staged images.

That's why it can be interesting to look at how brands like Volkswagen and Chobani use Pinterest. I've mentioned Chobani in previous chapters when discussing their use of Pinterest as a place to collect and showcase recipes created by their fans that include Chobani yogurts. This is a great way to showcase your product's potential while playing to the existing interests of Pinterest users.

Volkswagen takes a similar approach in several boards that highlight the love affair people have had with their VWs for decades (see Figure 11.20).

Figure 11.20 With boards like "Peace Love Volkswagen" and "Decorated Volkswagens," the Volkswagen brand has done an excellent job of using Pinterest to showcase devoted fans while boosting the iconic appeal of their vehicles.

The key to this approach is remembering to add value. There's nothing wrong with pinning content that features your product or services. There's nothing wrong with uploading your own tailor-made Pinterest content that features your product or services. Just make certain the focus on the post provides value beyond "hey, isn't our product supercool?"

Friday: Pinterest Best Practices

Pinterest is still a fairly new social media channel, but millions of users have been testing the water and establishing best practice in the two years since it first launched. Many of these best practice techniques arose because they have stood the test of time and consistently deliver strong results. Others exist simply because no one has taken the time to challenge the norm and discover a better way of doing things.

Use these best practices as a starting point for your strategies so you can establish a baseline of measurement for your Pinterest campaigns. But don't be afraid to deviate from them and to measure the positive or negative impact any changes have on the activity of your pins and pinboards.

Individual Pin Best Practices

Most of the things you'll want to do on Pinterest fall into the broader category of marketing best practices. Still, it's a good idea to take the time to familiarize yourself with what we already know works well on Pinterest.

Write engaging, keyword-rich descriptions for pins. Though it's the images that most often catch Pinterest users' attention, the description associated with them can play a powerful role in driving both click-throughs and repins.

Tag other Pinterest users when appropriate. Like Twitter, Pinterest allows users to @username other Pinterest users in pin descriptions. This can be a great way to draw the attention of another user or associate a pin with a specific account.

Always credit the proper source of an image. Never use someone else's image to link to your own content. Whenever possible, click through to ensure a pin or repinned content belongs to the site being linked to.

Focus on how products are used. Pin content supportive of your brand by showcasing how your customer base uses or adapts it.

Select or create high-quality images. When pinning content from a third-party site, select the highest-quality graphic that best represents the concept being pinned. When creating your own content, use the best-quality images possible.

Use proper sizing for instructographics and infographics. Make these images too large and Pinterest users will be able to digest their content in full without ever leaving Pinterest. Size them at about 2000–2500 pixels in height and Pinterest will shrink them enough to be tempting but unreadable without clicking through to the host site.

Watermark the images you own. Depending on the content you create and the market you are targeting, consider adding a small watermark or URL to your images. Doing so can ensure you retain credit for the photo, even if it gets reposted on other sites.

Add descriptive text to images you own. Though many images speak for themselves, overlaying an appropriate text description on an image can help ensure a proper title stays with the image, even if users change the assigned description when they repin your content.

Put more effort into pinning than repinning. Pinning takes more time and effort, but it also offers more value to the Pinterest community. Avoid the temptation to be lazy and repin other people's content. Try to add at least one fresh pin for every repin you make.

Pinboard Best Practices

Great pinboard curation is similar to great content curation. Take the time to focus on the end user and make certain you are providing valuable content in an easy-to-digest format.

Balance conversion with search when titling pinboards. Incorporate keywords, but focus on driving followers with descriptive pinboard titles.

Reorder pinboards based on current trends and seasonal content. Don't be afraid to reevaluate the order of your pinboard display on at least a monthly basis. Relocate past promotions and out-of-season content further down the page.

Leverage group pinboards when appropriate. Give consideration to hosting a group pinboard, keeping in mind the power of leveraging brand evangelists or hosting guest pinners.

Customize the showcase image for each pinboard. Pinterest allows you to assign a specific pinned image to a board's profile listing. Take advantage of this feature and select a gorgeous image that showcases the content of the board.

Don't be afraid to add or delete boards over time. Sometimes boards are seasonal, sometimes they're event based, and sometimes they are evergreen. No matter why they were created, you will always find boards that don't hold interest and underperform. Do not be afraid to remove these boards to free up time to pin to other boards.

Pinterest Marketing Best Practices

It should come as no surprise that marketing on Pinterest is similar to marketing on other forms of social media. It's essential to integrate it with your other channels and to set up plans to measure your efforts accordingly.

Balance pinning your own content with third-party content. Keep in mind that in social media, it's not all about you. Maintain a proper balance of pinning three to four times more content from other sites than from your own.

Support your brand with lifestyle pinboards. Consider the topics, ideas, and emotions associated with your brand. Create pinboards and curate content that is supportive of these concepts.

Build community with pinboards that highlight fans. Encourage fans to pin content related to your brand and to tag you in it by highlighting creative ideas and product usage within your own pinboards.

Promote your Pinterest activity across social media channels. Don't let your Pinterest account exist in a bubble. Drive traffic to your boards and boost contests and promotions by leveraging existing fans on other social media channels.

Create and measure Pinterest metrics. Never forget that Pinterest is a marketing channel. Understand your goals, have a plan in place to track progress, and continually adapt your strategy to deliver the best results.

Week 9–Using Pinterest to Engage with Fans

One of the single most powerful forces propelling Pinterest's phenomenal growth is the impressive ability of images to strike at the passion points of people's heartstrings. Millions of users have flocked to Pinterest because it opens the door to creativity and reminds them of the things they love in life. Pinterest is about enabling consumers to improve their lives.

For brands that recognize this power, Pinterest unlocks the door into the heart and soul of the consumer. It gives brands the chance to connect with consumers by sharing their passions with them. That's why an essential part of any Pinterest-based social media strategy is an understanding of how to leverage those passion points to better engage with customers and fans.

Chapter Contents

Monday: Play to the Interests of Your Audience

In many ways, Pinterest offers the chance to continue a trend we've seen executed effectively by companies on their blogs. For years, social media advisers have told companies to look beyond their own products and services and to write about topics their target audience might find interesting.

Food manufacturers were told to blog recipes, outdoor sporting goods stores were told to blog camping tips and features on the best fishing sites, and used car dealers were told to offer advice for teaching your teenager to drive or keeping toddlers entertained on road trips. This "related content" helped boost the credibility of the brand by allowing it to offer useful information and content that easily tied back to the products or services they sold. It also paved the way for better search engine optimization by increasing the amount of keyword-rich content and links associated with the site.

The same concept applies to Pinterest. It becomes the perfect place to reach out to your target audience by drawing them in with content that both appeals to them and supports your brand. It also becomes a great way to increase exposure and attract links and traffic back into the content you are creating on your own site.

Look for Natural Brand Tie-ins

One of the first things companies need to do when mapping out their Pinterest strategy is to spend some time brainstorming the topics and concepts connected with their brand. If your brand is already actively blogging, chances are high you've already done this and will have a good idea of what types of boards to create. If your brand is not blogging, it's a good idea to sit down and spend a little time brainstorming topics (see Figure 12.1).

Figure 12.1 A jewelry store might ask itself what occasions prompt jewelry purchases in an attempt to generate some ideas on possible Pinterest board topics.

Online jewelry e-tailer Gemvara.com does an excellent job of tackling Pinterest using this approach. Gemvara was already successfully keeping customers engaged with a blog that tackles celebrity fashion trends, gemstone education, creative wedding ideas, and more. They carry this strategy over to Pinterest flawlessly on many fronts, including curated boards that don't directly promote their products but that tie in to their brand through natural topical connections (see Figure 12.2).

Figure 12.2 With Pinterest boards like "Fit The Dress" Recipes and The Offbeat Bride, Gemvara.com does an excellent job of keeping its more than 2,000 Pinterest followers happy.

The key here is to make sure you are using these boards to reinforce your brand. Since Gemvara is known for offering unique collections of original and cutting-edge jewelry, their "The Offbeat Bride" board does a great job of showcasing the unique styles, trends, and ideas that appeal to its target audience.

Another brand that plays to this concept extremely well is Middle Sister Wines. Known for naming their wines with spunky names like Mischief Maker (Cabernet Sauvignon), Drama Queen (Pinot Grigio) and Sweet & Sassy (Moscato), Middle Sister has built their Pinterest strategy around reinforcing the attitude and imagery evoked by the names of their wines (see Figure 12.3).

Figure 12.3 Middle Sister Wines curates boards that share the name (and attitude) of their 12 types of wine.

Ask yourself whether topics and trends are a strong fit to reinforce your brand and consider launching new Pinterest boards on those topics.

Offer Activity-Inspired Discounts

In the world of social media, social sharing is one of the single biggest drivers of increased brand exposure and traffic. Pinterest, like other social media channels, offers another place for brands to motivate sharing activity in unique and creative ways.

Although many companies choose to test these waters using contests (a concept we'll explore more fully in Chapter 13, "Week 10—Pinterest Marketing Through Contests"), others test conversion and sales potential by finding creative ways to motivate pin activity.

One company doing this well is Gilt Group, a membership-based site that offers limited quantity "flash" deals on luxury brands in the clothing, jewelry, and accessory departments. Their Gilt Baby & Kids division focuses on selling these high-end items for pint-size consumers and their Pinterest boards reflect this focus.

In 2012, Gilt Baby & Kids tested a Pinterest activity-focused product campaign that required Pinterest users to repin a specific item from the Gilt collection in order to "unlock" a special sales price (see Figure 12.4).

Figure 12.4 Gilt Baby & Kids required 50 users to repin their product listing before "unlocking" a special price on this Halabaloo Flower Dress.

The listing quickly racked up 62 pins at which point the Gilt team opened up purchases on a limited quantity of the dress. Taking the social activity concept a step further, they also made sure to engage buyers in the comment window of the pin to invite them to post pictures of their tiny tots in the dress on the company's Facebook page (see Figure 12.5).

Jeannie Swanson Yay, I got one!!! Thank for the great deal! Too bad it's a handwash dress:(

Gilt Baby & Kids @Jeannie Swanson Oh happy day, congrats! Please share a picture of your little one in her party dress when your package arrives: http://www.facebook.com /Gil... We'd love to see her all dressed up!

Figure 12.5 Gilt Baby & Kids takes Pinterest activity marketing a step further by reminding happy customers to share images of their purchases on the company's Facebook page.

Measure Response to Test Boards

It's generally a great idea to look for topical and trend-based concepts to curate pins around, but it's also important to realize that not every related topic will play well on Pinterest. This is why it's essential to create a plan and then test it before going all out in your efforts.

Putting together a new board and carefully tracking both the followers and the amount of repin activity around it can be a smart way to know if it's worth building a long-term strategy around the concept.

Let's return to our Gemvara.com example and look at some of the non-jewelry-related boards they've launched on Pinterest. Checking each of these boards for things like the number of followers and the number of repins is a good starting point to gauge interest levels in a topic (see Figure 12.6).

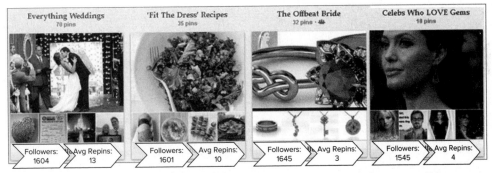

Figure 12.6 By looking at the activity surrounding brand-related topical pinboards, it becomes fairly easy to see which ones attract the most attention. In this case, Gemvara's "Everything Weddings" board far outperforms its "Celebs Who Love Gems" board.

While these basic numbers can go a long way toward helping you decide what types of content you may want to focus your Pinterest efforts on, they are only part of the equation. Keep in mind your overall Pinterest strategy also needs to focus on the amount and quality of traffic being fed to your website, a concept we covered more thoroughly back in Chapter 8, "Week 5—Track and Monitor Pinterest Traffic."

Tuesday: Featuring Content That Highlights Your Brand

At its heart, Pinterest is about inspiration and ideas. It's about allowing users to collect images of concepts and items that inspire them. It's about finding new and creative ways to enjoy the life they're living. Playing to this emotional touch point by offering inspirational content and suggestions for making their lives more enjoyable can be a great way to help keep your audience motivated, which in turn can help remind them to continue using your brand to help them reach their goals.

The 2012 Social and Mobile Commerce Study conducted by Shop.org, comScore, and The Partnering Group found that online U.S. consumers already follow an average of 9.3 retail companies on Pinterest. This is higher than the numbers on Facebook (6.9) and Twitter (8.5) despite the fact that those channels have existed longer.

In addition, the study dispels the fear that consumers follow brands *only* to gain access to discounts and coupons. In fact, nearly one-third of consumers claim they follow brands in order to gain access to current trends and how-to guides, and to interact with the brand about its products or services (see Figure 12.7).

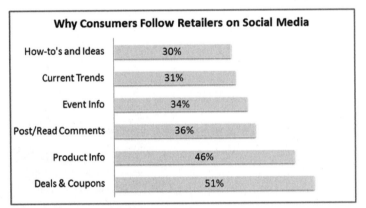

Source: 2012 Social and Mobile Commerce Study

Figure 12.7 The 2012 Social and Mobile Commerce Study shares valuable insight into the many reasons consumers choose to follow retailers on social media sites.

Pinterest provides retailers and brands alike with the perfect place to engage customers on each of these levels. That's why it's essential that brands consider how they might best engage Pinterest users in ways that highlight the value of their products and services.

Inspirational Content and Quotes

When we look at using Pinterest to spark inspiration, it's easy enough to think of the obvious tie-ins. There's Kodak offering heartwarming family photo ideas or Matador

Network pinning images from a traveler's bucket list. These are the ways brands keep consumers coming back for more: by visually reminding them of their passion points and by being the brand that continually draws them back in with reminders of what *can* be.

Using inspirational content on Pinterest is about tugging at the heartstrings of Pinterest users and getting them to connect an emotion to your brand. It's about cementing yourself in their minds as the brand that understands what matters to them and propelling your products forward as the solution to those wants and desires.

Companies like Diapers.com pull this off brilliantly by collecting (and sometimes creating) images for their "Mom Truths" board (see Figure 12.8).

Figure 12.8 Diapers.com curates a board targeted at moms that features cute quotes about the daily joys and struggles of parenting.

These types of boards play to the thoughts and emotions you know your target audience can relate to. This makes them highly effective in terms of attracting followers and generating repins. Create and pin a few of your own images to the mix like Diapers.com does and you can also reap the benefit of driving traffic and links back to your blog.

Educational Content and How-tos

With the 2012 Social and Mobile Commerce Study showing that 30 percent of consumers follow brands on social media specifically to gain access to how-to content and ideas, it can be highly effective to use Pinterest as an educational opportunity for your followers.

Consider the products or services you offer and how your customers might use them, and then create or curate content around those ideas. A nail polish company might feature creative nail design tutorials. A customer auto-parts retailer might show how to install nerf bars on a truck. A fashion accessory retailer might showcase the year's trendiest ways to wear a scarf. The possibilities are limited only by your imagination.

In the case of the American Heart Association, the focus is on educating consumers about how to reduce their risk of heart attack and stroke. This leads to natural tie-ins like heart-healthy recipes and fitness ideas, but it also opens the door for content aimed at helping consumers understand how the heart and brain work as well as identifying risk factors for heart disease and stroke (see Figure 12.9).

Figure 12.9 The American Heart Association shares infographics and links aimed at helping increase awareness of the risk factors for heart disease and stroke.

Sometimes what consumers are looking for in their education is a step-by-step guide showing how to build or fix something. That's the type of content home improvement giant Lowe's offers on their "Build it!" pinboard (see Figure 12.10).

Figure 12.10 Lowe's curates a variety of boards aimed at homeowners including a "Build it!" pinboard that attracts hundreds of repins per image.

Keep in mind that while images of finished products that link through to full tutorials and step-by-step image collages that help get people started on simple tasks can be a powerful way to gain repins and traffic from Pinterest, it's important not to overlook video content in this area as well. For brands that invest heavily in YouTube content, Pinterest can be an excellent channel to showcase your content while providing a nice change from the standard image-based pins.

Your Products in Action

For many companies, Pinterest provides the ideal location to showcase their products in action. Though this might require a brand to create content to pin, it might also simply mean searching for content that already exists online. For creative brands that proactively leverage social media, this might also mean feeding products into the hands of bloggers to spark the creation of Pinterest-friendly content like Chobani did in our example back in Chapter 9, "Week 6—Developing a Successful Pinterest Strategy."

Sometimes these tie-ins are perfectly suited to a brand because consumers have already taken to Pinterest to showcase their use of an item. A perfect example of this is OPI Nail products. Fashion trends were an early favorite of Pinterest users and continue to make up a large portion of activity on the site. Brands like OPI Nails simply need to take the time to find content featuring their products (see Figure 12.11), which they can then easily repin to their own topical boards.

Figure 12.11 Pinterest (and the Web in general) is simply full of fan-created product shots showcasing OPI Nail products in action.

Other companies use Pinterest to showcase specific products in an effort to drive increased conversions and sales. For beauty and lifestyle retailer Birchbox, that means curating a board of customer-uploaded images of their popular sampler box service.

Birchbox offers a limited number of $10-a-month subscriptions to customers, who then receive a customized box of samples each month. The boxes are a mystery until they arrive, and customers take great pride in taking and uploading photos of what their boxes contain each month. By finding and pinning these images, Birchbox is able to drive conversation around the contents of the box (see Figure 12.12).

Figure 12.12 Birchbox has attracted nearly 22,000 followers to its "Your Birchboxes" board. Unlike most branded boards, the pins here tend to generate plenty of comments as well as repins, making it an excellent tool for promoting their sample box subscription program.

Since customers must join a waiting list to gain eventual access to the sample service, Birchbox's pinned images of the shipped sample boxes and the comments associated with them serve as a great marketing tool to drive sign-ups for the service.

Wednesday: Promoting Other Sites' Content

Much like blogging or tweeting, a strong Pinterest presence requires a great deal of sharing content that is neither owned by you nor directly associate with your brand. The standard social media split of promoting 80 percent third-party content and 20 percent of your own content works quite nicely with Pinterest.

That's why it's important to spend time using Pinterest and not just publishing to it. Finding good Pinterest accounts to follow and regularly running searches for new pinboards and new Pinterest users to follow will help you stay on top of current Pinterest trends as well as help keep the quality of your content fresh.

The Value of Promoting Third-Party Content

It's extremely important to remember that Pinterest is not just another content feed for you to publish your blog posts, videos, and photos to. Though many companies do restrict their Pinterest activity to pinning content featured on their own sites, this goes against the way consumers use Pinterest and runs the risk of making your brand look "stingy" in the eyes of pinners.

After all, it's simply not realistic for any one brand or website to feature every single take on a particular topic. Sure, your party supply store may excel at generating creative ideas for kids' birthday parties, but there is no way you've put together your own content for every single idea on this topic. That's why pinning and repinning content from other sites can help you add to your own content to create a well-curated selection of ideas and inspiration for your audience.

Much like linking to other blogger's posts or retweeting links to great articles and videos, pinning and repinning content from other sites helps build your credibility as a resource among your customers.

Pin the Content of Evangelists

For many brands, repinning third-party content still does an excellent and effective job of promoting their own products. So far in this chapter, we've already looked at how brands like OPI Nails and Birchbox leverage fan content to fill pinboards.

For other brands, it's less about showcasing a product in use and more about promoting the overall tenets of the product or service. Popular weight loss program Weight Watchers hadn't yet joined Pinterest as of the time of publication for this book. However, a brand like Weight Watchers would have an easy time finding and pinning content that already integrates their popular points system into blogger-created recipes.

For example, the blog SkinnyTaste.com serves up several recipes a week to more than one hundred thousand loyal followers who pin and repin the recipes like crazy (see Figure 12.13).

Egg Tomato and Scallion Sandwich
Skinnytaste.com
Servings: 1 **Serving Size:** 1 sandwich • **Old Points:** 4 pts • **Points+:** 6 pts
Calories: 213 • **Fat:** 9.5 g • **Protein:** 13.5 g • **Carb:** 21 g • **Fiber:** 5.5 g • **Sugar:** 5 g
Sodium: 363 mg (without salt)

Figure 12.13 Popular food blogger Gina Homolka serves up Weight Watcher's friendly recipe adaptations at SkinnyTaste.com. Her recipes are among the most popular food-related pins to be found on Pinterest.

Since each of the recipes on the website feature Weight Watchers' Point calculations, this third-party content is ready made to be featured on a future Weight Watchers' account on Pinterest.

In some cases, pinning the content of evangelists means a direct promotion of your brand; in others, it simply means raising the overall profile of a topic related to your business. Consider the outdoor adventure retailer who repins content from a popular extreme geocaching blog, or the educational retailer who repins content from popular teacher and homeschool blogs.

Finding the evangelists within your industry and sharing their content with your readers is a great way to build relationships and keep your followers happy.

Promote Other Pinners and Bloggers

Social media is all about allowing a wide range of people to share their unique voices and ideas in an environment where anyone and everyone can gain access to them, a concept that plays out extremely well on Pinterest. A big part of social media is also pointing people toward the best resource or additional resources on a topic, even if that means sending them off to another blogger, Twitter user, or Facebook Page.

One way that several companies live out this concept on Pinterest is to feature curated boards of topical bloggers or even other Pinterest users. Similar to the "Follow Friday" collective campaigns on Twitter, these boards allow you to share the love (and traffic) with valuable Pinterest contributors while gaining additional credibility with your own followers for pointing them in the right direction.

Plaid Crafts, the makers of popular crafting glue Mod Podge, curates a pinboard titled "Craft Blogs We Like" (see Figure 12.14).

Figure 12.14 Plaid Crafts' curated board of their favorite craft bloggers does a great job of not only spreading the link and traffic love, but of helping their followers connect with bloggers who offer content the followers will enjoy.

Although it's not remotely uncommon to see individual pinners or even brands pinning links to their favorite bloggers, there's still a lot of space for companies to make a name for themselves by curating boards of great pinners. Pinterest users are always looking for fresh sources of new ideas, and getting a recommendation from a friend (or brand) who has taken the time to review the overall quality of a pinner's pins adds significant value to their Pinterest experience (see Figure 12.15).

Figure 12:15 Since most of my followers are interested in finding new healthy recipe ideas, I've built a pinboard where I can link to other food pinners.

Pinterest doesn't allow you to pin content from the Pinterest website itself. This means you'll have to do a bit of creative workarounds to set up a pinboard featuring other pinners. The easiest way to accomplish this is to take a screen capture of the pinner's avatar or Pinterest profile and then use the Add A New Pin upload feature to post it. Once you've uploaded the new image, you can go in and edit the URL to point to their Pinterest profile.

Thursday: Creating Crowd-Sourced Boards

As I've mentioned several times throughout this book, one of the primary selling points of Pinterest to busy social media marketing teams is how much less time it takes to curate than to create. Busy social media times don't always have the hours or staff available to properly compete on yet another social media channel. With Pinterest, the workload is much lighter.

For many companies, that means finding creative ways to leverage the content being created and uploaded by other users and presenting it under the banner of a familiar brand. Finding new and creative ways to gather Pinterest-friendly content from the masses is an important part of leveraging Pinterest without dramatically increasing your social media team's work hours.

Curating from Hashtags and Mentions

The idea of encouraging followers to upload content to be utilized by brands is nothing new. Brands and event planners have long leveraged hashtags on channels like Twitter and Instagram to help identify content related to a specific campaign, company, or event.

It's true you can just take a chance that consumers will include your company or product name in their Pinterest description. But proactively encouraging them to include a hashtag or mention in their description because you plan to feature fan content can go a long way toward helping you brand your campaign on Pinterest.

Though Pinterest does allow users to include hashtags as part of their pin description, it's important to note very few pinners were using hashtags as of this writing (see Figure 12.16).

Figure 12.16 The hashtags included in Pinterest descriptions are clickable and should take users to a Pinterest search page for the included hashtag.

Unfortunately, the lack of hashtag adoption by users combined with Pinterest's still floundering internal search algorithm often leads to fairly poor search results. Ideally, Pinterest will eventually list and prioritize hashtagged pins by the number of repins, likes, and comments they receive.

That said, Pinterest also allows users to "mention" other Pinterest users in the description or comments of a pin by including the @ sign and the user's screen name (see Figure 12.17).

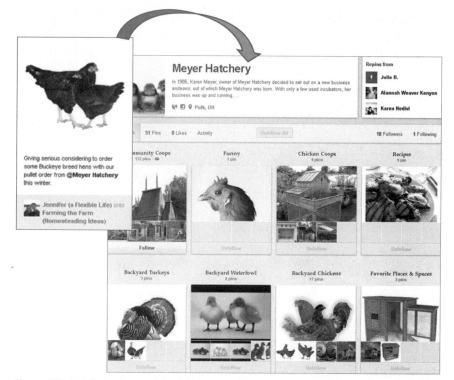

Figure 12.17 By including the @ symbol and a Pinterest user's screen name, it's possible to create a link to the user's account from the description of a pin.

Unfortunately, Pinterest was not sending notifications to users letting them know they had been tagged as of this writing. For now, the username tags only serve to allow people who do see the pin to click on the username and link to the named Pinterest account. This makes the mentions feature rather pointless as a notification system, but gives it some good potential as a Pinterest-specific branding system.

For this reason, promoting mentions as part of contest entries rather than hashtags is a preferred way to encourage pinners to notify you (and the general Pinterest population) of their participation in your campaigns and to create content for crowd-sourced pinboards.

Leveraging Content from Other Channels

The biggest problem with leveraging pre-pinned content is that you run the risk of curating a board featuring images your users have seen before. After all, if you found it while browsing Pinterest, there's a chance your followers found it too. One way to avoid this is by leveraging other social media channels to crowd-sourced content that can then be uploaded to Pinterest by your brand.

This is something The Weather Channel does extremely well. Their website features an area called iWitness Weather, allowing visitors to upload their own weather- and nature-related photos and videos (see Figure 12.18).

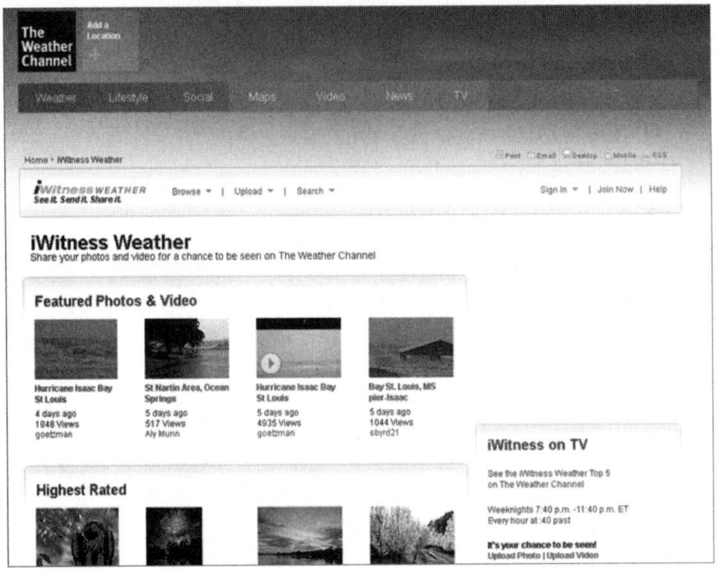

Figure 12.18 The Weather Channel leverages the iWitness Weather area of its website to collect viewer-submitted photos and videos of weather phenomena around the country.

Facebook fans also have the option of uploading their photos directly to The Weather Channel's Facebook Page, where administrators can in turn share them with The Weather Channel's followers. The uploads are then used on The Weather Channel's TV programming and featured on their Facebook Page. These images are then added to the iWitness Photos pinboard on The Weather Channel's Pinterest account (see Figure 12.19).

Figure 12.19 More than 2,000 Pinterest users follow The Weather Channel's iWitness Photo pinboard, which showcases compelling images taken by The Weather Channel viewers.

By taking the time to encourage viewers to upload and share their own content on other social media channels, The Weather Channel ensures it has a steady stream of great original images to choose from when curating this board.

> **Note:** It's important to remember that as with all forms of consumer-generated content you'll need to secure usage rights for the image. Make sure any system you set up for encouraging fans to submit images provides you with appropriate legal protection and usage rights as part of the submission process.

Leveraging Third-Party Pinners

Back in Chapters 9 and 10, we talked about the value of recruiting guest pinners to participate in group-curated pinboards. We explored the idea of how group boards work and then dove even deeper to figure out how to recruit new curators to the effort.

Now it's time to understand how companies are leveraging those teams and guest pinners. After all, they're not simply there to do your work for you—they are there to add a new dimension to your Pinterest presence and to help gain exposure of your brand to new audiences.

Leveraging a Team of Guest Pinners

As of this writing, very few brands were using teams of guest pinners as part of their Pinterest strategy. This is a shame because topical bloggers have been busy building collaborative boards that can attract thousands of followers (see Figure 12.20).

Figure 12.20 Nearly 3,500 people follow the more than 200 Pinterest users who contribute to the Yarn Love group pinboard.

Since board members' pins also show up in their personal Pinterest stream, these boards allow for a broad range of pinned content as well as raising awareness for the group pinboard. Companies and organizations can leverage these boards as a way to offer additional content, build relationships with evangelists, and increase exposure for their own Pinterest accounts. The key is to look for the natural tie-ins to your brand.

A company like Cricut or Sizzix who makes die-cut machines for scrapbookers could easily recruit scrapbookers who use their products to pin images of scrapbook layouts or creative paper crafts. A travel and tourism association could recruit local bloggers to curate topical boards about things to do in their specific locations.

The key is to treat your guest pinners as part of your social media evangelists campaign. Find and research the voices that are applicable to your target audience and cultivate a relationship with them that benefits both parties.

Leveraging a Solo Guest Pinner

Handmade and vintage marketplace Etsy was an early convert to Pinterest, building an active presence on the social media site before most companies even knew it existed. They've also led the way in their exploration of group boards and guest pinners, and launched a weekly guest pinner program in the late spring of 2012.

Etsy's program selects a "tastemaker" each week on Pinterest and sets them up as a contributor on a new Pinterest board that is then marketed via Etsy's blog. Each guest pinner spends a week curating a board on Etsy's Pinterest profile (see Figure 12.21).

Figure 12.21 Etsy's Pinterest profile includes a dozen or more guest pinner galleries.

These boards provide multiple benefits for Etsy's Pinterest account. First, it gives them a fresh source of original and unique content each week. Second, since each guest pinner pins content from the Etsy website, it provides direct traffic and conversion opportunities for the e-commerce site. Third, it provides increased exposure for Etsy's

Pinterest profile by recruiting high-profile pinners whose activity on the account will be broadcast to their own followers. Finally, it helps reinforce Etsy's reputation as a community-focused e-tailer.

Even for companies that do not have a standing history of collaboration with social media influencers, a guest pinner program can go a long way toward establishing goodwill and increasing exposure. Researching the influencers and evangelists within your vertical and partnering with them on short-term content can be a great way to cement yourself in pinners' minds as a solid part of the Pinterest (and social media) community.

Friday: The Value of Cross-Channel Integration

As with most areas of social media, it's important to look at your Pinterest activities as an integrated part of your overall social media efforts. Companies that allow their Pinterest channels to operate in complete isolation miss out on the chance to boost the power of their campaigns by attracting new followers from other social media channels.

That said, it's important to remember that cross-channel integration isn't only about attracting attention to your Pinterest stream from other social media channels. It's also about utilizing the content, relationships, and benefits of Pinterest to help make your efforts on other social media channels more effective.

We've already touched on the idea of pulling content from other social media channels to help boost your Pinterest activity earlier in the chapter. In this section, let's look at how your Pinterest content can and should be integrated into your overall social media efforts.

Highlighting a Featured Pinner

Earlier this week we talked about the value of recruiting guest pinners to help build both credibility and content for your brand on Pinterest. While it's true that a well-selected guest pinner can help attract new followers simply by giving your brand exposure to their own followers, it's also important to promote the guest pinner's activity as well.

In fact, a key part of leveraging this Pinterest tactic is making sure you properly promote your guest pinner across your other social media channels to help draw new Pinterest followers into the mix. Taking the time to highlight your guest pinners on your Facebook Page or blog can do wonders to raise awareness of the campaign (see Figure 12.22).

Figure 12.22 When luxury resort Calypso St. Barth recruited popular Pinner Christine Martinez to live pin a photo shoot, they included an interview with her and links to the pinboards on their site.

Promote the activity around your featured or guest pinners and use that promotion to attract even more followers to your pinboards. There are plenty of ways to do this. Put together a video interview with the guest pinner and share it on YouTube with links back to the pinboard on Pinterest. Share a photo and brief biography of your new guest pinner via Twitter or Facebook. Include a promo for the new pinboard or pinner in your email newsletter.

Promoting Pinterest Content on Other Channels

One of the great things about Pinterest that often gets overlooked by businesses and organizations is the sheer value of the content they might run across while building their own streams. Individuals use Pinterest to find inspiration for their everyday lives, so why shouldn't companies?

In fact, taking the content you find on Pinterest and leveraging it for other channels is a great way to use Pinterest to boost your overall social media campaigns. Depending on your industry and the way you use Pinterest, the possibilities are endless.

We'll wrap up this chapter with just a few examples of how different types of companies might turn Pinterest discoveries into a social media goldmine.

How-to Video Content

It's no secret one of the top reasons people head to Pinterest is for do-it-yourself ideas and step-by-step guides. The question many Pinterest users have is whether or not these methods work. Why not collect a few of the best and put them to work yourself with a video camera documenting your progress and results? (See Figure 12.23.)

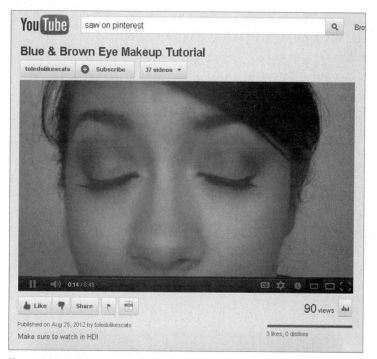

Figure 12.23 YouTube features hundreds of videos showing step-by-step walkthroughs of ideas found on Pinterest.

These videos could easily be uploaded to YouTube and then embedded in a company's blog and Facebook Pages as fresh content. With proper link credit back to the original idea source and pinner, these videos could also be used to build up good-will within the social media community.

As with most things social media related, it's always a good idea to offer a "hat tip" (a credit to the original source) when writing about or making a video of your own interpretation of an idea. These links tend to be greatly appreciated by the original authors and lend credibility to your own social media presence as well.

Sourced Ideas for Articles

In much the same way you can use Pinterest ideas to create videos, you can also lever-age them to write articles and reviews for your company's or organization's blog. Testing recipes, craft ideas, gardening tips, or home décor tutorials and then sharing the best of the best with your readers saves them time and builds your brand's cred-ibility. After all, Pinterest is absolutely full of pins claiming to be the "best way" or the "fastest way" to do something.

Why not test out their claims and provide some detailed information on whether or not these ideas really work? Even better, you can then use the article on your blog to feed content into Facebook, Twitter, and Pinterest itself to help complete the circle of social media activity and to ensure you're attracting followers from each of your active social media channels.

Pinterest Parties

One of the biggest potentials for companies in terms of offline to online tie-in is the idea of hosting Pinterest parties. Brick-and-mortar stores could use their buildings to host gatherings of Pinterest followers to collectively work on crafts or receive guidance on do-it-yourself projects. Even companies without physical locations could encourage followers to gather together regionally to test out ideas and projects showcased on Pinterest.

As with most of Pinterest's growth, its user base discovered this idea on its own, and groups of women around the country have already been curating group boards of project ideas for their next Pinterest party (see Figure 12.24).

Figure 12.24 Groups of women around the country are already gathering together for Pinterest parties to try out ideas together. They're even curating group boards to keep track of ideas for their next event.

Building on to this idea by hosting a brand-sponsored party could be a great way to attract new Pinterest users to your brand. In addition, if properly tied in to Facebook as events, attendees could be encouraged to check in to the party and post photos and videos of the results tagged with the company name.

Coming up in Chapter 13, we'll look at how companies are tying Pinterest activities to marketing goals by hosting contests and sweepstakes.

Week 10–Pinterest Marketing Through Contests

When new social media channels rise in popularity, marketers make their way to the playing field. It's not long after they arrive before they start searching for creative ways to get users to engage with their brands. Running contests is one of the most common ways to market via social media. As with other social networks, Pinterest is ripe for this type of marketing.

The great thing about Pinterest contest marketing is how many ways a company can creatively utilize the ways people are already using the site to build a brand boosting contest. This week, we'll explore the idea of Pinterest contests and how they can benefit your brand while we dig through several great examples of what some brands are already doing.

Chapter Contents
Monday: Understanding Pinterest Contests
Tuesday: Exploring Contest Examples
Wednesday: "Pin It to Win It" and Board Curation Contests
Thursday: Pinterest Scavenger Hunts
Friday: Pinterest Product Feature Contests

Monday: Understanding Pinterest Contests

Contests are one of the most popular forms of marketing via social media for a reason. They work. Of course, the challenge on many social networks is working around ever-changing rules and Terms of Service (TOS) to make sure your contests comply with each and every nitpicky detail of the social media channel in question.

For marketers, Pinterest is a contest marketing dream. With a wide open TOS and literally dozens of creative ways to engage followers, the potential is limited only by your marketing team's imagination.

Pinterest TOS

When it comes to running contests on Pinterest, there are two things you have to consider before you start doing any planning for your campaign: the current Terms of Service and the current Acceptable Use Policy. The link to these documents can be found by clicking on the About link in the top navigation bar of the Pinterest website (see Figure 13.1).

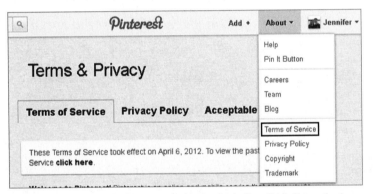

Figure 13.1 Pinterest's Terms of Service can be found under the About link in Pinterest's primary navigation.

As of this writing, nothing within Pinterest's published Terms of Service placed any restrictions on the type of marketing that could be performed on the Pinterest platform. For this reason, it's also important to read through Pinterest's current Acceptable Use Policy.

The Acceptable Use Policy

The Acceptable Use Policy breaks things down into one section outlining what types of content you may not post and another section outlining the types of activities you may not engage in on the site. Although it's essential to read the policy in full before proceeding with any marketing plan, you generally agree not to post anything illegal, hateful, or harmful to Pinterest users.

One area worth noting is Pinterest's policy on the use of third-party tools:

Attempt to access or search the Services, User Content or Pinterest Content or scrape or download User Content or Pinterest Content from the Services, or otherwise use, upload content to, or create new links, reposts, or referrals in the Service through the use of any engine, software, tool, agent, device or mechanism (including automated scripts, spiders, robots, crawlers, data mining tools or the like) other than the software and/or search agents provided by Pinterest or other generally available third party web browsers;...

As of this writing, Pinterest had not yet released a public API. This means any program, tool, or service that scrapes data from the site for marketing or reporting purposes is in violation of the Terms of Service and could end up getting blocked by the site. Though this doesn't restrict companies from dreaming up and running contests on the site, it does make it more difficult to run them and monitor them, since technically these feats would have to be accomplished manually.

Why Run Contests Through Pinterest?

The inability to use a contest management tool or a Pinterest analytics or monitoring tool without violating the site's Terms of Service might leave many companies wondering if it's worth investing the time in running contests on Pinterest. I'd challenge these companies to remember the early days of social media when there were no fancy content management tools to rely on. I'd also remind them that creative marketers are still finding ways to run measurable contests working around these limitations.

Traffic from Pinterest and the subsequent engagement or conversion levels can easily be tracked using any standard web analytics program. Additionally, as we talked about in Chapter 8, "Week 5—Track and Monitor Pinterest Traffic," individual pins carry a unique tracking parameter, which means that same analytics package can dig down fairly deep to better understand how specific entries within your contest performed.

Even outside of the ability to creatively track your campaign, keep in mind the other reasons so many companies are looking for creative ways to do contest marketing on Pinterest. These include:

A Rapidly Expanding User Base According to Experian's "2012 Digital Marketer: Benchmark and Trend Report" (http://go.experian.com/forms/experian-digital-marketer-2012), Pinterest is now the third most popular social network. Add to that a steady increase of users who spend an average of 90 minutes on the site per month and you've got a great foundation to build on.

A Naturally Viral Community Roughly 80 percent of the pinning activity taking place on Pinterest consists of repins. This means people are more likely to share information from the site than to post new information to it, a detail that bodes well for contest marketers.

A High-Engagement Traffic Source For targeted content that supports a company's brand image, click-through traffic tends to show strong engagement once they reach the destination site. Plan your contest wisely and the rewards can be high.

As with all forms of contest marketing, it's essential to plan your steps carefully, to target your message to your brand and audience and to have metrics in place for campaign measurement.

Tuesday: Exploring Contest Examples

Despite its relatively recent arrival in the crosshairs of marketers, Pinterest has already been leveraged by a wide range of companies using contest marketing. In fact, Pinterest was home to some of 2012's most creative social media contesting campaigns.

Before we explore the types of contests and campaigns that tend to do well on Pinterest, let's explore two of 2012's most interesting and innovative Pinterest contest campaigns.

bmi Pinterest Lottery

In March 2012, UK-based social media agency Rabbit helped British Midland Airways Limited (also known as British Midland International, or bmi) to launch one of the first publicly recognized Pinterest contest campaigns. The bmi Pinterest lottery gave consumers the chance to win a pair of return business class flights to the destination of their choice by repinning numbered images of cities bmi flew to (see Figure 13.2).

Figure 13.2 bmi Airlines curated boards featuring numbered images from popular destinations as part of their Pinterest Lottery game.

bmi launched five boards at the start of the three-month campaign, each one featuring a variety of pictures of a specific destination the airline flew to. Each image was numbered, and "players" were encouraged to pin up to six of their favorite images from the various boards (see Figure 13.3).

Figure 13.3 Each pinboard featured nine numbered images from the selected destination for players to choose from.

They also launched a Tumblr site to feature more detailed information and travel guides for the destinations featured in the contest. Each week, the airline selected a winning number from their boards, selected a random entrant who had pinned the image with that number, and announced them on the Tumblr site (see Figure 13.4).

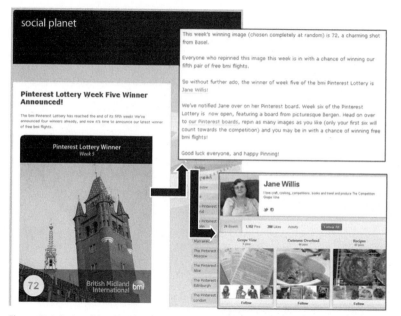

Figure 13.4 bmi used their Tumblr page to share details of the contest like newly added destinations and weekly winners.

The results were fairly impressive. According to Rabbit and the bmi team, they were able to measure a reach of over half a million social media impressions in the first two weeks alone. They also received a decent amount of activity on the site, attracting 650 followers and 3,500 repins over the course of a month. Those numbers might not seem outstanding in a world with millions of YouTube views and tens of thousands of Facebook followers, but it was a respectable number for a newly blossoming social media channel at the time.

Unfortunately, all the time and effort spent building up followers for bmi's Pinterest account and driving traffic to the campaign's Tumblr site seems to have missed the boat in regard to long-term marketing. bmi's Pinterest account no longer exists on the site and the bmi Social Planet Tumblr site hasn't been updated since the last winner was announced in May 2012.

That's a lot of social media capital to leave dangling in the wind with no further contact. The brilliance of bmi's outreach efforts could have carried far more long-term reward for the company if they'd directed traffic to a resource where they planned to continue communicating with consumers.

Simply keeping the destination blog online and continuing to add new destinations and new travel tips over time would have been a wonderful way to continue interacting with the fans created by the contest. Additionally, bmi could have required contest winners to take and post photographs of their winning trips to the bmi contest blog and to bmi's Facebook page. Simply discontinuing the content of the site leaves too much potential on the table.

Homes.com Spring into the Dream Contest

Another innovative contest that was run by a company in 2012 was Homes.com's Spring into the Dream, which partnered the company with popular home and lifestyle bloggers (and their readers) to curate hundreds of spring-related boards.

To launch the contest, Homes.com selected 20 popular home, crafting, parenting, and lifestyle bloggers and invited each of them to build a themed Pinterest board around getting ready for spring. The contest rules required them to pin a certain number of items from the Homes.com Pinterest boards and website to their newly created boards (see Figure 13.5).

Figure 13.5 Homes.com invited 20 well-respected bloggers to work with them on a seasonal Pinterest contest. The rules required participants to follow Homes.com on Pinterest and to pin some content from the Homes.com website.

Along with offering a $500 cash prize to the blogger they felt created the best pinboard, Homes.com also invited each blogger to encourage their readers to join the contest. Whichever blogger won would then be allowed to select her own favorite board from among her readers to award a second $500 prize to.

Homes.com has not released any data regarding click-through traffic, conversions, or how successful they considered the contest to be, but publicly available data looks strong. The 20 bloggers reached a combined total of more than 70,000 Pinterest users, and their followers generated nearly 500 additional pinboards for the contest that would have reached a second set of followers. With a $1,000 total cash prize, that works out to about $2 per branded pinboard being curated on the site.

Of course, these are just two examples of hundreds of contests that have now been run on Pinterest. In the rest of this chapter, we'll look a little deeper at the most common types of Pinterest contests and why any particular style might work best for your brand.

Wednesday: "Pin It to Win It" and Board Curation Contests

One of the most natural ways to integrate a contest into Pinterest is by utilizing the activities people are already doing on the site. Allowing the simple act of pinning a piece of content or curating a board on a specific topic to be the primary focus of the content not only reduces the barrier to entry, but it also helps integrate your content and your brand into users' lives on Pinterest.

How It Works

The two most common forms of contests on this front are the "Pin It to Win It" contests and board curation contests. We've already seen an example of board curation contests in the Homes.com blogger contest just described. For Pin It to Win It contests, it's usually a matter of asking users to pin a piece of content and tag it with the company's username as their entry.

Contest rules outline where the pin needs to come from, what hashtag or mention needs to be included in the description, and whether the winner is selected at random or by a panel of judges.

Why It Benefits Your Brand

For most companies, Pin It to Win It and board curation contests are all about building exposure and getting the brand in front of as many people as possible. It's also about getting contestants used to visiting your brand online and engaging with them on Pinterest in the hopes those interactions might continue after their contest participation ends.

For membership-based travel site Jetsetter, it was about expanding their reach among Pinterest users, signing up new members, and driving traffic to the travel listings on the site. Known as a site with stunning photography and gorgeous destinations, a Pinterest driven contest was a natural fit (see Figure 13.6).

Figure 13.6 Jetsetter's "Become a Jetsetter Curator" played off the Pinterest community's love affair with destination photos to drive increased exposure and traffic back to their website.

The rules were simple: Create a new pinboard with "Jetsetter Curator" in the title and make sure each pin included the #JetsetterCurator hashtag. The contest ran for roughly three weeks and attracted more than 1,100 entries. According to a case study published on Mashable.com, the average board owner pinned 40 images, carrying the contest's exposure to a total of nearly 50,000 hashtagged pins.

The engagement metrics are also impressive. Traffic to the Jetsetter web site from Pinterest doubled and the number of page views increased 150 percent. Combine that with lower bounce rates than average and it becomes clear that the Pinterest contest was extremely effective at sending highly targeted traffic into the site.

This is where pinning contests perform well; they create additional opportunities for exposure. When run over a period of time, they also help increase awareness within the community of the content your brand or website has to offer. If your campaign includes a focus on conversions, it also provides the opportunity for ongoing marketing to a new group of consumers.

Measuring Value

When it comes to pin-related contests, the primary motivator is exposure of your brand to the Pinterest community. It's about getting your images, your name, and your brand ideals out there into the mix by people who are already part of the community. There are several ways to measure value on these types of campaigns; mostly it depends on what your goals are.

If you are new to the service and trying to boost your presence, you might simply want to view the cost of any campaign as a way of "buying" exposure. Your metrics might focus on things like the number of new followers, the number of tagged images, the number of pinboards created, and the number of repins your content receives.

If you already have a strong Pinterest presence, you might wish to use these campaigns to drive traffic to your website or to boost conversions and sales figures. In these cases, you might view repins and followers as simply a step toward the ultimate goals of the campaign. Those goals might include the number of visitors the campaign drives to your site, the number of registrations for an email newsletter, the number of coupon or discount downloads, or the number of product purchases or service leads.

Thursday: Pinterest Scavenger Hunts

While getting Pinterest users to pin content from your website and curate boards around your brand is an effective way to engage them with your brand, it can be time consuming for users to take part in the games. An option that opens up the door to a quicker "game" style contest is the Pinterest scavenger hunt.

How It Works

For anyone who ever spent a crazy night in college running around asking people for strange objects, the concept of a scavenger hunt is pretty self-explanatory. Translating it to the world of Pinterest is as simple as requiring people to pin images of what they've found rather than stuffing those items in a backpack to be unveiled when the players get back to base.

There are a few different ways to pull off Pinterest scavenger hunts. Some brands like to send users on a wild goose chase through their website looking for puzzle pieces to pin to a contest-specific board. Some companies offer a list of requirements (for example, something you'd sit on, something you'd drink from, something you'd stand on) and allow the players to determine the content.

Others, like the team at America's Test Kitchen blog partial images from their pin-boards and ask contestants to go hunting for the full image. Once they found the image, they needed to email the contest coordinator with the link to the pinned image so they could enter a drawing for a copy of the Cook's Illustrated Cookbook (see Figure 13.7).

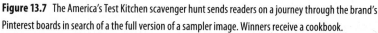

Figure 13.7 The America's Test Kitchen scavenger hunt sends readers on a journey through the brand's Pinterest boards in search of a the full version of a sampler image. Winners receive a cookbook.

There's also the potential to do an old-fashioned clue-based scavenger hunt where each pin leads to a web page featuring the clue for the next pin until players reach the final pin and are able to fill out their contest entry form signaling completion of the contest.

Why It Benefits Your Brand

If you are driving Pinterest users to a specific section of your site to hunt for contest images, you have the opportunity to expose them to new products and new content. You also have the ability to make sure that section of the site features tested conversion points for email newsletters, product specials, and membership opportunities.

Scavenger hunts present nearly unparalleled opportunity to push people deep into your site, so have a plan to take advantage of that activity. Giving people a reason to take a deep dive into the content of your website helps showcase the value of your content and can end up landing you a regular visitor or subscriber.

Even if you go the American's Test Kitchen route and ask consumers to dig through your Pinterest boards, you still increase the chance they'll spot (and pin) great content from your site during their hunt.

Measuring Value

With scavenger hunt–related contests, the focus is about getting Pinterest users to dig deep into the content on your site. It's about playing off their love of curation to drive that investment of time and energy it takes to immerse themselves in your content. The fact that the contest takes place on Pinterest opens up the potential reach of the contest activity.

For this reason, you'll want to look at things like engagement metrics on your site. Did requiring people to spend time digging through your site for the contest increase their time on site? Did you see a rise in number of page views per visitor? These contests also increase the potential for longer-term engagement by opening up the opportunity to place conversion points in front of participants.

Friday: Pinterest Product Feature Contests

There's no shortage of examples of companies using pin to win, board curation, and scavenger hunt–style contests. But one type of contest that hasn't shown up as often as I'd expect is one that highlights or features a brand or its products. In terms of building awareness and driving sales, this type of contest holds quite a bit of untapped potential.

How It Works

The idea behind product feature contests is to either showcase a specific product or to showcase the brand itself. In some cases, these contests ask fans to make blog posts and pin images of the new and creative ways they've put your products to use.

In others, they ask users to upload their own ideas and creations as they relate to your brand.

A nail polish maker might ask customers to create custom nail designs using the brand's colors and then post them to Pinterest as part of the contest. A tool brand might ask customers to post their home improvement projects or items they've built using the tools.

A popular brand like Lego might ask users to upload their own Lego-themed creations to the site and to designate them as contest entries by using the hashtag or mention feature. Brands could then either choose winners themselves, or narrow the field and encourage fans to vote on their favorites by using cross-channel promotions on social media sites like Facebook and YouTube as well as on Pinterest.

The truth is, Pinterest is already chock-full of users posting their own examples of brand interactions or brand interpretations. Lego-themed pins are extremely popular, with tons of consumers posting their own Lego-themed crafts or creative ways they've used the products (see Figure 13.8).

Figure 13.8 Pinterest is simply full of Lego-themed boards where users collect creative Lego-themed crafts, birthday party ideas, or even creative ways to display and make use of their favorite Lego items.

Developing themed contests like "Throw a Lego Birthday Party" or "Most Creative Way to Use a Lego Plate" could put Lego fans to work creating tons of new content that could be promoted and utilized on Lego's other social media channels.

Why It Benefits Your Brand

The benefits here are twofold: Contest entries tend to reinforce a love or passion for the brand, and they also tend to showcase creative ways to use a brand's products. Both of these benefits carry high potential for increasing conversation about a company via social media circles as well as having the potential to increase sales.

Using our Lego example, it would be easy for Lego to partner with the contest entrants to promote their content to craft bloggers, parenting bloggers, and geek bloggers to rekindle conversation about the brand.

Retailers have long known that buyers don't always use their products in the way they were intended. In fact, it's often consumers who discover new ways to use products that increase the value of those products. Putting your creative customers to work to help you understand the full potential of the things you sell can carry huge value for a brand willing to act on the knowledge they've gained.

Additionally, Lego could choose to partner with some creative crafters to add their creations to the ever-growing line of Lego-themed items and accessories (see Figure 13.9).

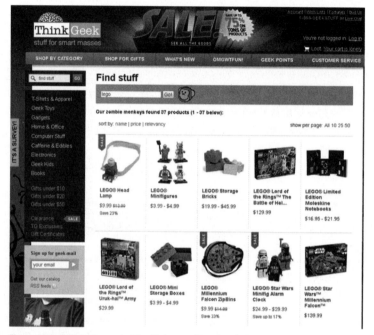

Figure 13.9 ThinkGeek.com already sells dozens of Lego branded items. Expanding the product line using ideas discovered on Pinterest could help Lego build additional revenue.

In the case of party-themed items, Lego could easily put together content on their website to help parents throw their own Lego-themed birthday parties for kids using ideas submitted to the contest.

Measuring Value

As with most contests, there are several types of metrics you'll want to measure to determine how successful this type of contest is. For the most part, your areas of value will fall into four categories; exposure, creative value, engagement, and direct sales impact.

In terms of exposure, you'll be looking at a potential increase across multiple social media channels. If you require contest entrants to post a YouTube video or blog post showcasing their idea before they pin it, you'll gain natural brand exposure on the chosen channel. There's also the chance other bloggers will pick up on the ideas and share them with their own readers or that Facebook and Twitter users will share the links to the ideas with their contacts.

Determining which exposure-based metrics you wish to tally prior to your campaign and having a plan in place to keep tabs on them will help demonstrate value for your brand.

In terms of creative value, you'll be looking at the quality of the idea being submitted and whether or not it's something you can go on to incorporate into your own sales and marketing efforts. For instance, if you've run a contest seeking out creative ways to wear your new line of scarves, have plans in place to feature the winning style on store mannequins and on models on your e-commerce site.

In terms of engagement and direct sales impact, you're measuring the standard metrics related to these concepts. You'll want to track things like how much traffic the contest drives to your site, whether social sharing of your content increases, whether order sizes increases, and so on.

Coming up in Chapter 14, we'll dive even deeper into the idea of measuring and refining your Pinterest efforts.

Week 11–Measure and Refine Your Strategy

As with any form of marketing, simply understanding how to put together a plan and execute it isn't enough. A sustainable Pinterest strategy requires you to frequently look over the results of your efforts and to make adjustments to your campaigns based on how they are being received.

Understanding how to set goals and measure results is the first part of this process. Using the knowledge you have of how consumers (and competitors) are using Pinterest is another part. Ultimately, it will be up to you to continually test new approaches in order to decide which strategies will perform best for your business or for your client.

Chapter Contents
Monday: Setting Pinterest-Related Goals
Tuesday: Analyzing Your Campaigns
Wednesday: Understanding Common Pinterest Problems and Their Solutions
Thursday: Continually Testing Your Approach
Friday: Learning from a Pinterest Case Study

Monday: Setting Pinterest-Related Goals

No amount of measurement, metrics, or analysis will help you if you haven't first taken the time to clearly lay out your goals. After all, if you don't know what you're trying to accomplish, no amount of data will tell you whether you've pulled it off.

Setting a Business Goal

Building a sustainable Pinterest marketing strategy has to start with the formation of goals. Don't misunderstand me here. I'm not talking about Pinterest-based goals like "get more followers" or "increase my repins." I'm talking about actual business goals you feel can be met based on the time and effort you invest in Pinterest.

For the most part, the goals you might have for your business fall into one of three categories: building the brand, increasing your presence, or driving conversions (see Figure 14.1).

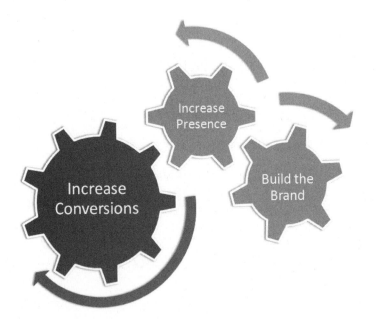

Figure 14.1 When thinking about your Pinterest goals, start by looking at whether you'd like to build your brand, increase your presence, or drive more conversions.

They key is to look at your business from each of these three perspectives to see where you might find a match. Are you looking to release a new product next quarter and need to find a way to spread awareness and drive sales? Your business goal will center on that idea and will end up being conversion related and exposure related. Are you looking to increase the traffic to your website because you are a content company generating revenue via advertising? Your business goal will likely center on building the brand and increasing your presence.

Ideally, as the person in charge of marketing for your company or organization, you should already know what your top business priorities are for the next few quarters. If you don't, this is the perfect chance to sit down with the team leaders in your company to find out what everyone has brewing.

Once you've selected a business goal to work from, you'll need to understand how that goal translates into business metrics and social media metrics. Take the example in Figure 14.2.

Figure 14.2 A business looking to launch new flavors into a popular line of yogurts will clearly desire to increase sales of the new flavors. Understanding how social media can help reach those goals is essential to creating strong campaign-related metrics.

In our fictitious example, we have a business that's looking to expand their line of yogurts to include several new flavors. Based on our understanding of social media, we know we can probably put some tactics in place to generate product reviews, increase conversation and buzz around the flavors, and even drive conversions by distributing coupons.

With a strong understanding of how to leverage Pinterest, it's simply a matter of outlining our options and figuring out the best approach to reach our goals. This is where tactics come into play.

Letting Your Goals Define Your Tactics

Once you've defined a business goal for your Pinterest campaign, you'll want to use it as a starting point to consider what you might be able to do on Pinterest to help accomplish it. To do this, take the high-level goal you've defined and break it down into smaller, supportive micro-goals that will help you reach the high-level goal (see Figure 14.3).

Figure 14.3 To put your goal to work, you've got to understand the steps you must take to reach the goal.

Once you've broken things down into micro-goals, it starts to get easier to see how social media fits into the equation. For instance, if you're looking to generate product reviews, you're going to need to research influential food bloggers to form a pitch list for product sampling and review posting. If you're looking to showcase the various ways to use the product, you'll want to develop content or partnerships that showcase the various ways to put it to work.

The key is to take these tactics and match them up with the micro-goals you've created. This will help the shape of your Pinterest campaign start to come together (see Figure 14.4).

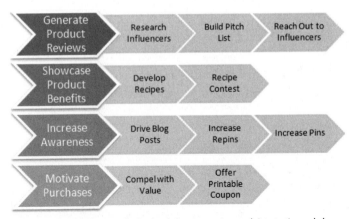

Figure 14.4 Taking the time to further break down your micro-goals into tactics can help you figure out your best course of action on Pinterest.

Putting It All Together

Once you've taken the time to move from business goal to micro-goals to tactics, you're ready to start looking at how Pinterest factors into the equation. In the case of our yogurt company, the plan would probably look something like the outline in Figure 14.5.

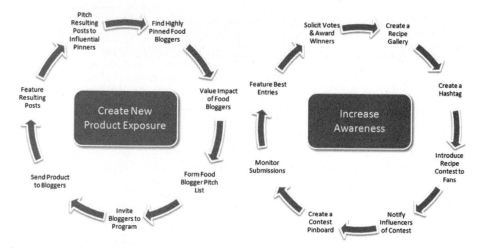

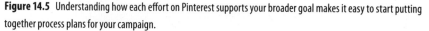

Figure 14.5 Understanding how each effort on Pinterest supports your broader goal makes it easy to start putting together process plans for your campaign.

The benefit of taking this approach is that while future campaigns may have different topical focuses, much of the groundwork for your process gets laid out ahead of time. Sure, you'll need to do your research to find out who the best-suited influencers are for any particular campaign. Sure, you'll need to develop a new hashtag, a new pinboard, and new promotional materials. In the long run, though, you begin to create a system that makes it easier for you to get the ball rolling on future campaigns.

You also make it much easier to measure the success of your campaign and to figure out where things went wrong if a campaign falters.

Tuesday: Analyzing Your Campaigns

Of the most important reasons for taking the time to clearly outline your goals on a channel like Pinterest is to make it simpler to set up your metrics. After all, if you aren't able to measure your efforts, it's extremely difficult to tell whether they're working.

Matching Metrics to Campaigns

Let's continue along with the campaign of our fictitious yogurt company from yesterday's section on Pinterest goal setting. There's immense value in using your business goal to come up with a course of action for your marketing team, but all that work could be for nothing if you aren't also developing metrics for your measurement team. (Or, let's be totally honest here for your small companies and say you'll need to have these plans and measurements in place so you can keep everything straight while you're doing it yourself!)

That's why, once you've taken the time to come up with your plan, you need to focus on creating measurement points (see Figure 14.6).

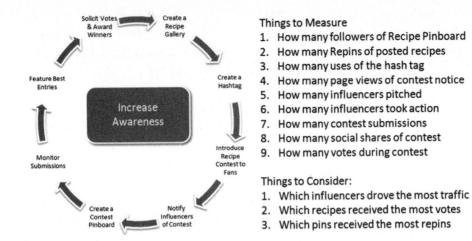

Things to Measure
1. How many followers of Recipe Pinboard
2. How many Repins of posted recipes
3. How many uses of the hash tag
4. How many page views of contest notice
5. How many influencers pitched
6. How many influencers took action
7. How many contest submissions
8. How many social shares of contest
9. How many votes during contest

Things to Consider:
1. Which influencers drove the most traffic
2. Which recipes received the most votes
3. Which pins received the most repins

Figure 14.6 Considering the plan of action you've laid out, ask yourself what is measureable. Give special consideration to which metrics provide valuable insight into the broader goals of campaign.

These measurement points are what you will need to use to see if your campaign is on task. You'll be able to use them to identify the areas where your campaign is lacking so you can refine your approach and improve the performance of your next campaign.

For example, let's say you're a few weeks into the campaign process. You created your hashtag, put up a post on your blog outlining the contest, and launched your new recipe contest pinboard. You spent a week compiling a list of over 150 highly pinned recipe bloggers and sent them each a personalized email outlining the contest and asking them if they'd be willing to participate.

Unfortunately, only 20 of your 150 bloggers responded and only a handful of them were willing to take part in the recipe contest. Because you are tracking that information, you can quickly determine there's a problem with your pitching approach. Perhaps you've accidentally targeted vegan bloggers. Perhaps you targeted sites that focus on cooking rather than baking. Maybe your pitch was poorly written. Whatever the cause, you can use the extremely low conversion rate of your pitching efforts to review your approach and expand your outreach to additional bloggers.

Perhaps your outreach efforts went extremely well and you ended up finding several dozen bloggers who were willing to create recipes and who each shared the campaign with their readers, generating hundreds more responses and entries. Although this is a wonderful start, you notice very few recipe pins showing up on Pinterest with the contest's hashtag, making it difficult to find contest entries.

This might spark an effort to double-check the contest announcements on your partner blogs to make sure they shared the hashtag with their readers. You find some who forgot to mention that detail and shoot them off an email asking them to correct their post and remind their readers of the need to include the tag.

You might also decide to switch gears a bit at this point because you notice the readers are sharing links to their own recipes in the comment section of the bloggers involved in the campaign rather than adding them to Pinterest with the proper hashtag. This might prompt you to invite your blog partners to co-curate the contest board, adding their own readers' recipes to the mix as they are shared in the comments.

The point of all this is that without metrics in place, your campaign can appear to have fallen completely apart when it was only just a small area of the plan that was struggling. The ability to identify these bottlenecks and correct them is the difference between campaign recovery and campaign failure.

Analyzing Campaign Details for Consumer Insight

As I've mentioned repeatedly throughout this book, one of the single biggest advantages Pinterest brings to the online marketer is the freedom to look into the mind of the consumer. Whether it's looking at the content being pinned from your website to take note of what's resonating with your audience, reading the names of the pinboards to understand the context in which a pin is viewed, or reading the descriptions attached to the pin to find out exactly what people think of it, Pinterest is chock-full of insight.

This is why it's also important to understand which metrics go beyond simply defining value for the current campaign. It's not enough to know the average yogurt-inspired recipe received 42 repins. You want to know which recipes garnered the most repins. You want to look for themes in the content to learn what plays well with the audience (see Figure 14.7).

Figure 14.7 Hmmm…pumpkin…pumpkin…pumpkin…anyone else noticing a common theme in terms of these high repin recipes?

If a single theme or usage regularly gathers a high volume of repins, ask yourself what you can do to generate more content of a similar nature. In the case of Figure 14.7, the pins with the highest number of repins from their Chobani Recipe pinboards are pumpkin focused. Not only could this knowledge be passed along to the product development team (pumpkin yogurt for next year?), it can also be used to develop and release seasonal content as part of next year's content marketing efforts.

Learning which influencers both responded positively to your outreach efforts and drove high levels of interest from their followers can also provide your team with valuable insight moving forward. It never hurts to know who can (and will) rally the troops around a great piece of content.

Wednesday: Understanding Common Pinterest Problems and Their Solutions

While we've spent the past 13 chapters walking you through the best ways to leverage Pinterest in order to increase engagement, traffic, and conversion from your target audience, there are still going to be times where it just isn't working. That's why it's important to understand some of the most common causes of poor performance from Pinterest accounts and how to fix them.

Lack of Repins

Repins can be a wonderful indicator of how well a piece of content is resonating with Pinterest users. At the same time, it's important to keep in mind that repins alone are not always a fair indicator of how popular a piece of content is. In fact, there are quite a few reasons why repins may be extremely low on a piece of content that performs quite admirably on your website.

The first question to ask yourself is whether the pin holds enough value to attract repins. If the content, photography, or concept is subpar, you can hardly expect the Pinterest audience to repin it. On the other hand, if you've done your research, created a high-quality piece of targeted content, and released it into your stream only to be greeted with crickets, you've got to dig a little deeper (see Figure 14.8).

After all, you might find that though the version you pinned isn't gaining much traction, the content on your website is being pinned repeatedly by your site's visitors. Visitors are getting exposed to the content on your site or Facebook feed rather than via Pinterest itself. Thus, you're getting a high volume of individual pins rather than a high volume of repins (see Figure 14.9).

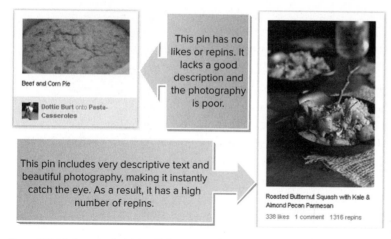

Figure 14.8 The image on the left is unlikely to gain much traction on Pinterest. The image on the right, however, is perfectly primed to garner a high volume of repins.

Figure 14.9 While none of these individual pins have attracted a high volume of repins (or any, really), the content itself has attracted a high volume of individual pins.

This isn't necessarily a bad thing and is common for sites that have a strong social media following as they first get into Pinterest. The goal, however, is to start seeing those individual pins boosting your exposure and attracting a new audience.

The best trick here may be to edit the default description that will attach to the images being pinned from your site. (We talked about how to set up the default image caption back in Chapter 7, "Week 4—Purposely Propagating Pins on Pinterest.") By including a call to action in the description of the pin, you can help push additional repins (see Figure 14.10).

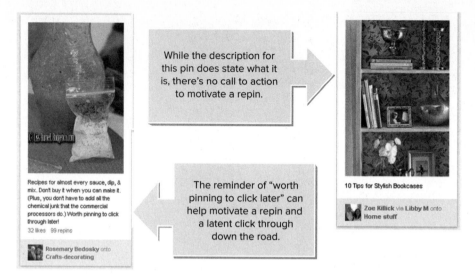

While the description for this pin does state what it is, there's no call to action to motivate a repin.

The reminder of "worth pinning to click later" can help motivate a repin and a latent click through down the road.

Recipes for almost every sauce, dip, & mix. Don't buy it when you can make it. (Plus, you don't have to add all the chemical junk that the commercial processors do.) Worth pinning to click through later!

32 likes   99 repins

Rosemary Bedosky onto
Crafts-decorating

10 Tips for Stylish Bookcases

Zoe Killick via Libby M onto
Home stuff

Figure 14.10 Simply reminding Pinterest users they can "pin now and read later" can go a long way to helping increase the number of repins on a piece of content.

The single most common reason a high-quality pin fails to attract a high volume of repins is lack of exposure. Since the Pinterest algorithm only promotes a limited number of pins from each user into the appropriate category stream, most pins will only be able to attract repins from the existing followers of the board it is pinned to.

To solve this problem, you'll need to work on finding and building a relationship with influencers who can help spread your content to a broader audience. Invest the time in researching pinners and bloggers in your vertical, and then work on building a relationship with them. This way, you can pitch your top-tier content to them for pinning the same way you might pitch a blog post or YouTube video.

Warning: Building a relationship with influential pinners can go a long way toward helping increase the exposure for your content, but make sure you pitch content sparingly. It's better to build a wide range of relationships and pitch each one only occasionally—no more than once every month or two. Otherwise, you risk the goodwill you've worked so hard to create by pestering them with self-serving requests.

Lack of Followers

Another primary problem when building up your Pinterest account is a lack of followers. After all, unless you are lucky enough to land key content in the category stream on a regular basis, scoring new followers is the primary way you're going to gain exposure for your content on the site.

Building up Pinterest followers clearly requires a time investment for building high-quality content, but this is not the Field of Dreams. You can't expect people to show up simply because you've built something.

This is where integrated marketing becomes critical. Consider your existing social media channels and how they might work to help you boost your followers. While you should already have integrated a "Follow Us on Pinterest" button on your website and blog, consider the other places where you can attract attention from your existing fan base.

We've had great luck pinning sampler content from a client's Pinterest boards to the client's Facebook page and encouraging Facebook fans to come connect with the brand on Pinterest. We've also seen good results from integrating a brand's Pinterest boards into the apps section of their Facebook page (see Figure 14.11).

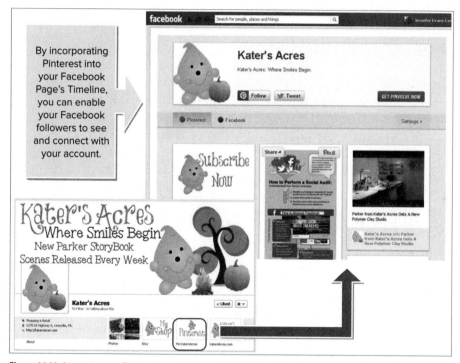

Figure 14.11 Integrating your Pinterest account into your Page's Facebook Timeline as an app makes it quick and easy for your Facebook fans to access and repin your content without even leaving Facebook.

Sending out an announcement of your new Pinterest boards via Twitter, Facebook, your blog, and email newsletters when you launch your accounts makes perfect sense, but don't forget to continue promoting over time. If you've added a new seasonal board or you've focused on curation about a specific topic, don't be afraid to send out another update via other social media channels to invite people to follow your new board.

Lack of Traffic

Perhaps you've had absolutely no problem attracting followers and driving pins and repins of your content. If the problem with your campaign is that despite stellar activity for the pin it's not driving any traffic through to your website, you've probably stumbled upon the problem of oversharing.

One of the most common mistakes associated with low-traffic, high-engagement pins is the simple sharing of too much information in either the image or the image's description (see Figure 14.12).

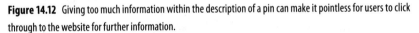

Figure 14.12 Giving too much information within the description of a pin can make it pointless for users to click through to the website for further information.

It's understandable to want to demonstrate the ease of an idea by highlighting the simplicity in a pinned description. After all, this type of information can help drive more people to repin the content. Unfortunately, this strategy can backfire on a brand if it's taken too far. If a user can understand everything they need to about an idea through the image and description, there's no reason for them to click through to the website to read the full description behind the idea.

Thursday: Continually Testing Your Approach

By this stage of the game, you should have a pretty good idea of what you need to do to get rolling with a strong Pinterest strategy. You should even have a pretty decent idea of how to start setting up metrics and measurement points to put value on those efforts and to help you refine your strategy over time.

It's important to keep in mind that even if things are going well, there's always value in testing to see what works best for your particular audience.

Test Topics and Concepts

The most obvious thing to be testing is the themes and ideas of the content you're pinning. It's not uncommon to expect one set of content to perform really well only to discover that a completely different set of content captures the attention (and traffic) from Pinterest.

For instance, my hobby blog has always featured blog posts of the bento lunches I make for my children. On Facebook, this has consistently been some of my best performing content. On Pinterest however, we've seen very little activity around the images. We saw even less click-through traffic happening. Upon speaking to some of my regular readers, I discovered that while they enjoy seeing them (and often click the Like button on Facebook) it's not anything they planned to make themselves, so there was very little reason to repin the images or click through to the site.

On the other hand, a few offhand blog posts I put up with some of the do-it-yourself projects from our backyard wedding absolutely exploded on Pinterest. These posts quickly gathered hundreds of repins and became one of the strongest traffic sources to my blog. Even the pins that didn't have a high volume of repins sent impressive amounts of traffic (see Figure 14.13).

Figure 14.13 Despite a lack of repins, this individual pin has sent a respectable number of visitors through to the site.

Additionally, the content flowing into my blog from these pins generally stuck around for quite some time and visited nearly every other post in the wedding section of my site. As soon as we discovered this pattern, we shifted gears and backed off the bento content to free up more time and effort for posting additional wedding content. The new wedding content has continued to perform strongly and has become one of the best producers of high-engagement traffic to my site.

This is why tracking your Pinterest activity is so important. Without a measurement plan in place, our analytics team never would have noticed the difference in traffic volume between our various topical focuses and we would have missed the opportunity to correct course to gain additional site visitors.

Test Descriptions and Calls to Action

Earlier in this chapter, we talked about the dramatic difference in traffic that can come from giving away too much information in the description of your pin. We also talked about the ability to help increase repins by including a call to action to repin within the description of the image.

Much like you should be looking at the broader topics and ideas being covered by your Pinterest content, it's also essential to keep tabs on what types of descriptions and calls to action drive repins, traffic, and engagement. Since any good analytics program will help show you which individual pins are producing traffic for your site (and subsequently allow you to measure the engagement rates of the traffic coming in from those pins), it's more than possible to measure which approaches work best with your audience (see Figure 14.14).

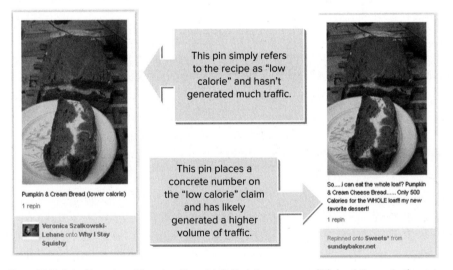

Figure 14.14 By looking at the traffic produced by each individual pin, you can see which descriptions entice the most viewers to both repin and visit the content.

It's important to remember that you won't always have control over what descriptions get attached to your pins. Whereas many pinners will leave the default description in place if it's descriptive enough, others will change it to add their own notes. In many ways, this is beneficial to you as a marketer.

The natural deviations present in descriptions on pinned content do a wonderful job of mirroring the way your target audience views and describes your content. By taking the time to look deeper at the pins that produce the best traffic for your site, you may come across selling points or descriptions put in place by your readers that you hadn't even thought to highlight, providing valuable insight for future pin descriptions.

Test the Best Time to Pin

We explored the idea of timing your pins for maximum impact back in Chapter 7. Thanks to multiple studies by marketers and advertisers, we are able to determine that most pinning takes place between 5 a.m. and 7 a.m. and between 6 p.m. and 8 p.m. EST.

That data can act as a good starting point for your campaign, but it's important not to rely too heavily on it. Your target audience may spend more time pinning during their lunch breaks or in the evening while watching TV or unwinding for the day. Additionally, you may find that the power pinners you are targeting do their pinning in early afternoon or even in the middle of the night.

That means it's important to take note of the repin activity for your pins and to look for patterns concerning the time of day they're posted. One late-night pin going viral might be a fluke. Half a dozen or more of pins going viral after 10 p.m. probably tells you you're on to something. Adjusting your pinning patterns accordingly could be a simple tweak that nets you a far more productive Pinterest presence.

Friday: Learning from a Pinterest Case Study

One company that understands the value of putting Pinterest measurement to work to refine your campaigns is Daily Grommet. Daily Grommet is the force behind Citizen Commerce (www.dailygrommet.com/products/about-us/citizen-commerce), a website aimed at supporting unique and innovative products and the companies behind them.

According to Community Manager Tori Tait:

We believe every purchase amplifies something in the world, good, bad or indifferent. At Daily Grommet we're creating a place for people who want their purchases to have meaning—to support what matters most to them: whether it's technical innovation, green or social enterprises, the creation of jobs, domestic manufacturing, or the preservation of craft.

Daily Grommet started taking note of Pinterest in the summer of 2011 when it began showing up as a referrer in their analytics reports. Tait had joined Pinterest about the same time and was immediately hooked. Curious about the traffic spike from

Pinterest, Tait ran a quick search on the Daily Grommet domain and was stunned to see dozens and dozens of products from deep within their catalog pages showing up as pins (see Figure 14.15).

Figure 14.15 Even before Daily Grommet launched their own Pinterest account, fans of the site were busy pinning and repinning their favorite products.

By the end of summer, Daily Grommet had set up shop on Pinterest and was working to engage with other Pinterest users while curating their own boards. From Tait's perspective, there were myriad reasons to build a presence on the service.

Users were pinning products into boards with titles like "Why Didn't I Think of That?" and "Must Have," denoting a passionate interest in the products being offered. Even better, pinners were often editing the descriptions of the products to include extremely insightful (and valuable) thoughts about the products and their experiences with them.

"We listen and learn a lot about how our community thinks about and interacts with our products and images," says Tait. "What boards they pin them to and the descriptions they leave can tell us a lot about how that person sees our products fitting into their lives." Daily Grommet also makes use of Pinterest to reply to questions and comments about the products, using Pinterest as another customer service channel for communicating with customers.

Daily Grommet had already been using social media as a channel to allow people to share the products they'd love to see featured on the site. While users had previously submitted products via Twitter, Facebook, email, and the site's Citizens' Gallery feature, Pinterest opened up the door to let them share awesome products with the company in a place where fans were already busy collecting cool ideas (see Figure 14.16).

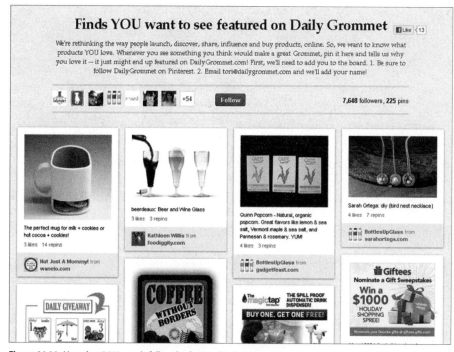

Figure 14.16 More than 7,500 people follow the dozens of Daily Grommet fans who contribute product ideas to the community sourced "Finds YOU want to see featured on Daily Grommet" board.

By creating a board titled "Finds YOU want to see featured on Daily Grommet" and inviting fans to join as board curators, Daily Grommet was able to attract dozens of guest pinners who quickly compiled hundreds of product ideas and attracted more than 6,000 followers. So far, the Daily Grommet team has sourced 6 new Grommets from the user-powered board.

Beyond using Pinterest for research purposes, Daily Grommet's efforts have proven extremely fruitful on the traffic front. Tait reports traffic increased by 446 percent in the two months after they joined the site and began curating boards. In fact, Pinterest has remained a top three referrer for them for the past year.

Note: The buy-in at Daily Grommet is coming from the C-suite as well. "As soon as we started using Pinterest, it was like coming home," said Jules Pieri, founder and CEO in a February 2012 interview with BostInno.com. "I told our Community Manager, 'whatever time you are spending on Pinterest, triple it.' Pinterest traffic rapidly turns into subscribers and customers. It's less of a walled garden than Facebook. It's a community built on curiosity, optimism, creativity and discovery like Daily Grommet. And it really helps that our Grommets are highly visual and exactly what Pinterest users celebrate."

According to Tait, one key contributor to the company's success on Pinterest has been its use of Curalate, a Pinterest analytics tool mentioned back in Chapter 8. Says Tait:

Curalate lifted the lid on the activity on Pinterest. Before we could see analytics around traffic coming from Pinterest, but the data in Google Analytics was difficult and time consuming to sort through. Curalate captures all the activity we would otherwise be missing; what products are getting pinned the most? How many repins are they getting? Which products are taking off on Pinterest? We can see that all now—easily. We're consuming the data and learning a lot.

Curalate helped put the pieces together for Daily Grommet, taking some of the work out of digging into individual pins and pinners and helping provide a bigger picture view of the data. Because Curalate works to aggregate all instances of pins and repins on a single piece of content, Daily Grommet could skip the math reports and focus on which pieces of content were performing the best (see Figure 14.17).

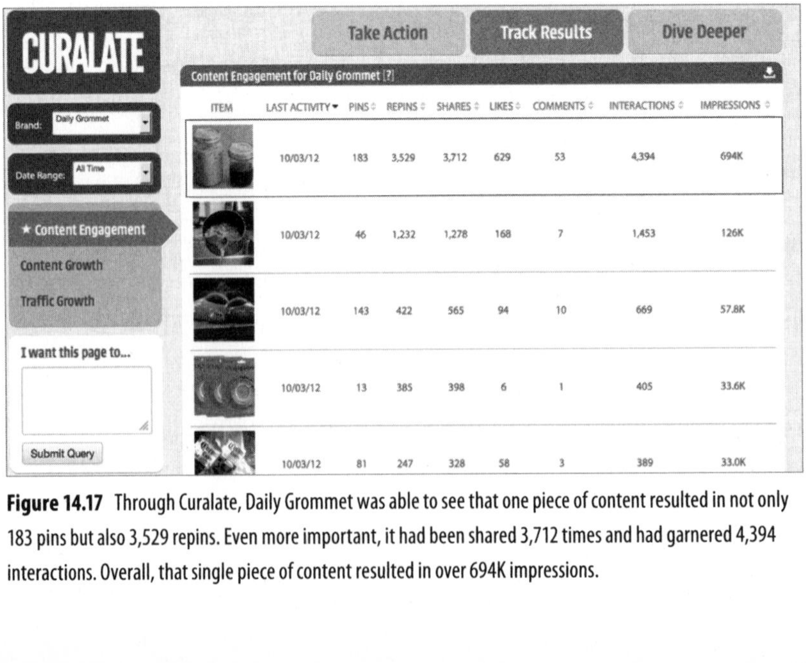

Figure 14.17 Through Curalate, Daily Grommet was able to see that one piece of content resulted in not only 183 pins but also 3,529 repins. Even more important, it had been shared 3,712 times and had garnered 4,394 interactions. Overall, that single piece of content resulted in over 694K impressions.

Tait has been able to use this data to help identify influential pinners, measure the reach of newly launched products, and gauge general consumer reaction to items they are considering for their retail efforts. Close and careful monitoring of the activity surrounding the brand on Pinterest has become an important part of their ongoing marketing strategy.

Perhaps the most telling thing about the Daily Grommet case study is the development of Pinterest as a tap on the pulse of the Daily Grommet's consumer. Because the team under Tait's leadership invested the time in learning how consumers were using the site to engage with Daily Grommet's brand, they were better able to utilize the channel to improve their marketing efforts.

Above all, Daily Grommet's approach to Pinterest proves the value of testing and analyzing the way your target audience interacts with your brand on Pinterest. Sometimes the results will perfectly line up with expectations; sometimes they won't. Either way, the knowledge gained through observation can be invaluable when it comes to leveraging your Pinterest marketing campaign to its maximum potential.

The Future of Pinterest Marketing

In the fast-moving world of social media, new channels come and go at a sometimes alarming rate. Even sites that win over the hearts of marketers and the media often only manage to stay in the game for a period of time. (Anyone remember Plurk? SecondLife? MySpace?)

The rarity in the world of social media is the site like Pinterest—one that has enough factors going for it to make its future appear uniquely bright. In this chapter, we'll wrap things up by exploring the likely future for Pinterest and by taking a look at just how heavily it's already influenced social media and web culture as a whole.

Chapter Contents
Pinterest Will Change the Web
A Future Pinterest API
Understanding the Pinterest Effect

Pinterest Will Change the Web

There's just something about Pinterest. It registers almost instantly as a channel of value with its target audience once they start using it. In fact, Pinterest managed to take hold with its target audience (middle American wives with young children) with hardly any help from the press or social media pundits. This is because it addressed a need they had and did it in a way no other site or service had yet managed to do. Giving women a place to organize their thoughts, ideas, and inspiration and adding a social component to the mix was like hitting the women's social media jackpot.

Pinterest has not only gained a foothold in terms of market saturation, it's also gained a foothold in the emotional value zone of its core audience. It's done this because it answered an unvoiced need in the minds of web-based content consumers: how do I find the best content on the topics that interest me?

For marketers, that means it's essential to see Pinterest as something bigger than what it currently is. It's about more than deciding whether or not your clients target women. It's about anticipating how Pinterest will change the way people will digest content and considering how you may need to restructure your content marketing efforts accordingly.

For marketers who have not yet taken the time to observe Pinterest and to understand how it's being used by its existing audience, Pinterest remains a site aimed at women in middle America. For savvy social media marketers and integrated marketing strategists, Pinterest is a game changer. It's not simply about recognizing the likelihood of Pinterest sticking around; it's about understanding how Pinterest will change the way people use the Web.

Of course, all this begs the question: Where is Pinterest headed in the next few years?

Beyond Browsing: Content Curation

We've already talked extensively about how Pinterest has changed the dynamic of the way people use the Web. It has not only removed the need to sort through legions of text-based bookmarks, but it has also allowed people to open the door of their collections to share them with their friends. It has taken the social sharing dynamic that was built on the backs of channels like Twitter and Facebook and has applied it to the practical and whimsical side of web surfing.

As Pinterest gains an even stronger foothold, there's a good chance we'll see this concept become more integrated into the way people use the Web. Saving content for later perusal will likely become more common and marketing departments will begin to consider the act of saving (pinning) content as a primary social media–based conversion point.

In fact, there's a very good chance that Pinterest will help shift Internet users from the mind-set of using search engines to find information each and every time they need it to the mind-set of using a service like Pinterest to archive topical information for future visitation. Search engines and social sharing will still play their roles, but content curation will allow users to create large databases of easily accessible content surrounding the topics that interest them most.

Of course, as this change begins to impact the way people use the Internet, it will also provide valuable data that will make it even easier for marketers and advertisers to reach out to consumers with targeted messaging.

Which leads to the idea of buyouts and partnerships.

Potential for Buyouts or Partnerships

Perhaps one of the biggest things Pinterest has going for it in the long term is the potential value it offers to the biggest players in the social media field. You've already watched Google gobble up social media services like YouTube, and you've seen Facebook purchase channels like Instagram.

There's no reason to believe either one of these players might not be interested in (or already working on) plans to buy and leverage Pinterest in the ongoing quest to rule the Internet.

Though a buyout could mean that Pinterest would simply end up being integrated into the existing offerings of a larger player, there's also a good chance the service would be integrated while still maintaining its independence, just as Google did with YouTube and just as Facebook has so far done with Instagram. After all, a strong, devoted, and ever-growing user base is not generally the type of thing companies like to mess with.

While my hope is that Pinterest will manage to stay independent, I can see several reasons why both Facebook and Google would be interested in acquiring it.

From Google's perspective, tremendous user data is available from Pinterest. From the search algorithm perspective, Pinterest does an amazing job of valuing and categorizing content from around the Web. Pinterest would give Google a further jump on measuring the social influence of a website and integrating that data into their organic search algorithms. From the targeted ad perspective, Pinterest also makes a tempting target for Google. Combining the pinning habits with a user's Google search profile could create a gold mine of advertising data.

From Facebook's perspective, the integration of Pinterest's interest graph with Facebook's existing social graph holds tremendous value. Facebook already has an amazing amount of data on how people are connected to each other online. They are also able to see which brands and websites not only attract followers on Facebook but also drive interactions. This relationship graph gives Facebook incredible data. It's what allows Facebook to prioritize the status update from friends and Pages that are most likely to capture the interest of Facebook users. Adding the layer of "what people are interested in" that comes with access to Pinterest's user data would catapult Facebook's targeting abilities.

The Archival System: Changing the Way We Engage with Content

As we discussed earlier in this chapter, Pinterest is poised to subtlety, but surely, change the way people access content online. It's poised to help people view individual pieces of web-based content as part of a broader topical theme and to have them get used to the idea of archiving that content appropriately. Traditionally, Internet users access and digest content in one of three ways:

- Through search engines
- Through sites they know
- Through recommendations

The biggest change Pinterest brings to the Internet in terms of content discovery is its ability to allow users to create their own collection of resources segmented by topic. There's no need to remember the name of the website the content came from or to ask around for recommendations. Pinterest allows you to save valuable content as you run across it during your every day Internet usage. This allows Internet users to absorb more information in a short period of time and to keep that information accessible for the future.

Consider the personal libraries of books you or your friends may keep. I personally have an extensive collection of recipe books and homesteading books. My mother keeps a large collection of gardening books, and a dear friend has a huge collection of theology books. These books provide an instant reference point when the need to dive deep into a topic arises.

Pinterest changes the way we collect and organize information by allowing web-based content to be collected and archived in the same way. Because I have a pinboard focused on raising chickens, I no longer have to rely on a single author for my information. I can pin chicken-based content to my pinboard and quickly and easily access it down the road. If my chickens aren't laying properly, I'll likely have at least a few articles pinned that address this topic. There's no need to visit a search engine, recall a site name from memory, or even ask a friend. Pinterest has allowed me to organize my own little topical archive from the Web. Better still, my friends can access my collection of information as well.

This represents a massive change to the way people are able to use the Web to find information. Forward-thinking marketers will look at Pinterest as more than just a place to target crafters and fashionistas; they'll view it as a service that could have a profound impact on how people access information on the Web.

Equally impactful is the creation of the "pin now, read later" mind-set. In the past, most web users read or at least skimmed content as they came across it. With this shift toward content curation, we're seeing a new conversion push within the Pinterest community to pin content before it has been read. This can lead to a high volume of content curation for later review. More and more Pinterest users are repinning content based solely on the image and description and then visiting their pinboards later to review, save, or delete the content they've been collecting. In a web-based world that shifted to almost instant gratification years ago, this could signal an interesting change in direction.

Pinterest's Effect on Search

One of the hottest topics in search engine optimization (SEO) circles right now is understanding how social media–based activity provides ranking signals to search engine algorithms. A true and impactful change from Pinterest is likely a few years off, but it's easy to see how the continued adoption and use of Pinterest could weigh heavily on future search engine algorithms.

Understanding Search Algorithms

It would take an entire book to fully explain the complexity of search engine algorithms, but every marketer should have at least a top-level understanding of how search engines value content. Although factors like the age of content, the words and phrases used in the content, and the coding of a website do figure into search rankings, outside indicators play a huge role in determining whether or not a piece of content will rank well for any particular term.

For nearly as long as search engines have been working to provide good content, they have looked past what appears on a page and have given heavy consideration to the quantity and quality of links pointing to the content from other websites. As social media channels began to spring up and social sharing became commonplace, search engines began to look to social indicators to help rank content.

After all, search engines are interested in valuing content in the same way humans do. They want to ensure your ongoing loyalty by providing you with reliable results that answer the questions and queries you type in. Being able to "see" a piece of content in the context of its social popularity can go a long way toward helping search engines deliver strong results. Being able to tie in the social connections of a particular user in an effort to weigh social and link activity from their friends and family helps take the search results to an even more effective level.

With Pinterest poised to make such a dramatic impact on how Internet users access, digest, and store content, it also has the strong potential to introduce a powerful level of data into future search engine algorithms.

What Makes Pinterest a Potential Game Changer for Search Engines

Just as Pinterest has the potential to change the way Internet users think about and access content, it also has the potential to heavily impact SEO. Search engineers work tirelessly to use social sharing data, linking data, and semantic technology to better understand how content topics tie together and how to value a particular piece of content.

Semantically, search engineers work hard to help the algorithm recognize that an American typing "Rental Car in Ireland" is probably looking for "Car Hire in Ireland." Understanding how words and phrases relate is critical for the future of responsive search. Pinterest has an amazing ability to factor into this equation by allowing search engineers to see how content is topically categorized by millions of web users.

With Pinterest, it becomes easy to start identifying patterns in content. Followers of the Paleo diet are often interested in gluten-free recipes, homesteaders with backyard chickens are often also interested in canning, and CrossFit devotees probably use a kettlebell at some point in time. Although it was certainly possible to identify some of these points of commonality from blogs and websites, the ability to explore the ways consumers bundle content together could prove extremely useful to search engines.

Add in the extra layer of interpersonal connections and Pinterest begins to give search engines a way to view content that has never before been possible on this level. We're likely still a year or more away from seeing this enter into the mix, but it's not impossible to foresee a world where segmented and socially connected content has a strong impact on how content is ranked by the search engines.

A Future Pinterest API

Despite multiple news stories in the first half of 2012 touting a soon-to-be-released public Pinterest API, as of this writing no public API has been made available.

Although this hasn't stopped numerous companies from working on building tools and service platforms for Pinterest, it has kept third parties from having full access and predefined parameters for interacting with the site and its data streams.

The Potential of a Pinterest API

When considering the idea of a Pinterest API and what it might mean to both the developer community and to users of the service, it's extremely important to understand the ecosystem that often surrounds popular social media channels.

The strongest social media services (such as Facebook and Twitter) tend to exist as a platform of features and services that attract a strong and loyal user base. From there, third-party developers are able to leverage the channel's API to create a secondary layer of features that add value to the original service.

At its most basic level, APIs allow users to do things like use their Facebook login to register for their Pinterest account, or to automatically publish their Instagram photo to their Facebook and Twitter accounts. At a more advanced level, they allow third-party analytics packages to fully understand how users move from a site like Facebook into a company's web page to enable better tracking and conversion analysis.

Developers basically use a service's API to improve user experience and introduce new and interesting ways to leverage the original platform.

The biggest and most obvious appeal to developers is the ability to create new tools and layers to improve the marketing and conversion potential of the service. However, there's also a strong chance that users will benefit from these new features and tools as well.

Speculation on the API Delay

With the enormous interest in Pinterest from marketers and developers, there's been quite a bit of questioning regarding why Pinterest hasn't yet released the API they claimed they'd have ready to go in early 2012.

Jay Yarow addressed this question with a strong theory in an article titled "Pinterest Is Scared of Having a 'Twitter Problem'" (`http://articles.businessinsider.com/2012-03-26/tech/31238519_1_mobile-apps-twitterrific-hootsuite`) in a March 26, 2012 article for *Business Insider*.

> *Twitter released its API when it was still an immature company, allowing developers to build applications with features that it was missing. When Twitter matured, and it wanted to control its platform, it began adding those features, thus damaging those developers.*
>
> *For instance, Twitpic, which built a way to share photos, is now threatened because Twitter added native photo sharing. HootSuite and Twitterrific, which build great mobile apps, were crushed when Twitter started putting more effort into its own mobile apps.*
>
> *As Twitter began competing with its developers, the developer community turned against Twitter. It didn't really trust Twitter.*
> *Pinterest doesn't want that to happen. It's a very young company and it's just getting started, says our source. It doesn't want developers to build features/applications that it plans on building, and then alienate those developers by building similar features.*

The idea that Pinterest wants to protect its relationship with developers and its ability to fully integrate new features itself is a strong one. Add in the reality that Pinterest has still not figured out how to fully monetize its user base and you have a company that's wise to work out a solid business plan for growth and monetization before opening the floodgates to let third-party players into the mix.

API Discussions for Developers

Pinterest features a contact form on their site for developers who wish to be notified when the public API is made available (see Figure 15.1).

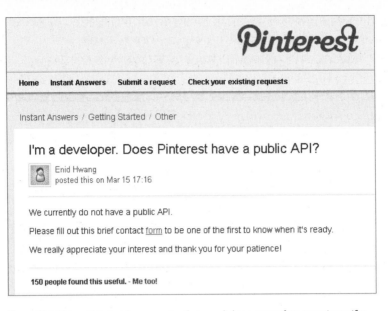

Figure 15.1 Pinterest's Instant Answers section features a link to a contact form to receive notification of the future API release.

It's also worth noting that several thousand developers have also gathered together in a private group on Facebook (`https://www.facebook.com/groups/pinterestapi/`) to discuss the potential and upcoming release of the Pinterest API.

Understanding the Pinterest Effect

Each of the major players in the world of social media has had a profound effect on both the way people use the Web and how marketers reach out to consumers.

The Impact of Social Channels Over Time

Blogs enabled web users to create a platform for sharing their thoughts and ideas and to build a following based on how well those ideas resonated with their audience. Even more so than the invention of the printing press, the creation of blogging platforms gave true voice to the masses and allowed them to attract and build a global audience around the topics of their choice. This led marketers to begin understanding the value of approaching bloggers in the same way they'd formerly approached news and magazine editors.

When YouTube arrived on the scene, consumers quickly realized they no longer had to rely on written words or images to get a full sense of a concept, place, or item. YouTube allowed both companies and consumers to create and upload their own walkthroughs, tutorials, and product reviews. This led marketers to begin exploring the need to offer visual documentation of their products and services. Just as blogging had handed the written word over to the masses, YouTube handed video to them.

Services like Twitter required consumers to condense those once wordy blog posts and video clips down to 140-character "Twitter-bites." Marketers followed suit with quick quotes, poll questions, and enticing lead-ins to motivate readers to click through to full stories and additional coverage. Facebook carried this concept further by incorporating the social connections that tie people together and adding layers of photos and videos on top.

Although the introduction of Twitter and Facebook to the mix allowed consumers to connect in ways they never had before (and allowed marketers to leverage those connections to gain unprecedented exposure to their products and services), it also had some negative consequences.

In a digital world where consumers were already drawn to the next shiny object flickering at the edge of their screen, it drove attention spans further into the gutter and required complex concepts and ideas to be boiled down into bite-sized pieces.

From the cynical perspective, the only logical place to go next was to a system that didn't even require the effort of writing down that handful of words to convey ideas to your audience. Enter Pinterest.

For better or worse, these days it takes only an image to compel a click and to get your message across to your target audience. On Pinterest, you don't even have the amount of time it takes to read that 140-character tweet to make an impression. It has to happen at a glance.

Within months of Pinterest catching hold, we began to see this same trend happening on Facebook. Individual users and Pages alike began sharing images and quotes integrated into images to catch the eye of the Pinterest-spoiled Facebook user.

Pinterest and the Future of Social Media Marketing

With Pinterest poised to change the way people use and access content on the Web, responsible marketers will need to adapt. A renewed focus on both content marketing efforts and on quality photography and images will have to be integrated into the marketing efforts of any site wanting to reach out to the Pinterest community. Longer term, content marketers will need to give careful consideration to how the concept of clustered content will be utilized by their target audience.

Pinterest drives a renewed focus on quality content. In a world that was shifting toward the bite-sized content of Twitter and the quick conversation style of Facebook, Pinterest's ability to drive interest in saving, sharing, and organizing quality content is a breath of fresh air. Add in its proven ability to drive traffic to sites themselves and you have a powerful new channel.

In the grand scheme of things, the addition of Pinterest to the world of social media channels that marketers must pay attention to is a good thing. It reminds us of the need to create great content and great imaging for our audience. It reminds us to keep tabs on what they like, what they share, and what drives them to take action. Above all, it reminds us that social media provides consumers with the ability to connect with each other and share the things that matter to them with the world.

As a business owner, social media pundit, or marketer, don't let those lessons pass you by.

Appendix: Pinterest Marketing Resources

*While I've done everything in my power to start you off with an excellent background in Pinterest marketing and Pinterest strategy, the world of social media moves fast. Savvy social media marketers understand the value of staying up-to-date on the latest tactics and techniques.*

This collection of websites, blogs, and even pinboards will arm you with the resources you'll need to stay abreast of the latest Pinterest news on the Web.

Pinterest Marketing: An Hour a Day Pinboard

http://pinterest.com/AFlexibleLife/pinterest-marketing-an-hour-a-day/

You don't think I'd take all the time to put together a book without bothering to create a pinboard to link to related content, did you? You can find and subscribe to the companion pinboard to this book on my Pinterest account. You'll find infographics, case studies, tips, and news articles related to the growth and use of Pinterest.

97th Floor Blog

http://colbyalmond.com/category/blog/

Blogger Colby Almond and the team at 97th Floor consistently put out great content on Pinterest. Keeping tabs on their blogs can be an excellent way to pick up breaking news and great how-to guides for leveraging the site.

Pinboard from PinnableBusiness.com

http://pinterest.com/pinterestbiz/pinterest-marketing/

This board is curated by the team at PinnableBusiness.com and features a ton of links to infographics, case studies, how-to guides, and other Pinterest-related content.

Marketing Land

http://marketingland.com/library/pinterest

The team of bloggers at Marketing Land does a great job of covering the site from all angles. Whether it's how Pinterest can be used to impact your local SEO efforts or which new features have been added to the site, you'll find great ongoing coverage here.

Pinboard from Team MarketingProfs

http://pinterest.com/marketingprofs/pinterest-marketing/

The excellent team at MarketingProfs.com does a great job of putting quality content out on the Web for online marketers, and their Pinterest-focused pinboard is no different. While the board isn't stuffed with tons of links, the content you will find is quality.

Social Media Examiner

www.socialmediaexaminer.com/tag/pinterest/

Another team-based contributor site, Social Media Examiner features several authors who cover Pinterest from both the social media news and social media marketing angles. You'll find a wide range of tips and case studies on this site.

Pinterest Marketing Articles Pinboard

http://pinterest.com/windhome/pinterest-marketing-articles/

While this board from Beulah Laster does include some articles related to Facebook and Etsy marketing as well, it does an excellent job of curating content related to improving your Pinterest marketing efforts.

Entrepreneur

www.entrepreneur.com/topic/pinterest#

It's not just online marketing bloggers who are focusing in on how Pinterest is changing the world of marketing—mainstream business sites like Entrepreneur are in on the fun as well. This site features regular articles and case studies on how companies and brands are using Pinterest to increase their reach.

Pinterest for Marketing Pinboard

http://pinterest.com/chic_geek/pinterest-for-marketing/

This excellent collection of graphics, articles, and tutorials from Lisa Anne goes beyond the standard Pinterest information. It also provides tips, tricks, and insight that isn't Pinterest focused, but will help you do well on Pinterest anyway. (For example, you learn which colors evoke which moods and how to optimize social media across the customer lifestyle.)

Mashable

http://mashable.com/follow/topics/pinterest/

When it comes to keeping tabs on the pulse of social media, few sites perform as well as Mashable. Checking in on a daily basis is a must for most social media marketers. You'll find plenty of Pinterest content, including news, tools, and case studies.

Appendix: Pinterest Tips from Top Marketers

As with any form of marketing, figuring out the best way to leverage Pinterest is a bit of an art form. Every marketer has their own way to approach it, and taking the time to brainstorm with other Pinterest marketers can be a great way to put a new perspective on your campaigns.

I sought insights from a wide range of experienced online and social media marketers who have been busy testing their own theories and ideas about Pinterest. Here, in their own words, are the invaluable tips and tricks these marketers shared.

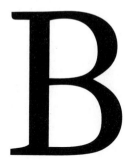

Ryan Sammy

Director of Web Promotion, BlueGlass Interactive (`www.blueglass.com`)

Pinterest isn't just another social media network to share your brand's message, products, or services. It's a medium that, if used well, allows you to build sentiment around your brand. It gives you the opportunity to interact with your followers and show off your brand culture through visual boards and pins. It also gives you the ability to see what's becoming popular in your niche, and what your audience wants.

One of the best ways to use Pinterest is to comment on users' pins. This isn't a common practice for most brands, so it will make yours stand out. Interacting with other users also gives prospective followers or customers the feeling they can directly interact with you and understand what your brand is about.

Searching for pinboards related to your brand or product(s) is a good way to find people to follow. If the user is already interested in your niche, you have a better chance of converting them into a follower, and then a customer. Sharing great content that isn't pushing a branding message is an easy way to create positive sentiment. Users will naturally relate your great shares to your brand.

The most important component of an individual pin is the image. Each pin should have a compelling photo that is easily viewable on the home page. Always include a small description, and that description should work with the image you choose to encourage the user to perform an action. Sometimes just asking people to share will be enough to have a pin reshared. When sharing a pin, know the best time for the brand. Try sharing at different times of the day until you can determine when you receive the most shares.

Remember to stay active and involved with your Pinterest followers. No one wants to follow a brand that's stagnant, and neglecting your Pinterest account can be seen by some as an indication of the kind of service you'd provide them if they were to become customers.

Prafull Sharma

Cofounder, HireRabbit (`http://hirerabbit.com`)

People want to win and that's why a Pinterest contest is an exciting idea. Contests provide an excellent way to encourage people to talk about your company or spread the word about your products and services.

So do contests on Pinterest really work, you ask? Yes, but only if you get it right. Contests can increase the number of followers and can also provide you with valuable customer information.

To create a successful contest:

- Identify your goals.
- Give away something that excites your audience.
- Use your existing audience to promote the contest to your email lists, blog, Facebook/Twitter, or other social media presence.

Pinterest can expose your brand to a large audience, given the viral nature of the images on Pinterest and a highly engaged Pinterest audience. Whatever you do, keep the contest simple and have fun!

Matt Siltala

President and Founder, Avalaunch Media (www.avalaunchmedia.com)

People who are using the site are actually turning into buyers. We all know that Pinterest sends amazing traffic, but Build Direct shared with me the average visitor from StumbleUpon stays about 10 seconds and views one page, whereas the average Pinterest visitor stays an average of 13 minutes and views 5 pages.

This is buyer behavior and makes Pinterest an amazing competitive intelligence tool. For any niche that I am in (or my client is in), I am going to monitor heavily every little thing my competitor is doing on Pinterest for this very reason.

If they are getting lots of pins, repins, comments, followers, and so forth, I am going to learn everything about them and target them and do better on my end. I will learn from what they do and I will do better (and more). Tools like PinAlerts and Repinly make this task even easier. I am seeing exactly (real time) when and what my competitors are pinning, seeing who is pinning them, seeing what boards they pin to, and so on.

Pinterest provides so much amazing research right at your fingertips in real time—all on a site that is driving *buyers*. You'd be crazy not to spend time researching and testing on Pinterest.

> *I use it as a place to keep anything that interests, inspires, and intrigues me. I think the most important thing for me has been to continue being true to my own voice regardless of what happens on Pinterest itself. At the end of the day, it is a reflection of who you are and what makes your visual senses go "ahhh."*
> —Satsuki Shibuya (designer, artist, curious explorer),
> www.satsukishibuya.com

Carrie Hill

Director of Online Marketing, KeyRelevance (www.keyrelevance.com)

My biggest piece of advice is "Don't Give Up!" I've had things go viral on Pinterest weeks (even a month or two) after I posted them. I repurpose my items by reposting them every week or two, sometimes with different labels and images, just to reach a fresh set of eyes.

Also, be prepared for success. Something can go viral instantly and your little-known site can get 100,000 visits with little to no warning, so be sure your hosting service can handle it.

Also, keep Jennifer's book on your desk, because you'll be referring back to it a lot!

Amanda Nelson

Manager, Content Salesforce Marketing Cloud (www.radian6.com/marketingcloud)

One of the ongoing challenges for social media marketers is staying on top of the ever-changing nature of social media. Pinterest is one of the latest shiny objects and it's changing the way companies think about how they graphically represent content. It's tailor-made for lifestyle brands and marketers with content that translates well to graphics.

In addition to creating more graphical content, we need to think about meaningful images. Infographics will work, but that's not enough. And where do those images link? People will click on an image looking for more information. It can't be just a link to the page hosting the image. This is a huge opportunity to present content in a way that has impact and that enhance our messages.

In other words, your content needs to be "pinnable." This can increase engagement and boost your brand's Pinterest presence. Whether it's an impromptu sketch, custom graphic, or an Instagram shot, use something that puts a unique stamp on your content and makes people take notice. Incorporate Pin It buttons to allow easy pinning of content. Make sure your photos are of high quality. The nicer the photo, the more likely people will want to share it.

In the end, social media measurement remains critical. Measure interest of your Pinterest page by reviewing how much traffic it brings to your website. Those Pin It buttons are measureable too—see which pins perform better than others. As results unfold, change it up, try new things, and most of all, keep on pinning.

Katie Laird

PR and Social Media Manager, Blinds.com (www.blinds.com)

You can't spell *Pinterest* without *interest*—make sure that your Pinterest boards are providing interesting, useful, and relevant content to your community to make it a worthwhile marketing activity.

For our brand, Blinds.com, we use our Pinterest presence (www.pinterest.com/Blindsdotcom) to market ourselves as window decorating experts. But to get that message across, we recognized early on the importance of presenting content that goes beyond our products and even our familiar realm of windows.

By sharing general home decorating and lifestyle content that's fun and shareable, we're placing our brand and products right smack in the center of a fun visual dialogue that's happening at a rapid pace between future customers. And the fact that this audience skews younger and is web savvy is hugely thrilling!

Another tip for aspiring Pinterest marketers is to regularly review your frequently pinned products to gauge product interest for future sales and promotions. While you probably have a good grasp on general shopping trends, watching your world through real-time Pinterest goggles can be eye opening. All it takes is a popular sitcom episode using a product or a splashy magazine spread with a similar style and *boom*! You just might find a niche item making waves on Pinterest—all the more reason to keep your website images highly shareable, to encourage this very thing.

Best of all, if you're noticing a trend in likes and pins on a particular product or style that's surprising to you, you're only a mere comment away from connecting with a Pinterest user.

The biggest mistake people make when trying to build an audience on Pinterest is deviating from their personal brand by pinning images or items they don't personally love. I only pin things that I actually want, would buy, or think are incredibly beautiful.

I also think it's a mistake to have too many boards. There are some people out there who have so many boards it makes me wonder if they are closet hoarders in real life. It sends a red flag that if I follow this person I'm going to get bombarded with images.

—Alexandra Evjen (Pinterest Power User) Fashion Stylist for AVE Styles
(www.avestyles.com)

Dirk Singer

Head Rabbit, The Rabbit Agency (www.therabbitagency.com)

Twelve months ago Pinterest was almost unheard of, driving around 2 percent of social media referral traffic to websites. Now (October 2012), that total is over a third with Pinterest sending more people to websites than Bing, Google+, YouTube, or Twitter.

Yet at the same time, bounce rates for that referral traffic is also higher than average.

Here are three ways to keep the traffic but stop people from leaving:

1. Tie into existing user behavior. This one should be obvious. Take a cross section of actual users relevant to your industry sector and see what they are doing. For example, if you are a travel company, what kind of images feature? Is it beaches? Hotels? Landscape images? That should then give you a steer toward what you should be doing on your boards.

2. Give people a reason to repin and share. "Repin to win" promotions are now fairly commonplace, and you'll get people pinning your images with a decent incentive. But are they then in turn sharing those images with their own networks via Facebook or Twitter? For that to happen, you'll need to be a little more creative.

    For example, for the bmi Pinterest lottery, we turned our promotion into a game of chance, with each pin having lottery style numbers. This made it more than just a straightforward promotion.

3. Where do they end up? One reason bounce rates are high is because people get directed to a standard home page that doesn't speak specifically to them. Think about having your pins go to a specific landing page instead. For the bmi Pinterest lottery we created a Tumblr featuring content about the different destinations we were promoting. As a result, people stayed for almost four minutes (four times higher than the average) with us, with the bounce rate a below-average 31 percent.

Megan Rivas

Associate Online Account Manager, aimClear (www.aimclear.com)

It's a dilemma many brands face: You want to kick it on the hottest social media platform but don't quite know how to fit in. Case in point: Pinterest, and companies with product lines outside the realm of fashionable clothes, adorable cupcakes, crafty DIY goodies, kittens, and so on.

If your company is finding it a tricky task to think up creative pinboard ideas, you are not alone.

Creative pin board titles are essential for getting attention!

Board titles are the first thing a user will see when they visit your Pinterest page. Children's Hospital in Phoenix, AZ features two pinboards that showcase artwork around the hospital and bald fashion dolls for children. Both of these boards are bold and truly intriguing ideas that would make me want to click into it and look around.

When a user clicks into one of your boards, they'll see the board description, right under your board title. This prime real estate offers you 500 characters with which you can explain what your board is about. You can say a lot in 500 characters, so take advantage! Tell people why you created this board: what makes it important, what's the incentive to click around? You can even take this opportunity to discuss your company and how it relates to the pinned content therein.

Jamie Grove

VP, Evil Schemes & Nefarious Plans (Marketing), ThinkGeek (www.thinkgeek.com)

Tell your creative team to go *epic* on every shot. Like any other social medium, Pinterest comes down to sharing truly great content.

Glossary

comment A note, link, or other comment left on a pin. Comments are publicly visible to other Pinterest users.

cover photo The pinned image designated by the board owner to serve as the default picture for a pinboard.

hash tag A word or phrase used to describe a topic, event, or idea in a way that makes it easy to tie concepts together. Hash tags are triggered through the use of the # symbol before a phrase (for example, #PinterestMarketing). Hash tags act as links on Pinterest and lead users to a listing of all other pinned content featuring the same hash tag.

like A way for Pinterest users to denote their appreciation of a pin without repinning it. A like on Pinterest works much the same way a like on Facebook does.

mentions The term used to describe the act of referring to another Pinterest user in a comment or description for a pin. Mentions are triggered through the use of the @ symbol before a user's name (for example, @aflexiblelife).

pin A piece of content that has been added to Pinterest.

Pin It bookmarklet This link can be added to the toolbar or bookmark section of any web browser to provide the ability to quickly pin content from websites that do not feature the Pin It button.

Pin It button The Pin It button is a social sharing icon that appears next to blog posts, images, videos, products, and other web-based content. It enables site visitors to have one-click access to pin content from the page where it's featured. The Pin It button can be added manually by inserting a section of code into a page's HTML code, or it can be triggered through the use of a social sharing plug-in.

pinboard A topical board created by a Pinterest user to house pins on a specific topic, concept, or theme.

pinner A person who uses Pinterest.

Pinterest A website allowing users to create image-based collections of topics and concepts and then share those collections with friends.

repin A piece of content that has been added to Pinterest by one user and then shared with a new audience by a different user.

Index

Been hearing about Pinterest and want to know how to REALLY use it for your business? Jennifer nails it! Read and learn all about using Pinterest to market your business in this definitive resource on using Pinterest for marketing.

—ANITA CAMPBELL, Editor in Chief, Small Business Trends

Everything I read in this book seems like common sense. The thing is, it's not actually common knowledge—it's just that Cario writes in such an accessible, clear, and open way that it seems like she's telling you something you already know. Other writing I've read on leveraging hot new social media trends usually feels already outdated, kind of hokey, or too slick and "salesy." This book does not fall into any of those traps. It is instead a totally refreshing take that resonates with my own experience as a Pinterest-user and gets me excited about expanding the way I think about the site's possibilities!

—KATE VAN WAGNER, social activist & owner operator of
BathsNotBombs.etsy.com

A practical guide to the fast-changing world of Pinterest. If you want to get in early and be successful, you couldn't ask for a better resource.

—JAMIE GROVE, VP Evil Schemes and Nefarious Plans (aka Marketing)
at ThinkGeek

What I love about Jennifer's style is that she always takes seemingly complex and daunting social media and marketing tools, and makes them accessible to everyone. With Pinterest, she makes the task of understanding this tool much easier and breaks it down into a step-by-step process that makes it far more manageable so all business owners can learn how to use Pinterest as an effective tool to connect with and engage their customers!

—MACK COLLIER, Social Media Strategist and author of *Think Like a Rockstar*

This book is a must for those learning how to market on Pinterest or trying to navigate the confusing world of Social Media Marketing and time management. Staying on task in social media, especially Pinterest, is something many marketers struggle with every day. Having a game plan that outlines each day's task is an invaluable marketing asset. Jennifer does a great job helping ever level of marketer from novice to pro. This text is a must have on the small business or agency bookshelf.

—CARRIE HILL, Director of Online Marketing at KeyRelevance

For brands the thought of managing another social platform with limited resources is daunting. What Pinterest Marketing: An Hour A Day does is show you the enormous potential of the platform, how it can impact your business, and a simple practical plan to use Pinterest as a tool to build and proliferate your brand's personality. The book

Advance Praise for *Pinterest Marketing: An Hour A Day*

With a concise yet engaging style, Jennifer Cario has created the ultimate guide to Pinterest for B2C, B2B and non-profit organizations of all sizes. Logically organized and easy to digest, Pinterest Marketing: An Hour A Day answers the who, what, where, when, why and – most importantly – the how of using today's fastest growing social media site to drive traffic, connect with fans and measure your success.
> —JENNIFER CARROLL, content marketing and social media strategist,
> Pole Position Marketing

This book delivered a firehose of creative solutions for a social channel that I clearly have underappreciated to date. Thanks for the splash of cold water in the face. How did I previously miss the immense data analysis opportunities and innovative solutions to create your brand personality and drive more traffic? I'm inspired to start using Pinterest more creatively...right now!
> —KAYDEN KELLY, Founder of Blast Analytics & Marketing

This is the ultimate "how-to" Pinterest guide for brands, content creators, and marketers alike. With effective pinning strategies broken down into easily digestible daily and weekly action steps, this book makes it super easy to jump in and leverage the massive opportunities for traffic, visibility and brand awareness that Pinterest has to offer.
> —AMBER WATSON-TARDIFF, COO at Legal Marketing Maven

Jennifer has created a resource beautifully designed to make effective Pinterest marketing achievable for anyone. This is one of those rare guides I will be getting all of my staff to read.
> —ROSS DUNN, Owner, StepForth Web Marketing

Jennifer Cario is the Queen of Social Marketing. In this book she provides easy actionable steps on how to use Pinterest to grow and expand your business. This is a must read for the professional looking to grow their brand!
> —SHAWNA SEIGEL, CEO at 1 Choice 4 Your Store

This is one of the first, detailed, foundational publications by a known Internet marketing guru that level—sets all expectations for Pinterest. Jennifer takes time to systematically educate, energize and empower readers with comprehensive information and techniques to get the most out of Pinterest.
> —CHRIS CAPUTO, President, Falls Digital